D0071009

VIETNAM

FOURTH EDITION

VIETNAM
Past and Present

D. R. SarDesai
University of California, Los Angeles

A Member of the Perseus Books Group

Copyright © 1992, 1998, 2005 by Westview Press, A Member of the Perseus Books Group

Second edition published in 1992 in the United States by Westview Press. Third edition published in 1998. Fourth edition published in 2005.

Books published by Westview Press are available at special discounts for bulk purchases in the United States by corporations, institutions, and other organizations. For more information, please contact the Special Markets Department at the Perseus Books Group, 11 Cambridge Center, Cambridge, MA 02142, or call (617) 252-5298 or (800) 255-1514; or e-mail special.markets@perseusbooks.com.

Library of Congress Cataloging-in-Publication Data
SarDesai, D. R.
    Vietnam, past and present / D. R. SarDesai.—4th ed.
        p.   cm.
    Includes bibliographical references and index.
    ISBN 0-8133-4308-9 (pbk. : alk. paper)
        1. Vietnam—History—20th century. 2. Nationalism—Vietnam—History. I. Title.
DS556.8.S24 2005
959.704—dc22   2004021785

The paper used in this publication meets the requirements of the American National Standard for Permanence of Paper for Printed Library Materials Z39.48-1984.

10   9   8   7   6   5   4   3   2   1

For ARNAV
With hopes for a humane and peaceful tomorrow

Contents

Tables and Maps

Tables

Maps

Acronyms

AFTA	ASEAN Free Trade Agreement
ARVN	Army of the Republic of Vietnam
ASEAN	Association of Southeast Asian Nations
BLDP	Buddhist Liberal Democratic Party
BOT	build-operate-transfer
BTA	Bilateral Trade Agreement
CEPT	Common Effective Preferential Tariff
CGDK	Coalition Government of Democratic Kampuchea
COMECON	Council for Mutual Economic Assistance
COSVN	Central Office of South Vietnam
CPP	Cambodian People's Party
DRV	Democratic Republic of Vietnam
EEZ	exclusive economic zone
EPZ	export processing zone
ESCAP	Economic and Social Commission for Asia and the Pacific
FDI	foreign direct investment
FUNCINPEC	National United Front for an Independent, Neutral, Peaceful, and Cooperative Cambodia
GDP	gross domestic product
GNP	gross national product
ICC	International Control Commission
ICP	Indochina Communist Party
ICRC	International Committee on Reconstruction of Cambodia
ICRF	International Commission on Religious Freedom
IMF	International Monetary Fund
ITC	International Trade Committee
JIM	Jakarta Informal Meeting
KMT	Kuomintang
KPNLF	Khmer People's National Liberation Front
KR	Khmer Rouge

KUFNS	Kampuchean United Front for National Salvation
MAAG	Military Assistance Advisory Group
MFN	most-favored nation
MIA	missing in action
MoCI	Ministry of Culture and Information
NEZ	new economic zone
NLF	National Liberation Front
NSC	National Security Council
NTR	normal trade relations
NVA	North Vietnamese Army
ODA	official developmental assistance
ODP	Orderly Departure Program
ORT	Operation Rolling Thunder
PCC	Paris Conference on Cambodia
POW	prisoner of war
PRG	Provisional Revolutionary Government
PRK	People's Republic of Kampuchea
PRP	People's Revolutionary Party
ROVR	Resettlement Opportunities for Vietnamese Returnees
SAM	surface-to-air missile
SEATO	Southeast Asia Treaty Organization
SNC	Supreme National Council
SOC	State of Cambodia
SOE	State-Owned Enterprise
SRP	Sam Rangsi Party
SRV	Socialist Republic of Vietnam
TEL	Temporary Exclusion List
UBC	Unified Buddhist Church
UNAKRT	UN Assistance to Khmer Rouge Trials
UNESCO	United Nations Educational, Scientific, and Cultural Organization
UNHCR	United Nations High Commissioner for Refugees
UNTAC	United Nations Transitional Authority in Cambodia
VCP	Vietnamese Communist Party
VNQDD	Vietnamese Nationalist Party
WTO	World Trade Organization
ZOPFAN	zone of peace, freedom, and neutrality

Preface

Vietnam has evoked more interest internationally among scholars and diplomats, militarists and peace activists, journalists and the public than most other countries in recent times. The spectacle of a small nation, with far less sophisticated weaponry than its opponents and hardly any air power, immobilizing the most advanced, militarily best-equipped nation, moved people across the globe. What motivated the Vietnamese men, women, and children to make such supreme sacrifices? Was it communism or nationalism—or a combination of both?

My interest in Vietnam was further aroused by numerous Vietnamese students at UCLA who had immigrated to southern California as "boat people" in the wake of the 1975 "fall" of Saigon. Their plaint about a persistent bias in most of the Western accounts about Vietnam and their plea that I write an objective history of the modern period in the perspective of its long historical past have been primarily responsible for this book. I have profited most from discussions with them, in particular Nguyen Dao Phan, who completed a thesis on the National Liberation Front under my supervision. My thanks are also due to Pham Cao Duong, whose scholarly insights into the agrarian policies and successes and failures of governments in Vietnam have benefited my understanding of rural Vietnam. For the recent period, I have drawn extensively from the most well-informed and fairly objective and analytical reports of Nayan Chanda, special correspondent and expert on Vietnam for the *Far Eastern Economic Review.*

I should acknowledge my debt of gratitude to Charlotte Spence, former Indo-Pacific bibliographer of the University of California, Los Angeles, for her unfailing assistance in locating materials; and to Dr. Ingelise Lanman, my former doctoral student research assistant, for her help in writing this book. I am very grateful to Jane Bitar, manager of the word-processing department for social sciences and humanities at UCLA, and Nancy Rhan, also in the word-processing department, for their professional expertise in the preparation of the manuscript. Finally, as always, I am beholden to my wife for providing consistent encouragement and inspiration in all my scholarly and writing endeavors.

D. R. SarDesai

Vietnam and Neighboring Countries

CHAPTER 1

Ethnicity, Geography, and Early History

The Southeast Asian littoral, the promontory at the extremity of mainland Southeast Asia, constitutes Vietnam. It extends from about 8° to 23°N and 102° to 109°E. The long coastline of Vietnam uncoils in the shape of an S from China's southern border to the tip of the Indochina Peninsula. It is bordered on the north by China, to the west by Laos and Cambodia, and to the east and south by the South China Sea. Nearly 1,240 miles long, the country extends unevenly at widths ranging from 31 to 310 miles and covers an area of 127,300 square miles. Vietnam is as large as the British Isles, smaller than Thailand, with a population estimated at 79 million in 2004, making it the thirteenth largest populated country in the world. Owing to heavy human losses during the long conflict, the population is young, with 70 percent under the age of thirty. The literacy rate is one of the highest in the world; 90 percent of those age ten and over are literates.

Vietnam's two fertile alluvial deltas—the Red River, or Song Ma, in the north and the Mekong in the south—have inspired the image of the typical Vietnamese peasant carrying a pair of rice baskets suspended at the ends of a pole. Connected by a chain of narrow coastal plains, the deltas produced enough rice before the war not only to feed the population but even to export. Since the late 1990s, Vietnam has become the second largest exporter of rice in the world. Although these delta regions make up only about a quarter of the country's area, they support almost 80 percent of its population. The rural population density in some of the provinces of the Red River Delta is as high as 1,000 per square mile. The Mekong Delta is the richer of the two and extends well into Cambodia. Both deltas are known for their intensive agriculture; the Red River Delta has long reached the point of optimum agricultural expansion. The country's historical, political, and economic development has taken place in these two separate areas partly because of a mountain range dividing the country. The Truong Son, or Annamite Cordillera, runs approximately north and south along the border of Laos and Vietnam, cutting the latter almost in two and also extending along the Vietnamese-Cambodian border. At certain points, the mountains have elevations of up to 10,000 feet.

Communications between Vietnam and Laos or Cambodia are possible through certain strategic passes. Of these, the more difficult ones are located in the north at an altitude of more than 3,000 feet at the head of the valleys of the Song Da (Black River), the Song Ma (Red River), and the Song Ca. Further south the communications are, by comparison, not as difficult. Thus the Tran Ninh area can be reached through the town of Cua Rao, whereas the Cammon Plateau can be reached from the Nghe An area through the Ha-trai and Keo Nua Passes at an altitude of more than 2,000 feet or further south through the Mu Gia Pass at a somewhat lower altitude. From Quang Tri one can traverse just north of the Kemmarat rapids through the Ai Lao Pass (at an altitude of about 1,300 feet), regarded as the gateway to Laos. Between the Red River Delta and central Vietnam, communications go through several passes and corniches at Hoanh Son, the gateway to Annam, at elevations of between 1,300 and 1,500 feet. The geographical configuration and the varied accesses are extremely significant for understanding the movement of people and armies in the military encounters in ancient as well as recent times.

Vietnam—The Nomenclature

For most of their history, the Vietnamese people lived only in the Red River Delta. During the first millennium of the Christian era, from 111 BC to AD 939, Vietnam was a directly ruled province of the Chinese empire. The separate kingdom of Champa, south of the empire's border in central Vietnam, existed until 1471, when most of it was overrun by independent Vietnam. The remnant of Champa was absorbed by the Vietnamese in 1720. Thereafter, taking advantage of an extremely weakened Khmer empire, the Vietnamese gradually expanded into the Mekong Delta, completing the conquest by the middle of the eighteenth century and reaching the modern borders of Vietnam.

Vietnam has had a succession of names, reflecting its rule by various people at various times. The Chinese called the country Nan Yueh and the Red River Delta the Giao. In the seventh century, after putting down a series of revolts by the Vietnamese, the Chinese renamed the territory Annam, meaning "pacified south." After the Vietnamese overthrew the direct Chinese rule in AD 939, the kingdom was called Dai Co Viet (country of the great Viet people). Through the centuries, as Vietnamese rulers extended the kingdom almost to the present-day borders, the three natural divisions of Vietnam— north, central, and south—came to be known to the Vietnamese as Bac Viet, Trung Viet, and Nam Viet, respectively. The kingdom as it existed in the sixteenth and seventeenth centuries covering north and central Vietnam was divided into two political parts and ruled by two families: the Trinh in the north and the Nguyen in central Vietnam, both of whom recognized the Le as kings (see chapter 2). The country was unified for the first time by Emperor Gia Long in 1802 and was named Vietnam. Because France conquered Vietnam in three different stages and later tried through official policies to submerge the nationalist identity and spirit of the Vietnamese people, the French referred to the three regions only by the names of their administrative units, insisting also that these corresponded to three separate cultural entities. Cochin China in the south was a French colony; Annam, or central Vietnam, with its imperial capital of Hué, was a protectorate; and Tongking, with Hanoi as capital, was regarded as a separate protectorate. The French vivisection of Vietnam was regarded as an insult by Vietnamese nationalists, who vowed to liberate their country from the French (and later from the Americans) and to bring about its reunification as the single nation-state of Vietnam. This they accomplished in 1976, after a relentless struggle lasting several decades.

The Human Fabric and Languages

The Vietnamese

The Vietnamese, who form 85 percent of the population, are a mixture of non–Chinese Mongolian and Austro-Indonesian stock who inhabited the provinces of Kweichow, Kwangsi, and Kwantung before the area was brought under Chinese rule in 214 BC. Further racial intermixture probably came about through marriages between the Vietnamese and a Tai tribe long after the Vietnamese had moved into the Tongking Delta.

The mixed racial descent of the Vietnamese is reflected in their language, which is both monotonic like the Malayo-Indonesian and variotonic like the Mongolian group of languages. It is also influenced by the Mon-Khmer languages in its grammar (no declension or inflection) and even more so in its vocabulary (up to 90 percent of words in everyday usage). Vietnamese owes its multitonic system as well as a large number of words to the Thai language. By the time the Vietnamese came under Chinese rule in 111 BC, they already had a well-developed language of their own. Thereafter, the monosyllabic Vietnamese language drew heavily on the Chinese for administrative, technical, and literary terms. For most of their history, the Vietnamese used Chinese ideographs for writing. In the twelfth century, the Vietnamese developed the Nom characters (literally meaning southern characters) independent of the Chinese. In the seventeenth century, a Jesuit missionary, Alexandre de Rhodes, developed a romanized system of writing. *Quoc-ngu*, as it is called, shows the differing levels of pitch as well as vocal consonant elements by diacritical marks. It was widely adopted for common use in the twentieth century.

The Tribals

Several tribal groups live in the extensive mountainous country to the north and west of the Red River Delta. The Meo, the Muong, and the Tai, all of Mongolian origin, are the most important and numerous. Together, all the tribals account for about 2 million people. The Tai speak languages closely allied to those of Thailand and Laos. Except for the 20,000 Muong, who use a language akin to Vietnamese, the other tribes speak dialects of Tibeto-Mongolian origin. The vast plateau and hilly areas of central Vietnam are inhabited by several ethnic minorities numbering nearly 1 million people and collectively called the Montagnards by the French. Six of the larger groups account for nearly half of the tribal population. These are the Rhade, Sedang, Jarai, Stieng, Bahnar, and Roglai, certainly a heterogeneous people, whose skin color ranges from brownish white to black and whose languages are drawn both from the Malay-Polynesian and the Mon-Khmer groups. They were pushed into the mountains by the Vietnamese moving south.

Traditionally, there is not much love lost between the tribal people and the plains people. Renowned as warriors and as masters of the strategic passes, the tribals have been able to move swiftly across the borders of Vietnam into Laos and Cambodia. They may be fewer in number than the Vietnamese and their weapons far less sophisticated, yet they were never completely subdued by the Vietnamese. Due to their bravery, skills, and knowledge of the terrain, the tribals were wooed by the Chinese as they considered an invasion of Vietnam, later by the French, and by both sides in the recent drawn-out war. The tribals have held all outsiders, including the ethnic Vietnamese, in contempt and have viewed them with strong suspicion. They do not have the Vietnamese enthusiasm for wet rice cultivation, preferring instead to burn the brush on the mountain slopes and resort to dry rice cultivation. Their ways of life, languages, dress, social organization, and house structures have all been distinct from those of the Vietnamese. Generally speaking, the Montagnards have never displayed a high regard for the law and government of the plains people.

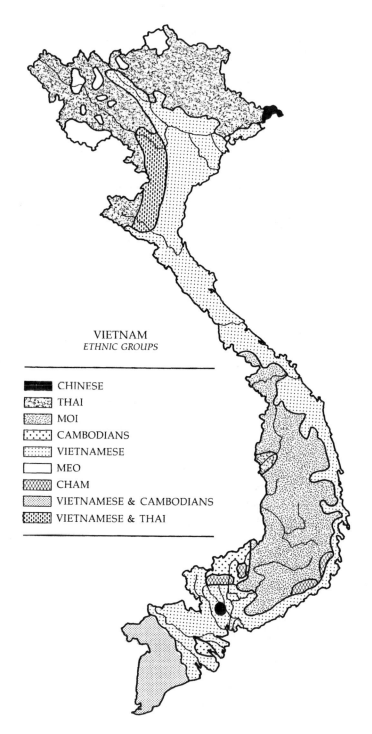

VIETNAM
ETHNIC GROUPS

- CHINESE
- THAI
- MOI
- CAMBODIANS
- VIETNAMESE
- MEO
- CHAM
- VIETNAMESE & CAMBODIANS
- VIETNAMESE & THAI

Vietnam's Ethnic Groups

Despite governmental efforts to better their lot, the tribal population of Vietnam still follows primitive ways of life, eking out a miserable existence exploiting the infertile and inhospitable terrain constituting four-fifths of the country's area. After 1954, the North Vietnamese government introduced several programs to improve their economic condition. This was perhaps because of the valuable assistance the tribals gave to the Viet Minh, who had operated from their hideouts in the mountainous territory of the northwest during the struggle against the French. The present government of Vietnam has a twofold policy toward the tribal population. On the one hand, it allows them autonomy, thus helping them to maintain their ethnic identity through retention of age-old social institutions and practices. On the other hand, it encourages assimilation through education and common participation in the life of the lowlands.

The Chams

Also in central Vietnam are the Chams, numbering about 40,000. The descendants of a former dominant and highly civilized people who controlled central Vietnam for nearly fifteen centuries, they are of Indonesian stock and have reverted to a tribal lifestyle. Their former kingdom, called Champa (or Linyi in Chinese records), was founded in AD 192 by a local official who overthrew the Chinese authority. Taking advantage of the weak Chinese control over Tongking in the declining days of the Han dynasty, the Chams extended northward. Although they controlled portions of central Vietnam at various times, Champa proper extended from a little south of Hué to the Cam Ranh Bay and westward into the Mekong valley of Cambodia and southern Laos. The history of the relationship between China and Champa was one of alternating hostility and subservience on Champa's part. With the reconsolidation of China under the Chin dynasty, Champa sent the first embassy to the Chinese emperor's court in AD 284. But whenever the Chinese authority in Tongking slackened, the Chams seized the opportunity to raid the northern province. During this early period, the center of the Champa kingdom was in the region of Hué.

Champa came under Indian influence around the middle of the fourth century AD, when it absorbed the Funanese province of Panduranga (modern Phan Rang). Funan was an early kingdom based in Cambodia, extending its authority over the Mekong Delta, southern Laos, Cambodia, and Thailand from about the first century AD. The political center of Champa had by then moved from near Hué to the Quang Nam area, where the famous Cham archaeological sites of Tra Kieu and Dong Duong indicate the profound Pallava impact of the Amaravati school of art. In the same area, the most notable archaeological site is that of My-son, a holy city whose art demonstrates Gupta influence as well as that of the indigenous pre-Khmer concepts of Cambodia. After the sixth century, the center of Cham activity moved south to Panduranga, where the south Indian influence increased, as is seen, for instance, in the towers of Hoalai. In the opinion of the eminent French scholar Georges Coedès, it was the Indianization of Champa that lent it strength against its Sino-Vietnamese enemies.[1]

Although the kingdom was divided into several units separated from each other by mountains, the Chams rallied dozens of times in the defense of freedom against attacks by the Chinese, the Vietnamese, the Khmers, and, later, the Mongols. In such conflicts Champa's mountainous terrain and easy access to the sea provided considerable scope for military maneuver. At last, after a millennium and a half of survival as an independent state, the Chams suffered a severe defeat at the hands of the Vietnamese in 1471. More than 60,000 Chams were killed and about half that number were carried into captivity. Thereafter, Champa was limited to the small area south of Cape Varella around Nha Trang. The remnant state lingered until 1720, when it was finally absorbed by the Vietnamese, the last Cham king and most of his subjects fleeing into Cambodia.

The Cham society was and is matriarchal, daughters having the right of inheritance. Following the Hindu tradition, the Chams cremated their dead, collected the ashes in an urn, and cast them into the waters. Their way of life resembled that of the Funanese. Men and women wrapped a length of cloth around their waists and mostly went barefoot. Their weapons included bows, arrows, sabers, lances, and crossbows of bamboo. Their musical instruments included flutes, drums, conches, and stringed instruments. Today about 40,000 southern Vietnamese and about 85,000 Cambodians claim Cham ancestry. Their social organization, marriage, and inheritance rules did not change despite their later conversion to Islam.

The Khmers

Not far west of Saigon and south of the Mekong live about 500,000 Khmers in what were once provinces of the Khmer empire (founded in the ninth century AD) and its precursors, the kingdoms of Chenla (seventh to eighth century AD) and Funan (first to sixth century AD). Like the Chams, the Funanese were of Indonesian race, whereas the Chenlas and the Khmers were kindred to the Mons of Burma. At its height, the Khmer empire extended over the southern areas of mainland Southeast Asia, including the Mekong Delta. The Funanese and the Khmers were extremely active as a maritime commercial power, serving as intermediaries in the trade between India and China. Both were Indianized kingdoms that adopted the Sanskrit language and Indian literature and religions and grafted Indian concepts of art and architecture to indigenous forms, producing (among others) the world-renowned monuments of Angkor. After the sack of Angkor by the Tais in AD 1431, the Khmers became subservient to the Tais but still retained control of the Mekong Delta. With the Vietnamese conquest of Champa and the final absorption of the Champa kingdom, the Mekong Delta region of the Khmer kingdom was exposed to the aggressive Vietnamese policies. The present-day Khmers of Vietnam are descendants of the population that chose to stay on in the Mekong Delta after its conquest by the Vietnamese in the eighteenth century. An indeterminately large number of them were used by the Vietnamese as an advance column in their march into Cambodia in December 1978.

The Chinese

Until the recent exodus, there were more than a million Chinese in Vietnam, mostly in the south and especially in Cholon, the twin city of Saigon (now called Ho Chi Minh City). Some of them are descendants of very old families, whereas ancestors of most others migrated in the wake of the French colonial rule in the nineteenth century, principally from the Canton area. As in most other countries of Southeast Asia, the Chinese dominated the economic life of their adopted country, acting as traders, bankers, moneylenders, officials, and professionals. They maintained close ties with relatives in their homeland. Due to their economic power, they invited the hatred and distrust of the Vietnamese people and governments, including the present Communist government. More recently, they became the target of official persecution in 1978–1979, resulting in their large-scale migration to China and as boat people to other destinations. A large number perished on the high seas.

One of the most persistent themes throughout Vietnamese history is a love-hate relationship between China and Vietnam. If the Vietnamese appreciated, admired, and adopted Chinese culture, they despised, dreaded, and rejected Chinese political domination. Such a mixture of envy and hostility is seen in the contemporary Vietnamese attitudes toward the ethnic Chinese in Vietnam, who have been by far superior to the Vietnamese in trade, commerce, and finance. Historically, Vietnam was the only country in all of Southeast Asia with close political and cultural ties to China, all the other Southeast Asian countries being heavily influenced by Indian culture, at least in the first millennium of the Christian era. As David Marr observed, "The subtle interplay of resistance and dependence . . . appeared often to stand at the root of historical Vietnamese attitudes toward the Chinese."[2]

The long history of Sino-Vietnamese relations was marked by significant Vietnamese absorption of Chinese culture both through imposition and willful adoption. Vietnamese intellectuals through the centuries have regarded their country as the "smaller dragon" and a cultural offshoot of China. Nonetheless, their history has been punctuated by numerous valiant efforts to resist the deadly domination of their land by their northern neighbors. Vietnamese nationalism has taken a virulent form whenever fear of Chinese takeover loomed large. Some of the greatest Vietnamese legends have been woven around the exploits of heroes who led the struggle against the Chinese. It is, therefore, no surprise that a significant section of the historical museum in Hanoi is dedicated to exhibits on the numerous instances of Vietnamese resistance to Chinese domination. The Vietnamese never allowed their culture to be totally overwhelmed by the Chinese, taking care periodically to review, rearticulate, and maintain their identity as a people distinct from the Chinese. The hostility born of long centuries of Chinese domination sharpened a militant nationalism against any alien rule.

Early Vietnamese History

The Vietnamese have attempted to give their country a history as hoary as China's. According to one of the numerous legends concerning the origin of their state, a Vietnamese prince named Lac Long Quan came to northern Vietnam from his home in the sea. He married a princess from the mountains, Au Co, who is also described as the wife of a northern (Chinese?) intruder, on the top of Mount Tan Vien some time around 2800 BC. Instead of the commonplace result of such a union, the princess laid 100 eggs, a son eventually hatching from each. For some unknown reason, the parents separated, the mother leading half the progeny across the northern mountains, where they became the ancestors of the Muong, and the father leading the remaining fifty sons to the sea, where they became ancestors of the Vietnamese. The most valiant of the sons was chosen to be the first of the eighteen Hung kings. Lac Long Quan, a prince of the sea, and Au Co, a princess of the mountains, are regarded by the Vietnamese as their primal ancestors. Does this imply that the Vietnamese were originally of the Malay-Polynesian, sea-oriented race who came to terms with the Mongolians of the southern Chinese plains?

The Dong-son Culture

The earliest name for Vietnam was Van Lang, founded by King Hung. Seventeen kings or generations, all styled Hung, succeeded him. They ruled throughout the Bronze Age, from Phung Nguyen in the Hong River valley (site of the Early Bronze Age, third millennium BC) to Dong Dau (site of the Middle Bronze Age at the midpoint of the second millennium BC) and Go Mun (peak of the Bronze Age, 1200–800 BC) to Dong-son (the most famous site of the Late Bronze Age, 800–300 BC). Although the archaeologist's spade has uncovered substantial quantities of bronze arrowheads in Dong Dau and Go Mun, a fairly centralized state probably did not emerge until the Dong-son period. The Hung era is rightly termed "legendary" by most historians inasmuch as no eighteen kings or generations could have spanned the nearly two millennia of prehistoric development in the Tongking Delta. It is possible that the rule of the eighteen Hung monarchs relates to the Dong-son period, which marked the displacement of the economic and social leadership of primitive agricultural practices by a monarchical apparatus responsible for the building and maintenance of an irrigation system of dikes and canals, providing against nature's vagaries of droughts and floods.

The new state, based on the irrigation system in the region of the three rivers in Upper Tongking, must have produced excess wealth, requiring protection against predator enemies from the exposed borders to the north and the south. Hence the need for extensive use of bronze technology for varied weaponry. By the Dong-son period, the kingdom of Van Lang extended to Hunan in southern China. The capital was moved to Vinh Phu, where the three rivers—Song Da, Song Ma, and Song Ca—meet.

The evidence of the bronze-using Dong-son culture is spread not only along the northern and central Vietnamese coastline but also as far away as Yunnan and Szechuan in China and in Malaya and Flores in the Moluccas. A large number of ornate bronze drums as well as hoes, axes, knives, spears, and plates of armor, among other archaeological artifacts, speak of a flourishing culture noted for agriculture, handicrafts, pottery, silk, music, and maritime activity on a considerable scale.

The Dong-son people were undoubtedly seafarers who built their own canoes for domestic communications but also modest-sized ships for distant trips, guiding their navigational movements with some understanding of astronomy. Their trading contacts with the outside world must have brought them the knowledge of metallurgy. The discovery of the Dong-son culture demolished the earlier theory that bronze was introduced by China (where iron was not used until the third century BC) and iron by India. As for religion, the art of Dong-son demonstrates the practice of ancestor worship and animism. Gods were related to agriculture; temples were built on hills or elevated platforms. The ashes of the dead were buried in jars or in megalithic dolmens, although the people seemed to believe that the dead passed away to some place in the direction of the sinking sun. In their elaborate cosmology, the dualistic elements of mountain and sea, winged beings and water beings, mountain dwellers and plains people provided the core themes. A substantial part of the Dong-son culture eroded among the Vietnamese during the subsequent long period of Chinese rule. Essentials of the proto-Vietnamese language of the Dong-son people have survived among the Muong tribal people, including the Dong-son title for princes—*quan lang*—used by Muong hereditary chiefs.

The reasons for the fall of the Hung rulers of Van Lang, known to us partly through the Dong-son cultural remains, cannot be established by historical evidence. By 300 BC, it seems the people in the region of Kwantung and Tong-king were divided into Tay Au, namely, Vietnamese of the highlands, and Lac Viet, Vietnamese of the plains. They were politically united into the kingdom of Au Lac by An Duong Vuong, about whom similarly little is known. It is not clear whether the Au Lac people were partly descendants of Van Lang or Dong-son or whether they were the Viets, "real" ancestors of the Vietnamese people who around 300 BC, under pressure from the Han Chinese, migrated from their habitat in Lower Yangtse southward into the Red River Delta.[3] Most scholars now accept that the Vietnamese are not descended from one single racial group but are instead a racial mixture of Austroasiatic-Indonesian and Mongolian races.

The capital of the new kingdom of Au Lac was built farther along toward the delta, at Co Loa, about 20 miles north of Hanoi. It was a fortified city, a model for later capitals, with three walls, the outer one nearly 9,000 yards long. Au Lac followed both land-based and water-based techniques of warfare in which the Tay Au and Lac Viet, respectively, specialized. Co Loa must have been involved with some very heavy fighting in its early days, judging from the thousands of bronze arrowheads found in the Iron Age layers under its ramparts. By the time Au Lac was overthrown by the Chinese general Zhao Tuo, it was already well into the Iron Age.

Vietnam Under Chinese Rule

With the first consolidation of the Chinese empire in the third century BC by Shih Huang Ti, the builder of the Great Wall, the Vietnamese living in the Kwangsi, Kwantung, and the Red River Delta areas came under increasing pressure. In 207 BC, Zhao Tuo, who commanded the Kwantung and Kwangsi Provinces, also brought the Red River Delta under his jurisdiction, carving out a wholly independent kingdom called Nan Yueh or Nam Viet (Nam meaning "south"). The capital of the new state was near modern Canton. Nam Viet was thus ethnically a composite Sino-Vietnamese state. Zhao Tuo encouraged local customs of the Vietnamese and promoted intermarriage between the Chinese and the Vietnamese people. The kingdom retained its independence for roughly a century.

In 111 BC, the expansionist Han emperor Wu Ti (140–87 BC) sent his forces against Nam Viet, liquidating its independence and turning it into a province of the Chinese empire. It took a long time, however, for the outlying provinces of the empire to be absorbed into the central administration. In fact, it was not until after the Trung sisters' rebellion in AD 39–43 that the Chinese seriously undertook to impose their culture on the Vietnamese. North Vietnam remained a province of the Chinese empire for the next millennium, until the ouster of the Chinese rulers in AD 939. For administrative purposes, the Han emperors divided Nan Yueh into three commanderies: Giao Chi (or Tongking), Cuu Chan (or Thanh Hoa), and Jenan (or Nhat Nam).

Two essential elements contributed to early Vietnamese social organization: the struggle against nature and the struggle against a mighty neighbor to the north. In the process, the Vietnamese developed into one of the most determined, persistent, and tenacious people anywhere. Frequent flooding of the Red River as well as disastrous droughts compounded the misery of the people of the Red River Delta. In a dry year, water may drop by five-sixths; in a year of heavy monsoons, the floods may raise the water level to forty times the normal height of the river. Early in Vietnamese history, possibly before the Christian era, the Vietnamese developed an elaborate system of dikes and canals and the rudiments of governmental authority to control and channel the supplies of water. The dikes cover an area of more than 1,500 square miles in the Tongking Delta today, assuring the peasants their sustenance but exposing them to the risks of an avalanche if the hydraulic installations are damaged. According to some scholars, the collective work on the building of dams and the regularly compartmentalized field system to provide protection against flooding were techniques introduced by Chinese rulers. They may have also brought the water buffalo and the plow to Vietnam and taught the Vietnamese how to use human excrement as field manure. The Chinese may also have introduced methods of intensive pig rearing and market gardening, which have contributed substantially to the alleviation of the peasants' financial woes in China and Vietnam to this date.

The millennium of direct Chinese rule accounts for numerous Chinese traits in the Vietnamese culture. Even before the Chinese rule began, as inhabitants of the composite state of Nan Yueh or Nam Viet, the Vietnamese had come into contact with the Chinese culture; once Chinese governors and county chiefs gained control, a certain amount of deliberate sinicization of Vietnamese culture took place. Further intensive and extensive introduction of Chinese culture came about in the first century AD, when floods of Chinese refugees poured into the Red River Delta. These were not needy peasants but accomplished scholars and officials who had fallen out with the Chinese government under the usurper Wang Mang (AD 9–23). They became agents of intensive propagation of Chinese culture through the introduction of Chinese classics, Confucian ethics, and Chinese ideographs. Vietnamese was the only language in Southeast Asia that used the Chinese characters and was therefore not alphabetical. Beginning in the fifth century AD, the Mahayana form of Buddhism was introduced to Vietnam by Chinese scholars and preachers, some of whom passed through Vietnam on their way to India for higher studies in Buddhism or for pilgrimage to Buddhist holy places. The Chinese traveler I-Ching attests that Hanoi had become a great intellectual center of Buddhism by the seventh century.

Early Nationalism

China's rule was punctuated by several violent expressions of hostility on the part of its Vietnamese subjects. A number of factors led to intense Vietnamese resentment of Chinese rule. The large numbers of mandarins, who flowed into Nam Viet in the wake of Wang Mang's ascendancy, occupied lands previously owned by high Vietnamese officials. The Chinese also made heavy demands for various tributes, maintained a monopoly on salt and iron, and embarked upon a program of Vietnamese conversion to Chinese culture.

Vietnamese revolts occurred during periods when the central government in China was weak and its authority consequently less effective in the outlying province of Tongking. The first of these uprisings took place in AD 39 and is notable for giving Vietnam two heroines remembered for their bravery and patriotism. A powerful local chieftain, Thi Sach, violently resisted the Chinese policy of acculturation and was executed at the orders of the Chinese governor, Su Ting, who wanted the event to serve as a warning to other recalcitrant chiefs. The Vietnamese reaction was exactly the opposite of what the Chinese intended. The chieftain's widow, Trung Trac, is said to have set aside her personal grief, not even wearing the traditional mourning headdress. Instead, she raised troops, boosting their morale with her oath:

> *I swear, first, to avenge the nation;*
> *Second, to restore the Hungs' former position;*
> *Third, to have revenge for my husband;*
> *Fourth, to carry through to the end our common task.*[4]

She and her sister, Trung Nhi, pushed the Chinese out and proclaimed themselves joint queens of almost all of Nam Viet for two years. It proved a short-lived liberation but was remarkable for its support not only by the nobility but also by the peasantry. When the Chinese retaliated and crushed the revolt, the two sisters committed suicide.

The Vietnamese later deified the two martyred sisters; for centuries, legends came to be woven in their memory as they continued to inspire Vietnamese resistance to alien domination. Many pagodas were built to honor the sisters, the most notable being the Hai Ba pagoda in Hanoi and the Hat Mon pagoda in Sontay Province. The government of Vietnam has proclaimed them national heroes. To this day, Vietnamese girls honor their memory on Hai Ba Trung Day in March, and troops marching to battle have been known to take along pictures of the two sisters to encourage them.

The Trung sisters' revolt was followed by a campaign of severe physical, psychological, and cultural suppression of the Vietnamese. Ma Yuan, the Chinese general in charge of the operation, pillaged and broke up Vietnamese feudal estates, executed hundreds of members of the nobility who were even remotely linked with the revolt, humiliated others, and exiled still others to South China. Chinese garrisons were set up at numerous strategic points to eschew the possibility of future revolts. Nam Viet was divided into three prefectures (*quan*) and fifty-six districts (*huyen*), all under the control of Chinese mandarins. A vigorous campaign was launched to further assimilate the Vietnamese into the Chinese culture through more intensive adoption of the Chinese script and education system, subordination of Vietnamese laws to Chinese jurisprudence, and, above all, enforcement of Confucian ethics of submission of subject to emperor, son to father, and wife to husband.

The Vietnamese proved diligent pupils, mastering the Chinese classics and quickly demanding posts in the civil service. But they were not readily or adequately rewarded for their industry and intelligence. The Chinese never intended to place them on equal footing; moreover, they resented that the Vietnamese scholars, despite adopting all the external trappings of Chinese culture, in fact managed to retain Vietnamese cultural traditions. Among the old customs that persisted even among the sinicized Vietnamese elite during the period of Chinese domination were tattooing, coating the teeth with black lacquer, chewing betel nut, and giving women a high place in society. Although the Vietnamese looked upon such customs as proud symbols of their cultural nationalism, the Chinese regarded them as barbarous practices that justified keeping the Vietnamese out of the Chinese civil service. The numbers of Vietnamese who managed to enter the civil service remained small until the Tang dynasty (AD 618–906).

Such "collaborators" were far fewer than those who consistently hated the Chinese rule and spared no opportunity to demonstrate the sentiment. Rebellions against Chinese domination were staged by nobility and peasantry alike and even by those Vietnamese who were conscripted into the Chinese army of occupation. The Vietnamese have recorded in extensive verse the exploits of their heroes in the struggle against Chinese rule. The Socialist Republic of Vietnam has enshrined the memory of such deeds in a special museum in Hanoi.

Among such revolts or wars of independence, the Trung sisters' rebellion was indeed the most notable. But there were others, too, that held down Chinese troops for long periods. Some of the more important uprisings were those led by Chu Dat in AD 160, by Luong Long in 178, and by Si Nhiep in 187. Si Nhiep had been a governor of Giao Chi under the Han and was successful in maintaining peace during times of trouble. After the overthrow of the Chinese, Si Nhiep made Nam Viet virtually independent from 187 to 226. In the middle of the third century AD, a major rebellion was again led by a woman. In 248, Ba Trieu, the nineteen-year-old sister of a headman in Thanh Hoa, helped her brother raise an army of more than a thousand for guerrilla training in the neighboring mountains. The guerrillas killed the Chinese governor of Chiao Chih (a port in central Vietnam) and resisted Chinese reinforcements for several months. In the end, superior Chinese forces crushed the resistance, Ba Trieu committing suicide on Tung Mountain, where a tomb and a temple perpetuate the inspiring memory of her sacrifice.

In the sixth century, Ly Bi, a Vietnamized Chinese of the seventh generation, led a revolt in Thai Binh Province. With considerable help from Vietnamese aristocracy and peasantry, he brought the country from Thai Binh (at the southern end of the Tongking Delta) to Langson (in the northeast, near the present-day border with China) under his newly proclaimed independent kingdom of Van Xuan. The independence lasted a brief four years before it was ruthlessly ended by the Liang emperor's army in 548. Bi's brother, Ly Thien Bao, continued to resist the Chinese in Cuu Chan. He was forced to withdraw into Laos, where he proclaimed himself the independent king of Dao Lang. Another of Ly Bi's associates, Trieu Quang Phuc, declared himself ruler of the Viets in the swampy area of Da Trach. A decade later, both he and Ly Thien Bao's cousin shared authority in most of Nam Viet. The exploits of Trieu Quang Phuc (also called Trieu Viet Vuong, or king of Viet), who seems to have successfully eluded the Chinese for three to four decades, stand out in the confusing history of that turbulent period.

The Tang dynasty, more powerful and centralizing, was noted for several revolts in Nam Viet and Laos, some of them involving non-Viet minorities. Notable of these was the rebellion of Ly Tu Tien, who in 687 succeeded in occupying Tong Binh and killing the Chinese governor. In 722, the Muong people of Ha Tinh, led by Mai Thuc Loan, revolted against the excessive economic exactions requiring delivery of lychee fruit to the Tang imperial court. The rebellion spread to Thanh Hoa, Nghe An, and Ha Tinh. Although Mai Thuc Loan also secured help from the king of Champa to the south to overthrow the Chinese governor and occupy the capital of Tong Binh, he was eventually defeated by superior Chinese forces and retreated to his mountain base, Ve Son. A citadel named Van An Thanh (Citadel of Peace) and a temple in Nghe An remind people to this date of Mai Thuc Loan's valiant fight against the Chinese.

Later in the century, two brothers, Phung Hung and Phung Hai, led a guerrilla movement in Ha Tay and succeeded in capturing Tong Binh and proclaiming their independence from Chinese control. Nam Viet's freedom under Phung Hung and his son Phung An lasted until 791.

In the last decades of the once powerful Tang dynasty, Nam Viet was attacked and held by the Tais (863–866) from Nan Chao in Yunnan. Although the Chinese rulers of Nam Viet were able to throw out the Nan Chao forces, the Tai takeover revealed the weakness of the Tang dynasty and its inability to control its distant southern province. When the Tang dynasty actually fell in 906, the Vietnamese would no longer recognize the suzerainty of the southern Han dynasty based in Kwantung. At this point, China was undergoing the rule by Five Dynasties (AD 906–960). First in 906, a Vietnamese notable, Khuc Thua Du, and later his son, Khuc Hao, and then Khuc Hao's son, Khuc Thua My, proclaimed themselves governor. The Khuc family did not want openly to confront the Chinese rulers with independence for Nam Viet. They had hoped that the disintegration of central Chinese rule alone would in time confirm Vietnamese independence. In 923, however, the last-named Khuc governor was replaced by a Chinese governor left behind by the invading forces of the southern Han dynasty. Less than a decade later, Ngo Quyen (son-in-law of Duong Dinh Nghe, a general of the Khuc family) truly ended the thousand-year Chinese rule. A brilliant strategist, he is believed to have used underwater iron spikes to wreck the invading Chinese ships. It gave a crucial victory to Ngo Quyen, who proceeded boldly to restore the country's name to Nam Viet, with its capital in the ancient city of Co Loa. The independence he established was conclusive despite the chaos caused by disputes over succession after Ngo Quyen's untimely death in 944. But for a short reinstatement of Chinese rule (1407–1428), the Vietnamese enjoyed virtual independence until the nineteenth-century conquest by the French.

Summarizing the complex Sino-Vietnamese relationship, King Chen noted, "Sino-Vietnamese relations in the past were an enterprise of mutual interest. Politically and militarily, China was for Vietnam an administrative tutor as well as an aggressor; economically, China was a promoter and an exploiter; and culturally, China was both teacher and indoctrinator."[5] It has been pointed out that thanks to the Chinese rule, the Vietnamese made substantial advances in technology and material life: use of the iron plow, the art of printing, minting of coins, silkworm breeding, porcelain manufacture, and a great involvement in international trade.[6] If we keep in mind the Vietnamese drive and dynamism of the Dong-son period before Chinese rule, though, we might well believe that the Vietnamese would have progressed in a number of these or other directions, to import technology and knowledge in a variety of fields of human endeavor on their own. The different Chinese roles were imposed on the Vietnamese, who preferred to be left alone to develop an independent state.

It is difficult, however, to estimate the depth of assimilation of Chinese culture by the Vietnamese. As in the other Southeast Asian countries, in Vietnam probably only the court and the elite were able to appreciate and absorb these alien cultural importations, whether Indian or Chinese. The Chinese mandarin system, with its Confucian values, helped the elite to erect a wall of authority that further buttressed their social and economic position vis-à-vis the peasantry.[7] Most of the hierarchical, bureaucratic positions were filled by the elite through a civil service examination, held as in China on the district, provincial, and imperial levels. The examinations were rigorous, requiring a long period of study of Confucian classics, which were highly regarded not only as scholarly works but also as a conceptual aid to finding solutions to contemporary problems; because only the elite could afford the luxury of a long-term education in the Confucian classics, the bulk of the people remained outside the pale of sinicization. The Chinese language written in Chinese characters remained the administrative and literary language of the elite. The masses retained the Vietnamese language, customs, and religious beliefs rooted in animism and ancestor worship. Vietnamese villages, with their closely knit families, helped preserve the distinct culture and remained firmly resistant to outside influences.

Yet the sinicization of the Vietnamese elite resulted in their desire and ability to acquire and retain their independence from China. As Joseph Buttinger put it, "The more they [the Vietnamese] absorbed of the skills, customs, ideas of the Chinese, the smaller grew the likelihood of their ever becoming part of the Chinese people. In fact, it was during the centuries of intensive efforts to turn them into Chinese that the Vietnamese came into their own as a separate people, with political and cultural aspects of their own."[8]

The phenomenon was not unlike what took place in the nineteenth and twentieth centuries, when Asian nationalism grew in the face of Western attempts to westernize the colonial peoples. Chinese rule and intensive efforts to sinicize promoted Vietnamese nationalism. Throughout its history, Vietnamese culture remained distinct enough for the Vietnamese people to resent and revolt against China's political domination.

CHAPTER 2

A Millennium of Freedom

In the tenth century, taking advantage of the fall of the once powerful Tang dynasty, the Vietnamese declared the establishment of an independent kingdom. Between AD 939 and the imposition of French colonial government in the nineteenth century, Vietnam enjoyed a thousand years of freedom from alien rule. The only exception was a short period of twenty-one years from 1407 to 1428, when the Ming rulers of China overran Vietnam and again brought it under direct Chinese control. Because the millennium of freedom from foreign domination followed a millennium of intensely hated Chinese rule, one would naturally have expected a revulsion for Chinese political and cultural institutions in the new era of freedom. The reaction was, however, mixed, not unlike what Westerners witnessed in the postcolonial, independent states of Asia and Africa, where a strong revival of indigenous values, traditions, and development of political culture took place within the general constitutional, administrative, economic, educational, and military frameworks inherited from the erstwhile colonial rulers.

As a mark of political expediency, Vietnam maintained formal though nominal links with the Chinese empire during the period by sending triennial tribute to the Chinese court through 1885. The expediency can be explained on several grounds. First, the long Chinese rule, particularly the liberal phase toward its end, had produced a Chinese-Vietnamese aristocracy with intellectual and institutional loyalties to a Confucian court. Such an elite perceived its vested interests to be more secure within the Chinese political system to which

19

they were by then accustomed than in a completely independent monarchy without any links whatever with the Chinese empire. Second, the new Vietnamese state had reason to be concerned about potential attacks from the Tai state of Nan Chao (in Yunnan), which had overrun Tongking in the eighth and ninth centuries AD while the latter was still under Chinese rule. Tongking had also suffered from a maritime invasion from the south, from the Sailendra kingdom of Java in the eighth century. And then there was Champa, the perpetual thorn in the Vietnamese side. The Vietnamese rulers believed that a Chinese connection established through the tributary overlord-vassal relationship would serve as a deterrent against any potential aggressive designs of its enemies, particularly the Tais.

The overlord-vassal relationship did not, as in Europe, necessarily obligate the vassal to send troops or funds to help the military adventures of the overlord. It did not really diminish independence except in a legal, formalistic sense. Yet the benefits of deterrence were real because a vassal could appeal to his overlord for assistance in times of need. Thus as late as 1884, when the monarchy based in Hué in central Vietnam was threatened by the French, the Vietnamese emperor appealed to the Chinese emperor, who sent his forces across the southern border to fight the French at Langson.

After the Vietnamese won their independence in 939, the leader of the independence movement, Ngo Quyen, moved the capital of his new kingdom to Co Loa (upstream from Hanoi), the base of the ancient kingdom of Au Lac. The decision to relocate the capital reflected the intense nationalist shift of the new leadership of Vietnam. The new kingdom was, however, plagued by internal conflicts from the very beginning because of rival claims to the throne made by ambitious chieftains. The first seventy years of independence saw the rise and fall of three dynasties, each of them founded by a man of great vigor and dynamism, who was, however, not followed by equally competent successors. Ngo Quyen, who was responsible for pushing out the Chinese rulers, lived for only five years thereafter. He had not had much opportunity to consolidate his kingdom and establish an institutional structure that would balance and contain the ambitions of numerous feudal lords. Twelve warlords divided the country among themselves not long after his death. It was reunited only in 968 by Dinh Bo Linh.

Dinh Bo Linh came from a peasant background and was by contemporary accounts a forceful person who put down the various ambitious and greedy feudal nobles, consolidated his kingdom, and called it Dai Co Viet, "country of the great Viet people." He tried everything possible to unify his people. To end the challenge to the country's integrity, it is said, he threw some of the recalcitrant nobles into cauldrons of boiling oil or to be devoured by his tigers. Unfortunately, Dinh Bo Linh, too, died early. His family having been murdered by certain nobles, the only surviving member was a six-year-old boy king; in 980 he was overthrown by the army chief Le Hoan, who ruled Dai Co Viet until 1004.

One significant legacy of Dinh Bo Linh was the triennial tribute to the Sung emperor of China in return for assurance that China would not interfere in Vietnam's internal affairs. Though this made him a vassal, Dinh Bo Linh still wanted to be designated emperor (*de* in Vietnamese, *ti* in Chinese). The Chinese preferred that the Vietnamese monarch be called governor. Realizing that it would be difficult if not impossible to reestablish control over their southern province, the Chinese finally agreed to a compromise: The Vietnamese ruler would be designated a vassal king of China; he could style himself emperor in relation to his own subjects and in dealing with his vassals.

Both the Ly (1010–1225) and the Tran (1225–1400) dynasties had excellent rulers, at least for the first hundred years of each dynasty. Several of the rulers had long reigns, the first four Ly kings ruling for a total of 117 years. The Ly rulers moved the capital to Thang Long (present-day Hanoi), renamed their kingdom Dai Viet, and gave it a strong centralized government. In order to facilitate closer administrative ties, a network of roads linking the provincial capitals to the royal capital was built by 1044. A postal courier service was also established by the middle of the century.

Although Vietnam had become an independent monarchy in the tenth century, it was only in the first half of the following century that major institutional changes came about. The power of the court and the civilization that the Ly dynasty created lasted for 400 years. The Ly rulers set up an elaborate apparatus to promote the Confucian cult at the court. During the last quarter of the eleventh century, they established a Confucian Temple of Literature and the Han-Lin Academy for Study in Confucianism at the highest level. In 1076, the national college was founded to train civil servants. Only scholars well versed in Confucian classics were able to pass the examinations. The principles guiding the government, then, were Confucian, and the mandarins who were regarded as social and intellectual leaders would, through their personal example, propagate Confucian values among the Vietnamese elite. The Ly rulers adopted the Chinese model of hierarchical bureaucracy in 1089, creating nine levels of civil and military officials. Thus, despite strong political hostility toward the Chinese, the Vietnamese rulers deliberately set their nation on a course of sinicization.

The Tran dynasty produced a number of great rulers, the most notable being Tran Thai Tong (1225–1258). The many innovative administrative, agrarian, and economic measures he introduced were extended more or less along the same continuum by his successors. Tran Thai Tong reinforced the Confucian-based civil service examination after the Chinese model, consolidated the hierarchy, and glorified it further by creating new, more impressive bureaucratic titles. He divided the kingdom into twelve provinces ably administered by scholar-officials. Tran Thai Tong revamped the taxation system by categorizing rice fields according to quality and imposing a land tax. Additionally, he introduced a poll tax payable by landowners. During his reign and throughout most of the Tran dynasty, public works were energetically pursued, embankments being constructed all along the Red River, down to where it emptied into the sea. Many other irrigation and water-control projects were undertaken to assure good crops and general prosperity.

A mighty achievement toward the end of Tran Thai Tong's rule was the repulsion of the Mongol invasion. In a bid to conquer all of China, the Mongols had taken over the southern province of Yunnan in 1253. In order to consolidate their southern flank against the Sung dynasty's armies, the Mongols sent ambassadors to Burma and Dai Viet demanding tribute. Both countries refused to recognize the rising Mongol political power, and Tran Thai Tong imprisoned the ambassadors. In retribution, the Mongol armies, under the leadership of Uriyangadai, swooped down and reached the Vietnamese capital in 1257. At this point, Tran Thai Tong and his heir apparent, Tran Thanh Tong, pushed the Mongols across the borders into China.

Mongols Invade Vietnam and Champa

After the conquest of China in 1279, the Mongol emperors became heirs to Chinese culture as well as Chinese political traditions. They followed the age-old policy of keeping a close watch on neighboring countries to see that they would remain weak and fragmented, never strong enough to attack China. They enforced the tributary system and at times insisted on a visit, in person, by the vassal kings at the court in Beijing (which the Mongols established as their capital). Most of the Southeast Asian monarchs lent a grudging cooperation. Champa was the most recalcitrant on mainland Southeast Asia; the Cham king, Indravarman V, sent tribute to Beijing but did not comply with the Chinese emperor's invitation to appear in person. Even the visit of the great Mongol general Sogetu, sent by the Chinese emperor to the Champa court in 1281, failed to persuade the Cham king to visit Beijing. At this rebuff, Kublai Khan sent a punitive expedition under Sogetu by sea because Dai Viet refused to allow Mongol troops to pass through its territory. Fortunately for the Chams, their relations with the Vietnamese were very cordial during the reign of Indravarman V. They perceived the common Mongol threat to their independence and decided to act in unison.

In the face of superior forces, the Cham king withdrew from his capital and for several years engaged two separate Mongol expeditions in guerrilla warfare from his refuge in the mountains, marking a precedent for similar struggles against a militarily superior enemy in recent Vietnamese conflicts against the French and US forces. Indravarman V proffered all kinds of excuses to avoid a personal meeting with Sogetu but showed readiness to send tribute and hold negotiations. In 1285, Kublai Khan sent a third expedition numbering 500,000 men under his own son, Prince Toghani; this time the Mongols traveled by land through the Dai Viet to help Sogetu's naval expedition, which landed directly in Cham ports. The Mongol troops suffered heavy casualties both in the Tongking Delta and in Cham territory. Cham guerrilla tactics and sudden ambushes paid off. The guerrillas killed General Sogetu; Prince Toghani suffered an ignoble defeat. Kublai's troops finally withdrew without getting the Cham king to appear in person at Beijing. Both Dai Viet and Champa, however, sent ambassadors to the Mongol emperor as they had done for previous Chinese emperors.

During the Mongol attack, the Vietnamese monarch vacated his own capital and repaired to the countryside to fight the invaders. Prince Tran Quoc Tuan's valiant exploits are among the most celebrated in the country's history of resistance against China. He repulsed the invaders three times, which has earned him undying admiration and gratitude of the Vietnamese, who still worship him in the historic Kiep Bac Temple in Hung Dao Commune in Hai Duong province. Through an annual celebration there, including a huge procession and a boat race, the Vietnamese recreate the prince's battles against the Mongols. Another major temple dedicated to him is the Phu Xa Temple in Dong Hai Ward in Hai-An district. The proud Vietnamese king refused to agree to Mongol demands that he send his sons as hostages to the Mongol court and supply troops for the Mongol army. Thereafter, the Mongols decided that discretion was the better part of valor and meekly accepted the Vietnamese and Cham triennial tribute in return for peaceful mutual relations.

Fall of Champa

Vietnam's relations with Champa did not always remain cordial. Three provinces to the north of the Col Des Nuages (just north of Hué and south of Vinh) long remained a bone of contention. Even a matrimonial alliance between the two kingdoms (the Vietnamese emperor's sister was given in marriage to the Cham king) in 1306 failed to bring an enduring peace. Finally, in 1312, the Vietnamese emperor Tran Anh-tong was able to inflict a major defeat on Champa, recovering the contested territory and making Champa a vassal state until 1326.

All through the fourteenth century, Vietnam and Champa were continually at war with each other. From 1369—when the Vietnamese emperor Tran

Du-tong died heirless—until the end of the century, the Vietnamese monarchy was beset with instability and palace intrigues that resulted in a series of uncertain successions to the throne. The king of Champa, the famous Che Bong Nga (1360–1390), took sides in these palace plots and attacked Vietnam by sea in 1372, 1377, and 1388, sacking Hanoi on the first two occasions. Champa was able to regain the disputed northern provinces. It would have brought the Tongking Delta under its rule but for a defense organized by Le Quy Ly, an official of Chinese origin who was related to the Vietnamese imperial family. From 1394 to 1400, he served as a regent while his infant cousin from the Tran family was the nominal king. The Tran dynasty had practically ended in 1394 but lingered in name until 1400.

A notable feature of the Tran dynasty was the rulers' tenuous relationship with China—the Trans never enthusiastically served as vassals of the Mongol rulers. In the fourteenth century, in the declining days of that dynasty and the beginning decades of the Ming dynasty (1368–1644), the Vietnamese sent no tribute to China. Champa, however, improved its relations with China largely to buttress its position vis-à-vis Vietnam. Recognized by the new Ming dynasty as early as 1369, the Chams kept the Ming rulers well posted on the succession disputes and rivalries in Vietnam in the last decades of the fourteenth century. The Champa kings openly sided with China in the ensuing Chinese invasion of 1407 because five years earlier the Chams had lost the northern provinces of the kingdom of Quang Nam again to the Vietnamese under Le Quy Ly.

In 1400, Le Quy Ly himself ascended the Vietnamese throne in a brand new capital, Tay Do, which he established in Thanh Hoa Province in the southern part of the Red River Delta. He assumed a new name, Ho Quy Ly. The Ho dynasty became the shortest in the Vietnamese annals (1400–1407).

Chinese Occupation and the Birth of the Le Dynasty

In the fifteenth century, Vietnam once again suffered Chinese invasion and occupation. The early rulers of the powerful Ming dynasty sought to augment Chinese influence in all of Southeast Asia. In 1407, Ming troops of Emperor Yung-lo entered Vietnam on the pretext of restoring the kingdom from the usurper Ho rulers to the rightful rulers, the Tran dynasty. Instead, the Chinese plainly annexed Vietnam to the Chinese empire. Ho Quy Ly and his son were captured and taken to China, where they languished and died. Vietnam witnessed the most intensive sinicization ever, as China made every effort to demoralize the Vietnamese. Chinese civil officials were imported and imposed on the Vietnamese. A Chinese-style census was undertaken to establish the basis both for conscription to the Chinese army and to levy heavy taxes. The Chinese system of *baojia* (collective responsibility) was rigorously enforced. Vietnamese ways of life and religious practices were banned, and the people—particularly the higher echelons—were compelled to adopt Chinese costumes: women to wear Chinese dress, men to wear long hair. The Vietnamese language was not allowed to be taught in schools. Vietnamese literature was confiscated and carried off to China. Those who resisted—about 100,000 Vietnamese intellectuals and artisans—were exiled to Nanjing, where they were drafted to serve the empire. A number of Vietnamese were also sent to various parts of Vietnam to procure precious metals, gems, pearls, and ivory for the Ming emperor. All Vietnamese were treated as suspect and were required to carry identity cards.

Such actions naturally provoked the Vietnamese spirit of nationalism and age-old hostility against China. Vietnamese reaction was swift and conclusive. By 1418, Le Loi, an aristocratic landowner from Thanh Hoa Province, had emerged to lead a guerrilla resistance that ended a decade later in the capture of Hanoi and expulsion of Chinese troops and civil officials. Le's proclamation of independence reflected the Sino-Vietnamese tensions as well as Vietnamese pride and patriotism:

> *Our Great Viet is a country where prosperity*
> *abounds. Where civilization reigns supreme.*
> *Its mountains, its rivers, its frontiers are its own;*
> *Its customs are distinct, in North and South.*
>
> *Trieu, Dinh, Ly and Tran*
> *Created our Nation,*
> *Whilst Han T'ang, Sung and Yuan*
> *Ruled over Theirs.*
>
> *Over the Centuries,*
> *We have been sometimes strong, and sometimes weak,*
> *But never yet have we been lacking in heroes.*
> *Of that let our history be the proof.*[1]

Though Le Loi liberated the country from Chinese rule, he could not liberate the peasantry from want of land and pangs of hunger. Le Thanh Thong (1461–1497) solved that problem by taking territory in the south at the expense of Champa in 1471. The conquest of Champa allowed the Vietnamese to expand first into central Vietnam and then eventually into the Mekong Delta in the eighteenth century. Le Thanh Thong also made Laos (then known as Lan Chang) a vassal of Vietnam. Although the Vietnamese thus received tribute from their vassals, they in turn sent tribute to the Chinese emperors, who recognized them as kings of Annam, the "pacified south."

Le Thanh Thong deliberately consolidated the Chinese system of administration, including its recruitment method, through the competitive, Confucian-style civil service examination. Whether this mode of cultural acceptance was simply designed to keep the Chinese out through flattery or whether it was born out of a genuine belief that such Chinese institutions lent social and political stability to a state will never be known. Under Le Thanh Thong, Vietnam adopted all the traditional Chinese cultural traits, such as language, the art of writing, the spatial arts, as well as Mahayana Buddhism. The central administration was patterned on the Chinese model, with six ministries—finance, rites, justice, interior, army, and public works. The civilian bureaucracy and military establishment were divided into nine grades each. A board of censors carefully watched over the bureaucracy and reported to the emperor any infractions of rules or procedures. The bureaucracy did not reach the village level. Rather, local affairs were managed through a council of notables, whose charge was to maintain order, execute official decrees, collect taxes for the imperial government, and recruit conscripts for the imperial army.

Recruitment to the civil service was dependent upon success in the examinations specially conducted for the purpose. They were based on the Confucian classics and held annually at the provincial level, triennially at the regional and national levels. As in China, the top candidates at the national level were granted an audience by the emperor himself and were given high positions in the administration. Because social and economic status was a factor of administrative rank, Vietnam became thereafter and until the nineteenth century a Confucian state dominated by the mandarins. The cultural impact of the system persisted until modern times. Even after the civil service examination was abolished in China in 1905, the system continued in Vietnam for several years longer. The Vietnamese intellectual elite was drawn from the Confucian-oriented families.

China's intense cultural impact on Vietnam was a mixed blessing. The system of civil service examinations produced an educated elite, encouraged a family-oriented hierarchical loyalty, and promoted a well-regulated mandarin bureaucracy, all resulting in a relatively stable social administrative order. Yet these same factors bred condescension toward people of other walks of life and a tendency to look to the past for precedents and for solutions to problems. The system discounted initiative, originality, and creativeness. The doctrine of the mandate of heaven underlined the ruler's moral responsibility to the people and allowed the people the right to revolt against inadequate or oppressive rule. Unquestioned loyalty to the emperor, father, husband, and older brother were mandatory in "normal times." A way of life and philosophy that regarded non-Confucian outsiders, including Westerners, as barbarians developed chauvinism and parochialism. This head-in-the-sand attitude could contribute only to the stagnation of political and social institutions, as it inhibited the adoption of scientific and technological knowledge from others. Vietnam's (like China's) relations with Western powers in the nineteenth century must be seen against this backdrop of constricting Confucian legacy.

Notwithstanding the administrative framework and the civil service examination that reflected such immense Chinese influence, Le Thanh Thong consciously sought to move away from Vietnam's intellectual bondage to the Chinese in at least one or two major aspects. The Code of Hong-Duc, promulgated in 1483, brought together within a single conceptual and legal framework all the laws, rules, and regulations issued from time to time by previous Vietnamese emperors. Another area of Vietnamese assertion was art. The Le dynasty witnessed a large-scale program of construction of temples, tombs, and ceremonial halls all over the kingdom, notably in Hanoi, Lamson in Thanh Hoa Province, and Hué. These edifices, along with steles, balustrades, and ornamental gateways, still survive, attesting partly to the continuing Ming influence but also to significant Vietnamese variations on traditional Chinese themes. The best example of such Vietnamese artistic assertion is seen at Hoa-lu (south of Hanoi), which had been the capital of the Dinh dynasty in the tenth century.

Vietnam's Partition

The annexation of the former Champa territories made the Vietnamese kingdom an administratively awkward unit. The southern portions of the kingdom hardly felt the impact of the central administration based in Tongking. At the same time, pressures of population in the Tongking Delta and an opportunity to fulfill political ambitions encouraged some Vietnamese princes and generals to move to the new territories in the south. The central government's authority weakened progressively. The reign of the last real Le ruler, Le Chieu Tong (1516–1526), was marked by rivalries for power among three families—the Mac, the Nguyen, and the Trinh. In 1527, the ruling Le family was deposed by General Mac Dang Dung, who seized power in Tongking. The Le family's cause was upheld by a loyal nobleman, Nguyen Kim, who fled to Laos, raised an army there, and in 1533 put a Le prince on the throne in Thanh Hoa. Nguyen Kim died in 1545 and was succeeded by his son-in-law, Trinh Kiem.

This series of events marked the beginning of a protracted civil war punctuated by intervals of truce that did not really end until the middle of the eighteenth century. The long periods of relative peace were made possible by the intervention of China, as Vietnam's overlord. The first such mediation (which the rival parties sought) brought about the initial "partition" of the country in 1540. China recognized the Macs as the rulers of Tongking, but it allowed the Le-Nguyens to make Thanh Hoa their capital and seek their fortunes in central Vietnam. The settlement was not as significant for its lasting value as it was for setting a precedent for Vietnam's future partition. The Mac rulers were stoutly opposed by Nguyen Kim's son, Nguyen Hoang, as well as his son-in-law, Trinh Kiem. By 1592, Trinh Kiem's son, Trinh Tung, overthrew the Mac regime in Tongking and restored the Le dynasty to the throne. He brought the nominal Le ruler from Thanh Hoa to Hanoi, thus unifying the divided kingdom of Vietnam. As the suzerain power, China undid the previous "partition," recognizing the Le dynasty as the only legitimate ruler of all of Vietnam.

In fact, there were two centers of power as before—the Trinhs governing in Tongking (with the Le as nominal rulers) and the Nguyens in the south also ruling in the name of the Le dynasty. The situation long remained fluid and tenuous. Technically, the Nguyens were self-appointed governors of the southern province, slowly carving out a kingdom for themselves at the expense of the Khmers. Yet they regarded themselves as loyal appointees of the Le rulers who were extending the Le empire. The Nguyens were generally well regarded by the Le rulers and, more important, by the people under their charge in the south; but the Trinhs—who had captured all the key posts at the capital, Hanoi (then known as Thang Long)—were considered usurpers. In 1620, an open conflict broke out between the Trinh and the Nguyen forces, the latter refusing to pay the Trinh taxes collected in the south in the name of the Le rulers. A military stalemate was eventually reached. In 1673, China worked out a durable peace. The territory was partitioned. A wall—some called it the "Small Wall of Vietnam"—was erected from the Annam Mountains to the sea near Dong Hoi, very close to the 17th parallel, which marked the dividing line under the Geneva agreements of 1954. The Nguyens were now officially recognized as independent rulers of the territory from Dong Hoi to Cape Varella, or Song Cau. The event ushered in an era of peace that extended for nearly a century.

The Tayson Rebellion

Once the Trinh threat was removed, the Nguyen power grew rapidly in the south. In the early eighteenth century, the Nguyens liquidated the remainder of the old Champa kingdom, thereby reaching the borders of the Khmer-controlled Mekong Delta. No major battles took place for the conquest of these rich and fertile lands. Vietnamese control came about like ink spreading on blotting paper. The Nguyen rulers encouraged their retired soldiers to establish colonies beyond the Vietnamese frontiers in Khmer areas. Minor skirmishes with Khmer authorities produced prisoners of war who, along with weaker ethnic communities, were used to help the Vietnamese cultivate the lands. By the middle of the eighteenth century, virtually all the Khmer territories of present-day southern Vietnam had become part of the Nguyen kingdom.

The last quarter of the eighteenth century was a period of great social and political convulsions for Vietnam. The old established regimes were overthrown in both the north and south. In 1773, three brothers from the village of Tayson in central Vietnam—Nguyen Van Nhac, Nguyen Van Lu, and Nguyen Van Hue (who had adopted the name of the southern ruling family)—raised the standard of revolt. They quickly became dominant in the provinces of Qui Nhon, Quang Ngai, and Quang Nam. The Trinh family ruling in Hanoi (with Le as effete emperor) took advantage of the situation, sent troops southward, and captured Hué in 1777. A decade later, feuds developed within the Trinh family, which gave the Tayson brothers the opportunity to capture central Vietnam and Tongking, eliminate the Trinh, and depose the Le dynasty. By 1788, the Taysons obtained control of all of Vietnam: Van Nhac was proclaimed emperor of Vietnam, with Van Hue and Van Lu in charge of the Red River and Mekong basins, respectively. In a sense, Vietnam was unified under the three brothers, though Vietnamese historians prefer to regard the Tayson revolt as a catalyst for the real unification brought about by Emperor Gia Long in 1802.

The Tayson success was helped by the public's disgust with the nepotistic, corrupt Trinh administration in Tongking and its belief that the Trinhs had lost the mandate of heaven; if in the north the Taysons were hailed as deliverers, however, in the south they were seen as unscrupulous usurpers. They were accused of taking advantage of the tragedy in the Nguyen family—the king having died without leaving an adult heir. The teenage prince, Nguyen Anh, received sympathy and secret support from large numbers of people in the Ca Mau Peninsula, where he had taken refuge. Nguyen Anh's adversity lasted slightly more than a decade. His family's numerous allies eventually enabled him to capture the environs of Saigon from the Taysons. The people believed the mandate of heaven had been passed from the Le and Trinh families not to the Taysons but to the Nguyens to rule all of Vietnam.

Unification and Consolidation

Among the supporters of Nguyen Anh was a French missionary, Pigneau de Béhaine, who regarded Vietnam as his second homeland. In 1787, he went to the court of Louis XVI with Nguyen Anh's son, Canh, to seek military assistance for restoring Nguyen Anh to power. Considering the domestic preoccupation and plight of the French monarch, it was a miracle that a Franco-Vietnamese treaty was signed, providing French military aid in exchange for a grant of monopoly of external trade and the cession to the French of Poulo Condore Island off the coast of southern Vietnam and the port of Da Nang. The French government directed its colonial governor of Pondicherry (in south India) to provide the military assistance, an order he failed to carry out. De Béhaine, however, raised 300 volunteers and funds in Pondicherry—enough to purchase several shiploads of arms. He arrived in Vietnam on June 19, 1789, barely a month before the fall of the Bastille.

French help was marginal to Nguyen Anh's success. Even before its arrival, he had captured Saigon in 1788; when he conquered Hué in 1801 and Hanoi a year later, there were only four Frenchmen in his army. Bishop de Béhaine, who himself participated in the military campaigns, died in 1799. The French helped in the construction of numerous forts, casting better and larger cannons and creating a navy. Vietnamese Communist historians have lambasted Nguyen Anh for accepting even this limited foreign assistance, comparing him with Ngo Dinh Diem and likening the French volunteers of the late eighteenth century to the US military advisory group of the 1950s and 1960s.

In 1802, Nguyen Anh proclaimed himself emperor of Vietnam, giving himself the title of Gia Long to signify the political unification of the Red River and Mekong Deltas. (The title itself was a contraction of Gia Dinh—the name of the region around Saigon—and Thang Long, that of the region around Hanoi.) In the following year, he sent tribute to the Chinese court; for the first time, China recognized the Nguyen dynasty.

Emperor Gia Long (1802–1820) is considered the first unifier of Vietnam. As remarkable a leader in peace as in war, Gia Long reorganized the entire country into three parts and twenty-six provinces. The traditional center of Nguyen power, Hué, became the capital of the kingdom. Tongking was divided into thirteen provinces, central Vietnam into nine, and Cochin China into four. The provinces were subdivided into districts, subdistricts, and villages. Gia Long allowed the Red River and Mekong basins considerable autonomy, a policy reversed by his son, Minh Mang.

Gia Long revived the imperial government as constituted by Le Thanh Thong in the fifteenth century, which was in turn based on the Chinese model. The emperor and six ministers constituted the Supreme Council. The civil service examination along Confucian lines was reinstituted, and a code of laws based on Chinese principles of jurisprudence was proclaimed.

Emperor Gia Long also devoted himself to reconstructing the country, which had been ravaged by three decades of civil war. The most urgent task was to restore the ancient, intricate irrigation system of the Red River Delta. Among his notable public works was the construction along the coast of the Mandarin Road (dubbed Route 1 in the 1950s by US soldiers from California), linking Saigon, Hué, and Hanoi. The road stretched 1,300 miles, which could be covered on horseback in eighteen days. Fortifications dotted the strategic points along the entire route to maintain firm control over most of the country. Communist criticism apart, such remarkable work has earned for Gia Long the undying gratitude of the Vietnamese people as their country's unifier and greatest monarch ever.

CHAPTER 3

The French Conquest
of Vietnam

Despite the long history of French presence in Vietnam, major French territorial conquests did not take place until the second half of the nineteenth century. Like that of the Portuguese, French activity in Asia began under royal patronage and with similar aims: God, gold, and glory. The first French expedition reached Asia in 1601. Two years later, an East India Company was formed in Paris. At least in the initial decades, however, its trading activities did not flourish, owing to persistently successful Dutch raids against French shipping in the Indonesian waters. An additional reason for the French company's failure was its official sponsorship by the royal court, which meant that its fortunes were dependent upon the whims of the reigning monarch and subject to court intrigues.

Vietnam and the French Missionaries

For the first two centuries of their presence in Asia, the French were far more successful in religious activities than in trade or acquisition of territories. In 1615, Jesuits opened a mission at Fai Fo, south of Tourane (Da Nang). Its most illustrious member was Alexandre de Rhodes, who beginning in 1627 spent nearly four decades in missionary effort. A great scholar, his most notable contribution to Vietnam was his invention of *quoc-ngu,* a method of writing the Vietnamese language in roman script instead of the traditional, cumbersome characters. De Rhodes's motivation, like that of many a missionary compiling glossaries, grammars, and dictionaries of different languages and dialects in Asia, Africa, and Polynesia, was to use the script to reach the masses more easily and convert them to Christianity.

De Rhodes had a checkered career in Vietnam. Born in Avignon, France, in 1591, he joined the Order of the Jesuits at the age of twenty and traveled to the East in 1619. Under instructions from the Vatican, all Catholic missionaries going to the East had to land first in Goa. After a short stay in Goa, Malacca, and Macao, de Rhodes received orders from the Vatican to proceed to Japan. While on his way, de Rhodes learned that there was an official ban on missionaries entering Japan. He therefore stopped in Vietnam. In 1627, he received the Vietnamese emperor's permission to work in the north, but by 1630, he was suspected of political links with Western powers and was expelled. A decade later, he returned to south Vietnam and was again expelled for similar reasons in 1649. After three years in Rome, he returned to France and established the Society of Foreign Missions (Société des Missions Etrangères) in Paris. The society sent scores of missionaries to Vietnam who were successful in converting thousands of people to the Catholic faith. By the end of the eighteenth century, French missionaries claimed about 600,000 converts in south Vietnam and about 200,000 in the north, mostly in the coastal provinces.

Successive French governments demonstrated a consistent interest in proselytization, and missionaries generally maintained close links with the French court right up to the French Revolution. As a French historian of Vietnam, Charles Maybon, noted:

> The history of the new Society [of Foreign Missions] is closely associated with the history of French influence in Indochina. One of its founders, Palu, tied the first knot of relations between the French and the Annamese royal courts. The most illustrious of all missionaries was the Bishop of Adran (Pigneau de Béhaine) who officially strengthened these ties: the acts of the Society's members provoked the first French armed intervention in Vietnam.[1]

Even though Bishop de Béhaine was posthumously given the honors due a duke of the Vietnamese kingdom, his role in converting the young Prince Canh during his visit to France was neither forgotten nor forgiven. Vietnamese monarchs no longer trusted the French missionaries. During Gia Long's rule, Christian converts received harsh treatment, their numbers dwindling by 60 percent.

Large-scale persecution of converts and missionaries began in the 1820s under Emperor Minh Mang (1820–1841) and was continued by Thieu Tri

(1841–1847) and by Tu Duc in the early part of his reign (1847–1883). The Chinese experience with foreigners (during the Opium War and its aftermath) and missionaries (the Taiping rebellion) had done little to reassure the Vietnamese court. There was a marked increase in hostility toward Catholics and foreign influences in general. Such an attitude was enhanced by continued missionary involvement in court politics. The close association of the missionaries with the semi-independent, rebellious governor of Cochin China, Le Van Duyet, who attempted to prevent Minh Mang's succession to the throne when Gia Long died in 1820, earned them the extreme wrath of the monarch. The revolt posed a serious threat to Minh Mang because Thailand took the opportunity to send its troops to Cochin China. The real reasons for the revolt were not so much religious as political. Contrary to his father's policy of devolution of power, Minh Mang had attempted to control Tongking and Cochin China from Hué, even though the one was 600 miles north and the other 600 miles south of the capital city. The Cochin Chinese rebellion was a protest against Minh Mang's ambitions. The emperor was, however, a forceful personality in religion and war. He pushed the Thai troops out of Cochin China and crushed the rebellion with an iron hand.

Minh Mang was an ardent Confucian who believed in ancestor worship. Missionaries encouraged Roman Catholics to oppose such practices. In 1833, the French missionary Father Marchand was suspected of involvement in an uprising in Cochin China led by Le Van Khoi. It was no surprise, therefore, that Minh Mang issued a series of proclamations to eliminate Catholic converts and their institutions. In 1825, Minh Mang forbade the entry of missionaries to his country because he regarded them as agents of an alien power and friends of his major political foe at home. Eight years later, an extremely severe decree ordered churches to be demolished and made profession of the Catholic faith an offense punishable by death.[2] Though the order was not literally applied, many Catholics, including priests, were killed. In 1836, almost at the same time the Chinese restricted foreign trade, the Vietnamese monarch closed his ports to European shipping.

If the Chinese experience held lessons for Vietnam, the British success in "opening" China emboldened the French, who employed similar tactics to open up Vietnam by using the excuse of religious persecution. French missionaries had made it a practice to ignore or violate the laws inhibiting travel in the interior of some of the Asian states, particularly China and Vietnam, and carried on their work of proselytization. As John Cady observed, "In the absence of any French Far Eastern commerce to protect, the missionaries constituted the only tangible aspect of national interest with which [French] naval officers could concern themselves."[3] In the 1840s, French merchant ships and the navy, whose presence in the South China Sea had increased following the opening of five Chinese ports, intervened to secure the release of some missionaries awaiting death sentences in Vietnamese prisons. In 1846, French ships blockaded Tourane (Da Nang) for two weeks and then bombarded the port, demanding the release of Monseigneur Dominique Lefèbvre, who had been condemned to death by the Vietnamese government. Estimates of Catholic casualties as well as descriptions of the French bombardment of Da Nang have been grossly exaggerated. Buttinger, for example, wrote, "In seventy minutes, French guns had taken a hundred times more lives than all the Vietnamese Governments in two centuries of religious persecution."[4] According to the US Catholic Digest, "In the persecutions of the last century, tiny Vietnam had 100,000 martyrs, far above any single nation's quota since the early Roman persecution."[5] Such hyperbolized accounts ignore the gap between the letter of the imperial edicts prescribing persecution and their actual implementation. It should be noted that during Tu Duc's reign—when the persecutions had been taken to a higher level through a decree ordering subjects to seize missionaries, tie rocks around their necks, and dump them into the sea—a Vietnamese Catholic, Nguyen Truong To (1827–1871), still served as a high court official. He was able to go with a missionary to Europe, see the pope, bring home Western books, and advise Emperor Tu Duc to institute reforms in Vietnam. He could not have survived if the imperial edicts had been strictly enforced.

Conquest of Cochin China

By responding to reports of persecution of Catholics, the French government of Napoleon III hoped to compensate for its fiasco in Mexico with success in Cochin China. The new French imperialism of the time was widely based on a coalition of diverse interests of the church and traders and manufacturers in search of new markets, and it was aided by the egotistic emperor's lust for colonies to augment national power and prestige. The business interests were aware that their position in Vietnam could eventually give them exclusive access to the lucrative markets of interior China. The opening of five Chinese ports in 1842 and eleven more in 1860 gave equal opportunity to almost all foreigners by virtue of the most-favored-nation clause in the treaties of Nanjing and Tianjin. French businessmen attracted by overseas markets supported the government of Cochin China because a base in Saigon could funnel South China trade from Singapore and Hong Kong.[6]

In 1858, a joint Franco-Spanish expedition proceeded to Vietnam to save the missionaries. In that year, two priests—one French and one Spanish—had been killed in Vietnam. The Spanish quit after the Vietnamese government gave assurances of nonpersecution, but the French continued the fighting for three years, until they secured a treaty from Tu Duc in 1862. The provisions of the treaty revealed the French intentions clearly: The Vietnamese emperor ceded three provinces in Cochin China—including Saigon—to France and assured that no part of his kingdom would ever be alienated to any other power except France, a clause the latter interpreted to mean that central Vietnam, or Annam (as the French following the Chinese practice called it), had agreed to be a potential French protectorate. Tu Duc further agreed to pay an indemnity of 4 million piasters in ten annual installments and open three ports in central Vietnam to French trade. Christianity would be tolerated in the future. Significantly, the treaty gave France the right to navigate the Mekong. Five years later, the French obtained the remaining provinces of Cochin China to enable it to establish full control over the Mekong Delta.

How does one explain French success in Cochin China? Most historians have based their analyses on French accounts, blaming the Vietnamese debacle on the inadequate and inefficient administration in the Mekong Delta. If this were so, it is difficult to comprehend how the Vietnamese imperial court directed a war that lasted more than three years against France, an enemy with far more sophisticated equipment and economic power than Vietnam.

In fact, what made the Vietnamese emperor capitulate in 1862 was the need to divert his forces and attention to putting down a rebellion that had just broken out in north Vietnam under the leadership of a descendant of the old Le dynasty. More accurate explanations have been provided by Bernard Fall and Lê Thanh Khoi. Fall attributed the French success to the alienness of the Vietnamese in Cochin China, which they had "colonized" only recently. In his view, there they were "the least secure in their social structure and institutions." Hence the comparative lack of resistance among the non-Vietnamese population to the colonial penetration in the south; the French found it more and more difficult as they advanced further north.[7] Lê Thanh Khoi, an eminent Vietnamese historian, held that the mandarins hid from the ruler, who was isolated from his people by the high walls of the Forbidden City, immune to "national realities as well as the gravity of the crisis in foreign relations." In Lê's opinion, it was their "blind pride as well as their narrowness of views which bears a large measure of responsibility for the fall of Vietnam."[8]

There is no doubt that along with Burma and Thailand, Vietnam was the most advanced administrative polity in all of Southeast Asia. The Confucian mandarinate recruited through the civil service examination was still capable of governing the country and conducting a war with the French. It continued to govern central and north Vietnam for another two decades until the French brought the rest of Vietnam under their control. Owing to the mandarins' habit of looking to Confucian classics for solutions to the challenges posed by the scientific and technological innovations from the West, a national debacle at the hands of an aggressive, Western power was only a matter of time.

De Lagrée-Garnier Expedition

Undoubtedly the most important provision of the 1862 treaty was France's right to navigate the Mekong, which was believed to originate in southwest China. That, and not the protection of Christianity, was the real reason for the occupation of Cochin China. After all, Vietnamese Christians were not located only in Cochin China. Within four years of the treaty, the privately endowed Paris Geographical Society sponsored the exploration of the Mekong under the leadership of two naval officers, Francis Garnier and Doudart de Lagrée. It is significant to note that the president of the society was Chasseloup Laubat, head of the Ministry of the Navy, who was intent upon securing the interests of the traders. The society itself was a front for business interests. In 1873, in cooperation with the Paris Chamber of Commerce, a Society for Commercial Geography was established that sponsored and financed future explorations overseas. Garnier, then a young naval officer, was a scion of a royalist family who, like Joseph François Dupleix before him in India, held grandiose visions of a French empire in the East rivaling that of Britain. Garnier's consuming personal ambition was born of a sense of manifest destiny that he was the divine instrument for elevating France's declining prestige in the world. He had been administrator of Cholon near Saigon for four years when he volunteered to join de Lagrée on the Mekong expedition.

In its exploration of the Mekong, the de Lagrée-Garnier expedition, which left Saigon in June 1866, soon had to pass through Cambodia. Unfortunately, Cambodia had been in grave political trouble for quite some time, and its kings had appealed to France for intervention. With the conquest of Cochin China in 1862, France claimed to have succeeded Vietnam as overlord of Cambodia. In the following year, the French offered to establish a protectorate over Cambodia, a proposal readily accepted by King Norodom, who had succeeded his father, Ang Duong. A Franco-Khmer treaty was drawn up on August 11, 1863.

There was one major legal hurdle before the treaty could be valid. Norodom had not been formally crowned: The royal insignia was in Bangkok, and the Thai monarch insisted on the coronation of his vassal king at his own hands. If Norodom were to become the vassal of Thailand, the French would not be able to establish a protectorate over Cambodia without Thailand's consent. French gunboats therefore blocked Norodom's way to Bangkok. Thailand then revealed a previous secret treaty between Bangkok and Phnom Penh confirming Thailand's suzerain rights and acknowledging the Cambodian monarch's status as Thai viceroy of Cambodia. The ensuing Franco-Thai negotiations finally produced a treaty in 1867 whereby Thailand gave up all claims to suzerainty over Cambodia in return for French recognition of Thai sovereignty over the two western Cambodian provinces of Battambang and Siem Reap.

Garnier's Tongking Adventure

The de Lagrée-Garnier expedition had reported on the unsuitability of the Mekong as a commercial artery into South China. The frequent waterfalls and gorges in northeast Cambodia and Laos impeded navigation on the Mekong. De Lagrée lost his life in the upper reaches of the Mekong. Garnier managed to proceed to Yunnan and return to Saigon via Hankow. In a two-volume report on his journey, Garnier recommended exploration of the Red River route. He had discovered while in Yunnan that the bulk of the south Chinese trade in silk, tea, and textiles passed through the Red River valley rather than Canton. Garnier argued that the exploration of the Red River route would offer France, in addition to commercial benefits, an opportunity to extend its *mission civilisatrice* (civilizing mission) to the Red River Delta and beyond.[9]

The serious domestic crisis in which France was engulfed following its disastrous defeat by Prussia arrested all plans for exploration in Indochina for some time. By 1873, however, a chorus of mercantile agitators in Paris and Saigon demanded that France strengthen its hold on Indochina and precipitate access to the markets of interior China before the other Europeans in the region did. Three principal actors of the drama to be enacted that year in the Red River Delta were Admiral Marie-Jules Dupré, governor of Cochin China; Francis Garnier; and a French adventurer-trader, Jean Dupuis.

Dupuis had been in Asia since 1858. An extremely able but unscrupulous man, he had established an official arms procurement agency for the Chinese government to enable the latter to suppress the series of revolts in south and southwest China following the Taiping rebellion there. Dupuis's interests soon extended to trafficking in minerals and salt between Yunnan and Tongking, violating the monopoly interest of Vietnamese mandarins in those items. In Hankow in 1868, Dupuis discussed with Garnier the possibility of opening the Red River route to facilitate the flow of trade. Both were eager to "take Tonkin for a French granary and obtain an opportunity to exploit the mines of Southern China."[10] Four years later, Dupuis enlisted the support of the French Ministry of the Navy, which agreed to have "a naval vessel to rendezvous with him off the Tonkin coast and provide him with information and at least moral support in his negotiations with the Vietnamese."[11] While in Paris, Dupuis also met the governor of Cochin China, Admiral Dupré, and apprised him of future plans.

In the decade before Dupuis's incursions into the Red River Delta, the Vietnamese emperor's hold over his northern possessions was at best tenuous. It had taken five years to suppress the anti-Nguyen revolt of 1862 in the Red River Delta, but a series of new disturbances had broken out in the almost inaccessible, mountainous terrain on either side of the Sino-Vietnamese border. Hordes of fugitive Chinese bandits and rebels who had participated in the Muslim rebellions of South China for more than a decade moved across the border, preying on the produce and property of Vietnam's Montagnard population. Two of the largest, best-organized bandit armies were the notorious Black Flags and Yellow Flags, who soon vied with each other for control of the trade and customs revenue collection of the upper Red River valley. Such a local context of "rebellion, banditry and social disorder" was further muddied by the activities of Dupuis, who was determined to open the Red River route to Yunnan to facilitate his illicit trade in salt, minerals, and guns.[12] In addition to some covert support from French officials, Dupuis had a well-trained and well-armed force of 150 men, loaned to him by the Chinese commander in chief of Yunnan.

Dupuis's force clashed with local Vietnamese elements in Hanoi in May 1873. The mandarins there were apprehensive of Dupuis's trading activities because they cut into their monopolies. They refused to allow the Frenchman to proceed upstream on his second attempt to deliver a cargo of salt and arms to China. Dupuis responded by occupying a section of Hanoi with the help of his Chinese troops and appealing to Governor Dupré for mediation with Vietnamese authorities. Unaware of the secret ties between Dupuis and Dupré, the Vietnamese emperor, Tu Duc, also appealed to Dupré to order the French intruder out of Hanoi. This was indeed a heaven-sent opportunity for Dupré, who wanted an excuse to fish in Tongking's troubled waters. He decided to send under Garnier's command a "mediation force" of two gunboats, two corvettes, and 100 men, including sixty marines, ostensibly to evict Dupuis from Hanoi. Garnier had resigned from the navy and, after receiving adequate funds from merchants in France for exploration of new trade routes, had returned to China.[13] He was in Shanghai when Dupré sent for him and entrusted him with the Tongking mission. Ever since he had become governor of Cochin China in 1871, Dupré had harbored an ambition to open the Red River Delta to French influence in order not only to be able to reach South China before the British did but also to help Cochin China's economy, which had been depressed for some time. He was so keen on achieving these objectives that he even disregarded a dispatch from the new minister of the navy and defense in Paris advising patience toward the Tu Duc government and specifically requesting him to abstain from any military involvement. In the absence of a flat veto from the minister, Dupré and Garnier decided to go ahead with plans to occupy the Red River Delta and present Paris with a fait accompli.[14]

Once in Hanoi at the head of a group of forty men, Garnier threw to the winds the assurances given to Emperor Tu Duc that he would evict Dupuis from Tongking. Instead, he joined forces with Dupuis, picked a quarrel with the local mandarins over the quarters provided for his men, and initiated other measures that were bound to infuriate the mandarins. On November 16, 1873, Garnier unilaterally declared the Red River open to international trade and revised the customs tariffs to make them more advantageous to foreigners. Five days later, in a brash action, Garnier stormed the citadel of Hanoi and proceeded to do likewise in all important towns of the Red River valley. Within three weeks, lower Tongking, including Haiphong and Ninh Binh, was under French military control, and Dupuis seemed well entrenched in Hanoi; but the spectacular success was too easy to last long. The mandarins, whose pride, position, and profit were hurt by Garnier's actions, used another group to get rid of him. Garnier had already declared himself opposed to the Black Flags then roaming and raiding the Tongking countryside. The mandarins instigated a Black Flag attack on Garnier. On December 21, Garnier lost his life during a skirmish with the bandits.

It is difficult to know whether Garnier and Dupré were acting on their own or as part of a skillfully disguised scheme of the French government, which could always disclaim the venture if it went awry. Ostensibly, at least, the news of Garnier's undertaking dismayed Paris. France officially denounced his actions, ordered Dupuis out of Tongking, and signed an essentially conciliatory treaty with Tu Duc. Nonetheless, a number of Garnier's objectives had been accomplished: The Red River was declared open to foreign commerce and three ports of the delta were also opened, with a French consul and garrison stationed in each. Both Garnier's death and the episode as a whole, however, were a serious setback to further French expansion for at least a decade.

Completing the Conquest of Vietnam

In spite of the Garnier affair and domestic strife within France, certain groups still advocated expansion in Southeast Asia. Those enthusiastic about increasing overseas markets and desirous of a predominant role in the international competition for colonies demanded immediate French initiative in Asia and Africa. Members of the emerging geographical societies were often the most ardent supporters of such an initiative, arguing that colonization projects would afford desirable outlets for surplus population and capital and help the reestablishment of French prestige and power. These geographical organizations, including the influential Paris Geographical Society, were critical of the lack of support for Garnier and Dupré's intervention in Tongking. They insisted that the area would not only be a commercial asset but would allow the French to pass on the benefits of their superior culture to the "barbaric" inhabitants.

By 1881, the exponents of imperialism had enlisted the aid of the new premier, Jules Ferry, who was prepared to take the risks of pursuing an active and aggressive policy in the Far East. A onetime, self-styled economic liberal, Ferry had changed his views on the value of colonies at the behest of colonial traders and investors interested in opening profitable markets. Maintaining colonies, he had come to believe, "is the best affair of business in which the capital of an old and wealthy country can engage."[15] He emphasized the importance of colonies to French commerce, which was then suffering from the prevailing depression. For his own efforts toward the conquest of the Tongking Delta, he gave another reason: "It is not a question of tomorrow but of the future of fifty or hundred years; of that which will be the inheritance of our children, the bread of our workers. It is not a question of conquering China, but it is necessary to be at the portal of this region to undertake the pacific conquest of it."[16]

The treaty of 1873 gave France the rationale for its subsequent action. The French alleged that the Vietnamese court had contravened the protectorate clause implicit in that treaty by continuing to send the traditional, quinquennial tribute to China. Besides, the Vietnamese mandarins had hindered a French expedition led by Henri Rivière to push the piratical Black Flags out of the Red River valley. The Vietnamese emperor was forced to sign further treaties in 1883 and 1884 that made Vietnam a French protectorate, gave France administrative control of Tongking Province, and turned Hanoi and Hué into French residencies. The powerless emperor appealed to his Chinese overlord for help in stopping further French encroachments on Vietnamese territory.

As the French approached the Chinese borders, frequent clashes took place between the Chinese and French troops. With the defeat of French forces at the border post of Langson on March 28, 1885, the Ferry ministry collapsed. France struck back by attacking Keelung in Formosa, capturing the Pescadores Islands, and blockading the port of Fuzhou, crushing the Chinese navy that defended it. Ultimately, the well-armed French troops overcame the ill-equipped Chinese forces. At Tianjin on June 9, 1885, the Middle Kingdom signed a treaty recognizing the French protectorate over central Vietnam (Annam) and Tongking, permitting French traders in South China, granting preference to France

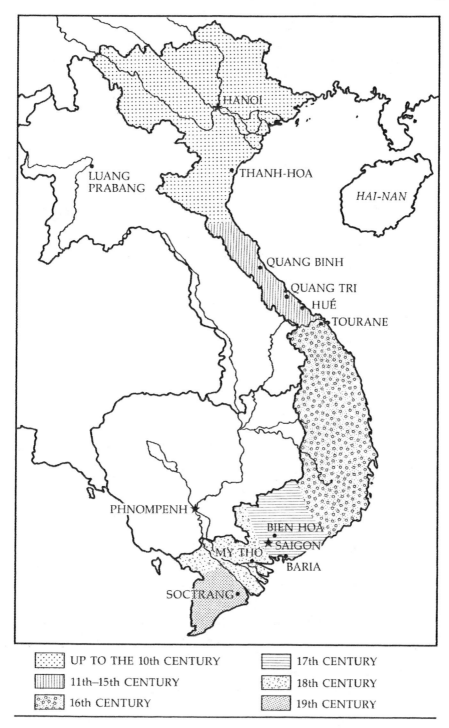

LUANG
PRABANG

HANOI

THANH-HOA

HAI-NAN

QUANG BINH

QUANG TRI
HUÉ
TOURANE

PHNOMPENH

BIEN HOA
MY THO ★ SAIGON
BARIA

SOCTRANG

UP TO THE 10th CENTURY   17th CENTURY

11th–15th CENTURY   18th CENTURY

16th CENTURY   19th CENTURY

Vietnamese Southward Movement

over all other European powers in Yunnan, and allowing France to build a railway paralleling the Red River valley from Hanoi to Kunming. The treaty brought to an end the subordination of Vietnam by China that had lasted nearly 2,000 years—and completed the French conquest of Vietnam.

Although Vietnam had been unified under the Nguyen emperors since 1802, the French divided it into three administrative units: Cochin China, Annam, and Tongking. With the conquest of three provinces of Cochin China in 1862, the French governed the new acquisition as a colony. Its administration was placed under the navy, which had been responsible for its conquest in the first place. Until 1879, its governors were appointed by and accountable to the Ministry of the Navy and Colonies. Meanwhile, in 1867, a protectorate had been established over neighboring Cambodia, where the old court and nobility continued to have nominal authority, though the French nominee at the Cambodian monarch's court exercised real power.

The annexation of Tongking and central Vietnam (Annam) to the French empire was also effected through treaties of protectorate concluded with the Vietnamese emperor in 1874 and 1883. In 1885, they were ratified by China, thereby terminating Vietnam's status as a vassal state of the Chinese empire. In 1887, four French acquisitions—Cochin China, Cambodia, Annam, and Tongking—were brought under a new colonial entity called the Indochinese Union. It created a French governor-general, headquartered in Hanoi, with authority over all four French units. Cochin China was treated as a direct colony under a French lieutenant governor; a French official styled the "resident" was placed at the courts of the emperor at Hué and of his viceroy at Hanoi. A resident was similarly accredited to the Cambodian king's court at Phnom Penh. Although the newly established Indochinese Union appeared to be a combination of direct and indirect rule, in effect, power came to be increasingly concentrated into the hands of the governor-general in Hanoi.

Further centralization of authority over Indochina came about under the strong-willed Paul Doumer, governor-general from 1897 to 1902. A few years before his arrival, the French had brought the kingdom of Laos under its protection. In 1897, Doumer abolished the post of Vietnamese viceroy in Tongking, instead appointing a French "resident superior" to represent that region in Hanoi. Another French resident superior at Hué would exercise all authority in the name of the emperor. A resident was also placed at the court of the king of Laos; there was no change in Cochin China's status. By the end of Doumer's administration, all semblance of indirect rule had disappeared, though the Vietnamese emperor and the kings of Cambodia and Laos were allowed to maintain their courts and advisory councils.

CHAPTER 4

The Nationalist Movement

The Vietnamese are a freedom-loving people who have often had to fight to obtain and maintain their liberty. As Marr observed, "The continuity in Vietnamese anti-colonialism is a highly-charged, historically self-conscious resistance to oppressive, degrading foreign rule. Possessors of a proud cultural and political heritage, many Vietnamese simply refused to be cowed."[1]

Vietnamese nationalism began as opposition to the direct Chinese rule from 111 BC to AD 939 and again from 1407 to 1428. As late as the end of the eighteenth century, the Chinese emperor Jianlong lamented, "The Vietnamese are, indeed, not a reliable people. An occupation does not last very long before they raise arms against us and expel us from their country. The history of past dynasties has proved this fact."[2]

Despite a policy of sinicization of Vietnam, whether enforced by the Chinese rulers or voluntarily adopted by the Vietnamese emperors, Chinese culture failed to obliterate the Vietnamese social traditions, particularly in the countryside, where the bulk of the people lived. Sinicization affected mainly the upper classes. Left to themselves, the villagers continued to worship village genies, ancestors, mountains, and rivers in rites that predated the advent of Chinese culture. Chinese domination never threatened the traditional modes of Vietnamese social behavior as much as did French rule, especially toward the end of the nineteenth century.

The French administration destroyed the Vietnamese peasant civilization that had survived with nominal foreign interference for two millennia. Before the French conquest, each bamboo-fenced Vietnamese village was an almost autonomous social entity governed by a council of village notables who collected taxes on behalf of the central government, assigned agrarian chores, distributed the rice, and dispensed justice. The imperial government intruded only to take census or to recruit soldiers. The rural folk believed that the laws of the emperor were less significant than the customs of the village. The French disrupted the village system, instituting regular registration of births and deaths to allow more accurate tax polls and more efficient tax collection and generally establishing a tight control over fiscal matters. Later they substituted elections for co-optation of council members. The right to vote was based on education in French and high property qualifications, which limited the benefits of the new system only to Western-educated individuals, who had neither a traditional following nor influence among the peasants. The changes made the traditional notables join the ranks of the opposition.

Early Resistance to French Rule

Under diverse leaders, including peasants, resistance to French rule began almost as soon as it was introduced in Cochin China in 1862 and expanded to revolutionary scale after the French conquest of central Vietnam (which they called Annam) in 1885. The pacification program, as it was called, like its British counterpart in Burma, reached its height in 1895 but extended until 1913. In one especially brutal campaign from 1909 to 1913, the French tracked down resistance leaders such as De Tham (the Tiger of Yen Tre), killing them one by one. Peasants sheltered the leaders of the resistance movement, among them the Vietnamese scholar-gentry class. Before 1900, the mandarins were under the illusion that although French occupation of their lands might mean loss of political control, the Vietnamese would retain cultural and spiritual independence. A new generation of mandarins, however, was aware of the pervasive educational and cultural impact of colonial rule; they feared *mat nuoc* (losing one's country) and were taken aback by the attitudes of the collaborator mandarins and the royal family, who had fallen prey to French temptations and imitated their ways. The mandarin class could thus be divided into three groups: those who had collaborated with the French, those who retreated to the villages in a kind of passive noncooperation, and those who battled to bring new meaning and ethnic salvation to their country.[3]

Two major events in Asia changed the direction of the Vietnamese opposition to French rule from an urge to restore monarchy and the status quo ante to a demand for popular democracy either through a constitutional monarchy or republicanism. One was Japan's spectacular rise as an industrially and militarily strong nation. The other was the 1899 Boxer Uprising against Western presence and domination of China, followed by China's reform movement and overthrow of the decadent Qing monarchy. The reform movement in China was led by Kang Youwei and Liang Qichao. The latter's writings inspired the Vietnamese and led them to read and absorb Chinese translations of great Western political philosophers, notably Locke, Rousseau, and Montesquieu. Numerous Vietnamese intellectuals were also influenced by Sun Yat-sen and his revolutionary leadership in overthrowing an autocratic, decadent monarchy in China and introducing a republican government with individual rights to freedom.

Phan Boi Chau and Phan Chau Trinh

The happenings in East Asia had a direct impact on two Vietnamese anticolonialist leaders, Phan Boi Chau (1867–1940) and Phan Chau Trinh (1871–1926). A member of a scholar-gentry family, Phan Boi Chau passed the regional examination in 1900 and soon became familiar with Liang Qichao's writings. In 1902, he published *Ryukyu's Bitter Tears,* which used the transfer of sovereignty of the Ryukyu Islands to the Japanese as a metaphor for the Vietnamese loss of freedom under the French. Two years later, Phan Boi Chau and some of his pupils and associates founded the Duy Tan Hoi (Reformation Society) to foster revolutionary monarchism based on the model of Japan, whose emperor had allowed the development of a constitutional government in response to the challenges of the West. Supported by Prince Cuong De, the group decided to obtain outside assistance to achieve its nationalistic ends. In 1905, Phan Boi Chau made a secret trip to Japan, where he met Liang Qichao and, through him, Sun Yat-sen and other Chinese revolutionaries from whom he learned the techniques of starting a revolution. Liang also introduced Phan Boi Chau to the Japanese leaders, who promised liberal scholarships to Vietnamese students but no military assistance to overthrow the French rule. Soon afterward, Phan published *The History of the Loss of Vietnam,* which went through five editions in China and circulated clandestinely throughout Vietnam. The book had tremendous impact both among scholars and common people in Vietnam because of its nontraditional style and translation into *quoc-ngu,* romanized Vietnamese. Influenced by Phan's work, scores of Vietnamese students enrolled in Japanese institutions, including military academies.

Meanwhile, Phan Boi Chau had made Canton his base for revolutionary activity in Vietnam, establishing for the purpose the Viet Nam Quang Phuc Hoi (Association for the Restoration of Vietnam) in 1913. In 1914, the association passed a resolution to organize a "restoration army." Phan Boi Chau was thereupon put behind bars by the governor-general of Canton at the instigation of the French colonial government. In 1917, the restoration army attempted an uprising on the Vietnam border but failed miserably. Later in the same year, Sun Yat-sen's exertions resulted in the release of Phan Boi Chau.

Phan Boi Chau spent the next few years in Canton and Shanghai. He was responsible for getting forty Vietnamese admitted to the Whampoa Military Academy, where Chinese nationalists and Communists worked together. Despite the nationalist-Communist honeymoon (1924–1927), Phan Boi Chau got into trouble with the Communists. In 1925, Phan Boi Chau was kidnapped in Shanghai, presumably by Communists, and "sold" to the French concession there for 100,000 piasters.[4] Phan Boi Chau was brought to Hanoi and sentenced to life imprisonment, though later, owing to widespread public protests and the somewhat liberal policy of the new socialist governor-general, Alexandre Varenne, the sentence was commuted to house arrest. The great patriot languished and died in 1940.

On the occasion of Phan's death anniversary, October 29, 1990, the Vietnamese government opened a memorial for Phan Boi Chau in Nam Dan, the place of his birth and early childhood. The memorial initially consisted of the house in Dan Nhiem village in which he lived from the age of three to thirty-eight. In 1967, the Communist Party rehabilitated his house and collected his memorabilia to establish "the Phan Boi Chau Relic Site" in Dan Nhiem to mark his birth centennial. Twenty years later, the "Site" was removed to Nam Dan town, his real birthplace and a location less prone to flooding.

For Phan Chau Trinh, however, monarchy as an institution had become outdated. He was a firm believer in democracy and an advocate of a Western-style republican constitution. He led a tax-resistance movement in 1908, was arrested, and was later deported to French prisons, where he remained until 1925. A few months after his release, he managed to reach Saigon, where he perceived that politics had changed so much during his long absence that he could not take part in the nationalist movement even if he wanted to. His death on March 24, 1926, however, unwittingly fueled the nationalist movement. Nguyen An Ninh, a reformer and editor of *La Cloche fêlée*, wrote a eulogistic obituary for which he was arrested and his paper censored. The arrest provoked strikes among students and bank and postal employees. Several hundred students were expelled from colleges and universities for defying the ban on wearing mourning bands to honor Phan Chau Trinh.

Beginnings of the Modern Nationalist Movement

In the second decade of the twentieth century, the purpose and leadership of the nationalist movement gradually changed as the results of French education began to show. Many young individuals from well-to-do families who had been trained in Vietnam and France became nationalist leaders. Large numbers of Vietnamese youths went to China after the revolution of 1911. In 1913, these expatriates instigated small uprisings in Tongking and Cochin China. They had short-lived success despite the assistance of Emperor Duy Tan (1907–1916). In 1916, a more serious revolt was severely suppressed by the French authorities, sending Duy Tan and his father, Than Thai, the former emperor, into exile. That, in a sense, marked an end to the conservative, restorative, monarchical phase of the nationalist movement. Following the exile of Duy Tan, no Vietnamese nationalist presented restoration of the Nguyen monarchy as a feasible alternative to French rule. After 1916, the alternatives were clearly populist, republican, or revolutionary. The immediate inspiration was provided by the Chinese republic, established after the overthrow of the Qing dynasty in 1911.

The shift toward a wider, popular base for the nationalist movement was also helped by the events of World War I. Many of the more than 100,000 Vietnamese soldiers and workers who saw wartime service in France returned home full of new aspirations for freedom that were, in the French view, subversive. Some of them joined the nationalists in making modest demands for participation in the councils and for greater accommodation in civil service positions. These were the moderates in politics, who were further inspired by pronouncements of Western leaders, such as those of US president Woodrow Wilson, whose Fourteen Points included the right of self-determination of nations. Even a would-be radical revolutionary such as Ho Chi Minh was apparently so impressed by the promise of self-determination that he attempted to seek a meeting with Western leaders gathered at the Versailles conference. In the aftermath of the war, frustrated nationalists, who were fascinated with the success of the Russian Revolution, turned to Marxism as a means of liberating their homeland from colonial rule.

Many Vietnamese Communist and non-Communist youths received their initial intellectual, organizational, and revolutionary training across the frontier in China. Although a good number of non-Communist leaders had been educated in French schools in Vietnam and France, almost all the Communist leaders (with the major exception of Ho Chi Minh) were trained in China. The exploits of the Kuomintang (KMT), or Nationalist Party, as well as of Communist leaders in China inspired the Vietnamese nationalists. A more distant but nevertheless potent source of inspiration was India, where a virulent and popular mass movement had been launched by Mahatma Gandhi, challenging the continuation of British rule on the subcontinent. A Vietnamese nationalist, Duong Van Gieu, met Jawaharlal Nehru at the Brussels meeting of the League Against Imperialism and for National Independence in 1927 and attended the meeting of the Indian National Congress the following year.

The 1920s proved to be a decade of tremendous political, intellectual, and ideological ferment over most of Southeast Asia. In Vietnam, a new class of educated young people had replaced the old mandarin class. The French themselves sought to create a new type of Vietnamese, "yellow gentlemen," who would accept French beliefs, standards of deportment, and values. The colonial educational system mirrored metropolitan models for reasons of both pride and pragmatism. The needs of colonial administration as well as those of the new economy, particularly of the French enterprises, required large numbers of French-speaking, indigenous, subordinate staff. The Vietnamese did not, however, limit themselves to such a rudimentary level of education, mastering as well French writings in politics and economics.

The new Vietnamese elite consisted of government employees, professionals, French-trained college and university students, educated landowners, and businesspeople. They were articulate enough to inspire the support of noncommissioned army officers and skilled workers. Vietnamese intellectuals quickly and clearly saw the contradiction in the French profession of the hallowed principles of equality, liberty, and fraternity and their practice of denial of fundamental freedoms in an atmosphere of official repression. They would soon demand important positions in high administration as well as legislation equating the Vietnamese status with that of French settlers. Above all, they demanded freedom of speech, association, and press.

The educated Vietnamese, particularly those schooled in France, perceived the difference between metropolitan France, where even the colonials could enjoy the democratic freedoms, and Vietnam, where they were denied such rights. They also noted that the colonial civil service, which was far inferior to that in France, was marked by unequal pay and unequal standards of eligibility for the Vietnamese, who were discriminated against irrespective of their competence. Vietnamese businesspeople rankled against the government regulations that favored French-owned enterprises over indigenous ones. The lack of representative institutions inhibited the efforts of the intelligentsia and business class to voice their grievances or make suggestions for improvement. The new elite produced a leadership that would articulate the problems of the semiliterate and skilled workers and organize the economically dissatisfied peasantry and, in so doing, promote nationalism among the masses.

The VNQDD

The most prominent of the non-Marxist organizations of the 1920s was the Viet Nam Quoc Dan Dang (Vietnamese Nationalist Party, or VNQDD) founded in Hanoi in 1927. Its organization modeled after the Chinese Kuomintang, it adopted Sun Yat-sen's principles of nationalism, democracy, and people's livelihood and committed itself to overthrowing French colonial rule with the KMT's help. A preparatory conference of the VNQDD had invited Phan Boi Chau to lead the new party. His arrest put Nguyen Thai Hoc, a twenty-three-year-old teacher and revolutionary, at the head of the party.

The VNQDD was dominated by its leftist wing, which used terrorism as a political weapon. A number of such "terrorists" infiltrated the Vietnamese units in the army, inspiring and provoking them to oppose their French commanders. Contemporaneous with the rise of the VNQDD was the growth of a number of Marxist groups—Communists and Trotskyites. They would be brought together in 1930 in Hong Kong by the most dynamic of their leaders, Ho Chi Minh. Even so, at that point the VNQDD held far greater appeal among the masses than did the Communists.

The Uprisings of 1930–1931

On February 9, 1929, the French director of employee recruitment for rubber plantations, indirectly linked to the French government, was killed by a Vietnamese youth, possibly at Communist instigation. The French authorities suspected the VNQDD and immediately imprisoned several VNQDD supporters and launched a thorough but clandestine investigation of the VNQDD's underground activities. Fearing that French retaliatory action could destroy the VNQDD, its leader, Nguyen Thai Hoc, ordered preparations for nationwide insurrection a year later, on February 10, 1930. When at the last minute the date was changed to February 15, chaos broke out. The military garrison at Yen Bay, unaware of the postponement, led its own uprising on February 10, killing French officers. Although the VNQDD expected the Yen Bay uprising to spark a nationwide revolution, only sporadic peasant uprisings in certain provinces took place. The French police easily suppressed the disturbances and essentially destroyed the VNQDD, many of whose members fled northward to China. Others were arrested and executed. The VNQDD underwent gradual attrition in Yunnan, where for some time it faced competition from another non-Marxist Vietnamese organization, namely, Phan Boi Chau's Association for the Restoration of Vietnam. At the end of World War II, a remnant of the VNQDD would be brought by Chiang Kai-shek's troops to Vietnam to fish in the troubled waters of Vietnamese politics. The French destruction of the VNQDD accounted for the lack of strong and effective non-Communist leadership among the Vietnamese nationalist ranks in the post–1930 period, opening immediate opportunity for the Communists and virtually guaranteeing their ultimate control of the movement. The leader of the Vietnamese Communist movement was Ho Chi Minh.

Ho Chi Minh

Ho Chi Minh was born to a modest mandarin family in 1890 in Kim Lien village in Nghe An Province. His given name was Nguyen Sinh Cung, which he changed several times both out of fancy as well as to conceal his real identity.[5] Such aliases included Nguyen Tat Thanh (Nguyen Who Will Succeed), Nguyen Ai Quoc (Nguyen the Patriot), and Ho Chi Minh (He Who Is Enlightened). His father, Nguyen Sinh Huy, was a scholar and a revolutionary who had passed the civil service examination and held the mandarin's title of *pho bang*. Ho's schooling was very sporadic, though records indicate his enrollment at Quoc Hoc (National Studies) College in Hué.

Ho Chi Minh left Vietnam as a cabin boy on the merchant vessel *Amiral LaTouche Treville* in 1913. After many odd jobs in England and France as kitchen help, photographic retoucher, and painter of French-made "Chinese antiquities," Ho established a reputation as a pamphleteer in leftist circles in Paris. During a stay in London (1913–1917), most of it at the Carleton Hotel as an assistant to the famous French chef Escoffier, he studied English and learned the activist ropes as a member of the Overseas Workers' Union, a secret anticolonial body, primarily under Chinese leadership.

In 1919, Ho Chi Minh appeared outside the Versailles peace conference intending to present to the statesmen assembled there his eight-point program leading to the right of self-determination for his country. His demands were a general amnesty for Vietnamese political prisoners, equal rights for French and Vietnamese, abolition of the criminal court misused as an instrument for persecution of Vietnamese patriots, freedom of the press and of thought, freedom of association and of assembly, freedom of movement and of travel abroad, freedom to go to school and to open technical and vocational schools for the Vietnamese, substitution of the system of law for that of decrees, and appointment of a Vietnamese representative in Paris to settle questions concerning Vietnamese people's interests.[6]

Ho Chi Minh soon discovered that the doctrine of self-determination Wilson propounded was to be applied only to East European nations created by the breakup of the Austro-Hungarian Empire. His disillusionment led him directly to the Marxist fold. As Ho himself averred, until then he understood "neither what was a party, a trade union, nor what was Socialism nor Communism."[7] Afterward, he became very active in the French Socialist Party, attending its congress in 1920 and voting with the majority for the Third International and for changing the party's name to the French Communist Party. Yet not until he had read Lenin's *Theses on the National and Colonial Questions* was Ho drawn to communism. To quote Ho, "At first, patriotism, not yet Communism, led me to have confidence in Lenin and in the Third International."[8] One can reasonably assume that it was the French intransigence that pushed many frustrated Vietnamese nationalists into the Communist fold and that most of them, like Ho Chi Minh, remained nationalist first and Communist second.

In 1923, the French Communist Party sent Ho Chi Minh to the Soviet Union for further training at the newly opened University for the Toilers of the East. Ho also represented the French Communist Party at the Peasants' International (or Krestintern) meeting in October 1923. He was elected a member of the executive committee of the Peasants' International for the next eighteen months. From June through July 1924, Ho was a delegate to the Fifth Congress of the Communist International. His performance there caught the attention of the Soviet hierarchy, and later in the year he was sent to Canton, ostensibly as a translator to assist Mikhail Borodin, adviser to the KMT, but really to organize the Communist movement in Vietnam.

A year later, Ho Chi Minh formed Thanh Nien (Association of Vietnamese Revolutionary Youth) in Canton, which had attracted numerous fugitive revolutionaries from Vietnam. Although many of them already belonged to other existing nationalist associations or groups, Ho managed to persuade some of the younger activists, including many members of the Hanoi Students' Movement, to join his organization. For six months, Ho taught his followers Marxist revolutionary techniques. The movement progressed slowly, the major problem being paucity of funds. In order to further finance the movement, some Thanh Nien members resorted to robbery and violence. Several publications, both scholarly and polemical, have charged that Ho Chi Minh himself betrayed his early youth idol, the great nationalist Phan Boi Chau, to the French for a reward of 100,000 piasters, a sum he used for developing the Thanh Nien organization. Many years later, Ho's associates explained away his action on grounds that Phan Boi Chau was a spent force, that he was too old to lead the movement and that his arrest could only help the nationalist cause through the wave of protest and hostility against the French that his arrest would surely arouse in Vietnam.

The 1999 publication of Phan Boi Chau's autobiography clearly removed this slur on Ho Chi Minh's character.[9] Phan wrote his autobiography in 1928 and ended it with the kidnapping incident in Shanghai on that dark day, July 2, 1925, when he arrived by rail from Hangchow at North Station (Shanghai) and was pushed into a "luxurious automobile" by four "Westerners" and whisked away to a French warship in the French Concession and taken to Vietnam. Phan records that the person who betrayed his movements to the French was Nguyen Thuong Huyen, "a man who lived with me and was supported by me."[10] All references to Ho Chi Minh in Phan's autobiography are to Nguyen Ai Quoc, the name Ho used in those years. Moreover, Nguyen Thuong Huyen is not one of the numerous aliases Ho used in his long life.

During the following two years, Ho Chi Minh trained about 250 men, got some of them enrolled in Whampoa Military Academy, and sent others to the Soviet Union to study Marxism. Most of these young men later made up the leadership of the Indochina Communist Party and the Democratic Republic of Vietnam. One of the trainees Ho sent to Whampoa was Pham Van Dong, who had been expelled from Vietnam by the French and who later became Ho's right-hand man and prime minister of Vietnam. In 1927, conflicts between the Chinese KMT and the Soviets obliged many Comintern members in China, among them Ho Chi Minh, to leave for Moscow. Owing to these developments, the Communist movement among the Vietnamese was driven off the course the Comintern had charted.

Two years later, the Comintern sent Ho Chi Minh to Bangkok, where the Comintern South Seas Bureau had been established. Ho worked there among the Vietnamese immigrants for a time, trying to win converts to communism. By that time the Thanh Nien and the small number of Communists in Vietnam itself were divided into several groups. In 1930, Ho fused the three prominent Vietnamese Communist factions in Hong Kong into a single Vietnamese Communist Party. The name was quickly and significantly changed to the Indochina Communist Party (ICP), although there were hardly any Communists then in Laos and Cambodia. Because he was so successful, Ho was appointed head of the Far Eastern Bureau of the Comintern. By 1931, the ICP claimed 1,500 members besides 100,000 peasants affiliated in peasant organizations.

Undeterred by the VNQDD failure and, in fact, to offset the VNQDD's relative popularity among the masses, the ICP decided to exploit the prevalent peasant unrest brought on by successive crop failures and the economic depression. Strikes in plantations and factories were organized beginning May Day 1930, and soviets were established in the provinces of Nghe An and Ha Tinh. Although Ho Chi Minh did not favor an immediate major uprising, advocated by the majority of the hard-liners in his party, he relented. The ICP met the same fate as the VNQDD at the hands of the French police. Hundreds were killed, many more arrested. Ho fled to Hong Kong, where he was arrested by the British police on June 30 of the following year. He was later admitted to a Hong Kong hospital for tuberculosis. In 1933, Ho suddenly disappeared and for the next eight years remained practically incommunicado. Except perhaps for a few senior members of the Comintern, no one knew Ho's whereabouts. During Ho's absence, the French Communist Party acted as the intermediary between Moscow and the Vietnamese Communists.

The two uprisings—the VNQDD's and the ICP's—had a tremendous impact on the Vietnamese masses, whose resentment against French rule multiplied manifold. According to Vietnamese nationalists, more than 10,000 of their compatriots had been executed, tortured to death, or killed with bombs or bayonets, grenades or guns during the two violent uprisings. The bombing of unarmed marchers at Vinh, which took several hundred lives, was unconscionable, as were the several hundred guillotinings without trials. Some French legionnaires were known to have rounded up suspected villagers and shot nine out of ten before interrogating the sole survivor. Prisoners were brutalized in the worst imaginable manner, having parts of their bodies cut off and being left to die. Many Communists were interned in the crowded dungeon cells on the Poulo Condore Island, their ideological beliefs and zest for independence hardened further in reaction to the brutal treatment there.

The two uprisings also affected public opinion in France, leading some liberal colonialists to advocate reforms in Indochina. In September 1932, Prince Bao Dai was brought back from France at the age of eighteen to head a reformed monarchy with a moderate nationalist, Pham Quynh, as his chief of cabinet. That was an opportunity for nationalists such as Ngo Dinh Diem, Bao Dai's new minister of the interior and chief of the reform commission, to push the reformist movement ahead. Diem came from an illustrious Catholic family with excellent connections. He was given to understand by Governor-General Pierre Pasquier that the newly constituted emperor's council would have genuine authority to carry out reforms. In a few months, he was to realize that the French colonials, for neither the first nor last time, could not be trusted. The disillusioned Diem left Bao Dai's cabinet and went into virtual political retirement, whereas the frustrated young emperor sought solace in the life of a playboy monarch, spending more time on the beaches of southern France than in Vietnam—a failing Diem never forgave him.

The VNQDD apparatus had been crushed by the French repression, but the ICP was soon able to reassemble its party machinery, thanks to its superior organization and party discipline. Its greater fortune lay also in the politics of the period of détente (1936–1939) in France, when the Popular Front recognized the ICP. In the early months of 1936, the Popular Front released all political prisoners, including Communists. The other Vietnamese parties remained without a coherent program or organization, but the ICP took advantage of the political situation to organize a broad Democratic National Front, under the leadership of Pham Van Dong and Vo Nguyen Giap, aimed at uniting all social classes and political groups—with the exception of their staunch enemies, the Trotskyites. With the outbreak of war, the Popular Front government fell in France, the honeymoon with the Communists ended, and the ICP was banned. Most of its cadres went underground; some fled to China.

Birth of the Viet Minh

In August 1940, following the lead of the collaborationist Vichy government in France, the governor-general of Indochina signed a general accord with Japan, which allowed the French administration to continue in Indochina in return for placing the military facilities and economic resources (rice, coal, rubber, and other raw materials) at Japan's disposal. Toward the end of 1941, the Japanese used Indochina for consolidating their land and sea forces to launch massive attacks against Malaya, Hong Kong, the Philippines, and Indonesia. The Japanese interned the French in March 1945, just before the war ended. The subservience of the French and their humiliation at the hands of an Asian nation completely obliterated the image of European colonial invincibility. Never again were the Vietnamese to regard the French with awe. When the French returned in September 1945 at the behest of the Allies, many, particularly those who had spent a lifetime in Vietnam, were shocked at the new attitude of insouciance, self-confidence, and challenge among their Vietnamese subjects.

The war made for strange political bedfellows, the Soviet Union and nationalist China joining the Anglo-American forces in a common struggle against the Japanese. Ho Chi Minh was released from a Chinese prison at Chiang Kai-shek's orders to enable him to lead a resistance movement in Vietnam against the Japanese-dominated Vichy government. Military and other supplies were made available to him by the US Office of Strategic Services.

Meanwhile, the ICP's central committee met in southern China in May 1941 and decided to subordinate its plans for agrarian reform and class revolution to the immediate goal of independence and freedom for all Vietnamese. A new organization, the Viet Minh (short for the Viet Nam Doc Lap Dong Minh Hoi, the Vietnam Independence League), was launched in September 1941 to bring all Vietnamese, irrespective of party or ideological affiliation, into a common front to fight for independence. Salvation associations were to be organized throughout the country to encourage popular participation in politics. The Viet Minh, though led by Communists, chose to seek a broader political base of patriotism and nationalism. They had a two-stage plan that called for a nationalist uprising to be followed by a Communist revolution.

It was easier for the Vietnamese Communists to play down their doctrinaire loyalties during World War II and make it appear to the nationalists that they placed nationalist and democratic interests above those of communism. This was because of the alliance between the Soviet Union and Western powers. Parenthetically, it may be observed that to the Vietnamese, the doctrine of capitalism had manifested itself as the control of the economy by white foreigners. Democracy represented to them a vague idea that looked attractive but that, whenever it was tried, had been easily suppressed by the French. Thus capitalism had come to be equated with French interests, whereas the democratic forces had shown themselves too weak to stand up to repressive French policies. A nationalist movement led by anticapitalist Communists who could harass the French through their underground, terrorist, revolutionary techniques therefore won favor with a large number of people yearning for the country's liberation. Further, despite the early intervention on the part of the Soviet Union in the 1920s and 1930s through Ho Chi Minh, the Communists escaped the label of foreigners during World War II because of the peculiar international situation in which the Soviet Union was one of the Allies. The Communist-led Viet Minh thus gained acceptance by the Vietnamese people as the viable representatives of nationalism.

Notwithstanding its perceived nationalist stance, the Viet Minh was not readily acceptable to many non-Communist Vietnamese nationalists. Nor did the Kuomintang believe its claims of being a nationalist organization. During 1941–1942, the KMT rejected the Viet Minh's proposals to join forces against Japan. So distrustful was the nationalist Chinese government of the Viet Minh that toward the end of 1941 it arrested its leader, Ho Chi Minh (then still known as Nguyen Ai Quoc), and detained him in a prison in South China until the end of the following year.

The Chinese government called a meeting in South China in October 1942 to which all Vietnamese organizations functioning in exile in that part of the country were invited. Some Viet Minh leaders (but not Ho Chi Minh) were allowed to attend. At this meeting a new organization named Viet Nam Cach Minh Dong Minh Hoi (Vietnam Revolutionary League) was created by bringing together ten different Vietnamese parties and groups, including the Viet Minh, in the hope that it would organize within Vietnam an effective opposition to the Japanese. The Dong Minh Hoi failed utterly in its mission. At the end of 1942, in the hope that Ho Chi Minh's organizational abilities would make Vietnamese resistance to Japan possible, the Chinese government resolved to release him and make him head of Dong Minh Hoi. Though Ho entered Vietnam in that capacity, he quickly gave up the Dong Minh Hoi and instead mobilized the Viet Minh to provide effective assistance to the Chinese forces struggling against the Japanese. Dong Minh Hoi thereafter retained an insignificant existence mostly in South China, whereas the Viet Minh became the principal organization of Vietnamese resistance against the Japanese and (after 1945) the French.

The Viet Minh employed guerrilla strategies from the very beginning. In December 1944, with thirty-four men, Vo Nguyen Giap formed the first platoon of a guerrilla force. Its weaponry was limited to one light machine gun, seventeen rifles, fourteen flintlock rifles, two revolvers, and a modest amount of ammunition. Within a decade, in time for the battle of Dien Bien Phu, this platoon would grow into a well-trained and well-equipped army of six divisions.

The psychological and military guerrilla strategy used in this early period was similar to that used later to defeat the Americans. The Viet Minh would select for attack small isolated outposts of the French, keeping in mind exactly how many men and weapons awaited them. They would always make surprise attacks with superior numbers and in places where they were sure of success. They were eventually able to arm their growing army with weapons captured from the enemy. This strategy wore out the French and later the Americans, who were unfamiliar with Vietnam's mountainous areas and marshy terrains and untrained in dealing with guerrilla warfare.

By September 1944, the Viet Minh had an army of 5,000 men and the three mountainous provinces of Cao Bang, Langson, and Bac Kan under their control. Ho Chi Minh could clearly see that the day of his country's independence was not far away. From the jungles of northern Vietnam, he wrote,

> Zero hour is near. Germany is almost beaten, and her defeat will lead to Japan's. Then the Americans and the Chinese will move into Indochina while the Gaullists rise against the Japanese. The latter may well topple the French Fascists prior to this and set up a military government. . . . Indochina will reduce to anarchy. We shall not need even to seize power, for there will be no power. . . . Our impending uprising will be carried out in highly favourable conditions, without parallel in the history of our country.[11]

Ho's crystal-gazing powers were later proved substantially right. In March 1945, the Japanese took over the direct control of administration, interning French officials. During those critical months, the Viet Minh received tremendous public support, the situation ironically helped by a gross human tragedy. A terrible famine stalked north Vietnam, killing 2 million out of an estimated population of 8 million. Neither the Japanese administration nor the restored French officials in south Vietnam took steps to rush rice to Tongking. Much of the relief was organized instead by the Viet Minh. Taking advantage of the situation, the Viet Minh quickly established guerrilla bases and administration over three more provinces.

In the meantime, the Japanese had asked Emperor Bao Dai to abrogate the 1884 protectorate treaty with France and declare Vietnam independent. A puppet cabinet was appointed under Tran Truong Kim, a respected old scholar, as prime minister. The Japanese promised to transfer all general government services to the Bao Dai government by August 15. The Japanese also asked the kings of Laos and Cambodia to declare their independence.

Establishment of the DRV

When Japan surrendered to the Allies on August 7, 1945, the Viet Minh emerged from the sidelines to the center of politics. A national congress of the Viet Minh met at once and elected a national liberation committee, which was like a provisional government, headed by Ho Chi Minh. A ten-point plan approved by the congress involved seizing power, gaining independence for the Democratic Republic of Vietnam (DRV), developing the army, abolishing inequitable taxes, promulgating democratic rights, redistributing communal lands, and maintaining good relations with the Allies. There was no mention of any major agrarian reform or nationalization of any kind of property. It was a nationalist, not a Communist, program. On August 25, after the Viet Minh took over Hanoi, Bao Dai abdicated, handing over the sword and seal—the signs of sovereignty—to the provisional government and thus providing the new administration with legitimacy. He was made supreme counselor of state. A week later, on September 2, 1945, an enthusiastic crowd of half a million in Hanoi heard Ho Chi Minh proclaim the birth of the Democratic Republic of Vietnam. On that occasion, Ho Chi Minh read out his declaration of independence, which contained passages lifted directly from the American Declaration of Independence. It was a nationalist victory but with a strong base of power for the Communists inasmuch as ten members out of the fifteen in the new cabinet were Communists, though they did not openly admit their ideological affiliation. Ho Chi Minh himself successfully strove to project the image of a nationalist leader. In order to give his government a nationalist appearance, Ho invited Ngo Dinh Diem, among others, from his hideout in Tongking. Diem was not the only one to refuse to join a Communist-dominated government. The nationalist ranks were thus divided soon after the birth of the DRV.

The new republic was not recognized by any country. The Allies, meeting at Potsdam, had decided to reestablish the status quo ante and to that end asked nationalist China to occupy Vietnam north of the 16th parallel and Britain south of it. France maintained that the future of Indochina was an exclusively French concern. The Chinese forces arrived in north Vietnam in early September; the British troops under General Douglas Gracey arrived in Saigon on September 12. Gracey immediately released the French from prison and put them in charge of the administration of south Vietnam. Liberated France was, ironically enough, planning to reassert its colonial rights in Indochina despite an impassioned appeal to General Charles de Gaulle from Emperor Bao Dai.

> You would understand better if you could see what is happening here, if you could feel the desire for independence which is in everyone's heart and which no human force can any longer restrain. Even if you come to reestablish a French administration here, it will no longer be obeyed: each village will be a nest of resistance, each former collaborator an enemy, and your officials and colonists will themselves ask to leave this atmosphere which they will be unable to breathe.[12]

The Viet Minh could not easily establish themselves in the north because of the presence of the Chinese troops and the members of the VNQDD and the Dong Minh Hoi, who had accompanied them to Tongking. By September 16, Hanoi was divided, the central and southeast suburbs under Viet Minh control and the northeastern parts held by the pro-Chinese nationalists, who also controlled several provinces. In south Vietnam, the Viet Minh, organized as the Committee of the South, acted swiftly against the religio-military sects Cao Dai and Hoa Hao. The French treated south Vietnam as a separate unit, much to the consternation of the DRV leaders, who maintained that Vietnam was a single entity. After the French took over the south, the Viet Minh continued to pressure the government through guerrilla warfare, but their advances were not spectacular until at least a year later.

Ho Chi Minh therefore took several measures. First, on November 11, 1945, to the surprise of the non-Communists, he announced the dissolution of the Indochina Communist Party; it was clandestinely replaced by the newly formed Association of Marxist Studies.[13] Second, he offered the VNQDD seventy seats in the upcoming "free" elections to the National Assembly in January 1946. Power was ostensibly shared in a new cabinet composed of members of the Viet Minh, Dong Minh Hoi, VNQDD, and other parties. On March 6, along with the vice president (a Dong Minh Hoi representative) and minister of foreign affairs (a VNQDD member), Ho Chi Minh signed an agreement with the French allowing a limited number of French troops to enter north Vietnam to replace the Chinese in exchange for French recognition of the DRV as a "free state having its own government, its own parliament and its own finances, and forming part of the Indochinese Federation and the French Union." France also agreed to sponsor a referendum to determine whether Cochin China should join the union and to withdraw its troops gradually from all of Vietnam. The agreement was to be followed by negotiations for the resolution of other outstanding issues.

Why did Ho Chi Minh agree to the return of the French to Hanoi? He acted principally to get rid of the Chinese troops, who had rampaged the countryside in a campaign of loot, plunder, and rape. With their withdrawal, the power of the VNQDD and the Dong Minh Hoi could then be easily broken. Finally, he believed that it would be easier to oust a distant power such as France than the closer, traditionally dominant China. On this matter, Ho is reported to have remarked to a friend, in his customary earthy fashion, "It is better to sniff the French dung for a while than to eat China's all our lives."[14] Besides, he knew he could always blame the agreement itself on his VNQDD and Dong Minh Hoi colleagues—and he did.

The First Indochina War

Meanwhile, the French attempted to strengthen their military and political position. Having no desire to give up its sovereignty, France hesitated, hedged, and finally reneged on most of the assurances. It is possible that the French were reluctant to share power and eventually to relinquish it because the Viet Minh was led by the Communists. Ho Chi Minh tried to convince them that he and his associates were primarily nationalist but to no avail. He also pointed out that the Americans were about to grant independence to the Philippines and that the British were planning to transfer power in India, but the French were hardly ready to give up their empire in any part of the world.

Negotiations between the French and the DRV continued through most of that year, neither side yielding ground and both sides preparing themselves for what seemed like inevitable open warfare. In November, a French attempt to take over the customs department in Haiphong met with Vietnamese resistance. The French demanded that the Vietnamese lay down their arms. When the Vietnamese refused, the French used their cruiser *Suffren* to bomb the Vietnamese quarter of Haiphong on November 23, 1946, killing more than 6,000 civilians in a matter of hours. Negotiations failed, and the Viet Minh attacked the French troops stationed in Hanoi on December 19, 1946. That became a signal for the outbreak of general hostilities between the Viet Minh and France. The DRV leadership and its army of 40,000 trained troops withdrew confidently to the same limestone caves in northwest Tongking from which they had descended only seventeen months earlier. The First Indochina War (1946–1954) had broken out all over Vietnam, and the French had to face the Viet Minh at once on scores of fronts.

The French intransigence had led to the popularity of the Viet Minh, although its Communist nature was known to many Vietnamese nationalists. Having officially dissolved the party in November 1945, the Communists maintained that they were, first and last, nationalists. The devotion and dedication of the Viet Minh cadres to the cause of independence and their ascetic way of life had won over large segments of the population, whose only other alternative was the French-backed, largely self-serving and servile nationalist coalition. Besides, time seemed to be on the side of the Viet Minh. As Milton Osborne observed, after decades of disorientation, the people were predisposed to change.[15] The old feudal values of the mandarinate had been shattered, as had the impression of French invincibility. The new leaders had demonstrated their willingness and ability to work with the peasants to alleviate the problems that had been pressing upon the rural population for generations. During its brief tenure in office, the DRV had grappled with the famine in the north, mobilizing the people to cultivate quick-growing crops on every spare inch of available space. The Viet Minh had also held relatively fair and free elections in central and north Vietnam and won handsomely. It was true, however, that the Communists among the Viet Minh had employed terror tactics against non-Communists within the Viet Minh and even murdered most of the prominent opponents. Quite a few people were turned away from the Viet Minh because of such excesses. Yet the vast majority, at least in Tongking, seemed to approve of the DRV government's actions, and indeed they resented the restoration of French rule at any cost.

On March 8, 1949, France announced the Elysée agreements between French president Vincent Auriol and Emperor Bao Dai under which Vietnam, along with Laos and Cambodia, would be an associate state within the French union. It made very little difference in practice because the major instruments of power were still under French control. Even nationalists, such as Ngo Dinh Diem, refused to cooperate with the new government. France had shown some softness in policy due to the tremendous losses in men, money, and materiel caused by the "dirty war," as it was called in France. The war annually killed as many officers as were produced by Saint-Cyr, France's military academy. French reluctance to transfer real power was in part due to its lingering concept of national glory, in part because doing so would set off a chain of events in France's other colonies, and most important owing to its substantial economic interests, particularly in rubber and rice. But as long as the French showed no genuine desire to part with power, the Vietnamese masses would not endorse their political moves.

The year 1949 must be considered crucial to the Vietnamese freedom struggle. The establishment of the Communist regime in China in October 1949 altered the complexion of the Vietnamese movement. Almost immediately the Communist elements in the Viet Minh asserted themselves, openly admitting their affiliation with international communism. In August 1949, when the Communist victory in China appeared imminent, Ho Chi Minh told an American journalist that "it changed the center of gravity of power in Asia" but that "Vietnam is as always relying on its own strength to win its independence."[16] Similar discretion was not demonstrated by his colleagues, some of whom took measures to strengthen control over the non-Communist elements within the Viet Minh. In November 1949, some of them attended the famous Beijing meeting of the World Federation of Trade Unions of Asia and Australia, at which China's Liu Shaoqi exhorted the colonial countries to adopt the Chinese path in their "struggle for national independence and people's democracy."[17] The Vietnamese Communists returned from China with directives from their Chinese counterparts as to how to conduct their fight for freedom from French rule. In December, the moment of gloating glory came for these extreme elements in the Viet Minh when the Chinese Communists reached the Vietnamese frontier and unfurled the red flag at the international bridge linking Mon Kay and Tunghing.

From that point on, despite Ho Chi Minh's protestations and even genuine reservations, the Viet Minh subordinated nationalism to international communism. The shift did not necessarily benefit Ho Chi Minh's movement; if in earlier years the French had played into his hands and helped him secure sympathy from former colonial peoples, the Viet Minh now played into French hands. At a time when the French were stalemated in Indochina, weakened militarily and economically, with little prospect of extensive foreign support, the Viet Minh made them a present of large-scale US aid against the Vietnamese nationalist movement—not to maintain French colonial rule, which the United States had no particular reason to uphold, but to fight communism. The Indochina War thereafter became part of the worldwide struggle between Communist and "free world" forces.

In January 1950, with the recognition of the DRV by the Soviet Union and China, the cold war lines were clearly drawn. Bao Dai's Vietnam became an outpost of the Western bloc, protecting all of Southeast Asia against eventual expansion by China. US secretary of state Dean Acheson declared that Soviet recognition removes "any illusions as to the 'nationalist' nature of Ho Chi Minh's aims and reveals Ho in his true colors as the mortal enemy of native independence in Indochina."[18] The United States recognized the Bao Dai regime in the hope that the Elysée agreement would form the "basis for the progressive realization of the legitimate aspirations of the Vietnamese people." France was already receiving US help indirectly under the Marshall Plan, thus allowing France to release francs for military expenses in Indochina. But from early 1950, with the signing of a mutual assistance program, US aid to the French effort in Indochina was to be direct. It amounted to $3 billion by 1954. The Indochina situation was becoming internationalized, and for the first time the cold war seemed to extend into Asia.

It is difficult to get through the maze of propaganda and identify the real reasons for the Viet Minh's military successes and the French defeats. Both sides made blunders costing heavy casualties, the French generals hardly knowing how to fight a nonconventional guerrilla war and the Viet Minh forces lacking experience in pitched battles. After the cease-fire in Korea in 1953, the Communist countries concentrated on Indochina. Large amounts of Soviet and Chinese ammunition and weapons came across the northern borders to strengthen the Viet Minh supply position. By early 1954, the French forces were thoroughly demoralized, particularly by the public opinion at home, which overwhelmingly pressed for ending the war. Cabinets fell rapidly until the prime minister of the twentieth government to hold office since the end of World War II, Pierre Mendès-France, who became premier on June 17, 1954, vowed to resign his office if a settlement in Indochina were not reached by July 20, 1954.[19]

Dien Bien Phu

The last French commander, Henri Navarre, the fifth commander in as many years, pledged "to break up and destroy regular enemy forces in Indochina." For years, French military officials had consoled themselves that the ill-clad, "cowardly" Viet Minh succeeded because of their hit-and-run tactics and that in a close battle of the conventional type, which the French armies were trained to fight, the Viet Minh would be crushed. The battle of Dien Bien Phu was contrived not so much by General Giap as by General Navarre. His plan was to lure the core of the Viet Minh forces into a set-piece battle in the remote valley of Dien Bien Phu, close to the Laotian border, deemed strategically very important. He expected the Viet Minh to pass through the valley in early 1954 for a second attack on Laos. With their air superiority and better firepower, the French expected an easy victory and large-scale destruction of Vietnamese forces, which had no aircraft, no tanks, and hardly any means of transport fit for mountain warfare. A major defeat of Giap's forces there would be crippling to the Viet Minh's military effort. The French general had, however, underestimated the Viet Minh's ability to transport large cannons on human backs and ordinary bicycles and to position them in the surrounding hills, besieging the French troops. Logistically, the valley of Dien Bien Phu was the most indefensible site, leaving the French troops directly within the long range of Viet Minh artillery fire. The only way to supply the French troops was by air, which was also made extremely hazardous by the Viet Minh guns directed at the airplanes.

In April and early May 1954, the use of nuclear weapons seemed to US secretary of state John Foster Dulles to be the only way to save the beleaguered French garrison from total extermination by the Viet Minh. But the United States would act only jointly with Great Britain, and the latter firmly refused to go along and thereby open the prospect of a third world war, the action probably bringing massive Soviet retaliation. The situation enabled General Giap to register his greatest triumph at Dien Bien Phu on May 7, the eve of the Geneva conference on Indochina. The losses on both sides were colossal. Of the 15,000 French troops, 1,500 were killed and 4,000 wounded, and of the 51,000 Viet Minh troops, 8,000 died and 15,000 were wounded. The Viet Minh's victory completely demoralized the French troops in Vietnam and the French politicians and diplomats at Geneva.

The Geneva Settlement of 1954

The Geneva agreements of July 21, 1954, temporarily divided Vietnam along the 17th parallel into two zones; the question of reunification was to be decided by a Vietnam-wide election in 1956. The Viet Minh accepted the settlement most reluctantly under pressure from their Communist allies, the Soviet Union and China, who were at the time espousing a global policy of peaceful coexistence with capitalist powers. China had another reason of its own: its historical policy of discouraging political consolidation among its neighboring countries. The Soviet Union was possibly concerned that in the event that an agreement were not reached by the deadline set by Premier Mendès-France, the French might resume fighting, and the United States might enter the fray directly on the French side. To the United States, it appeared the Viet Minh would soon take over the southern part of Vietnam. It refused to sign the declaration of the Geneva conference and proceeded to support the government of South Vietnam, of which Ngo Dinh Diem had been appointed premier on June 16.

The Viet Minh or Communist leaders had urged a division of Vietnam at least along the 14th parallel and wanted the proposed elections for the reunification of the country to take place no later than six months from the signing of the agreements. If negotiations are to some a continuation of war by other means, to the Vietnamese Communists they represented a big power game that had snatched a sure political victory from their hands. The Geneva conference sounded the death knell of French colonialism in Southeast Asia without, however, assuring freedom to Vietnam as one nation and without guaranteeing continued peace to an already war-weary land.

CHAPTER 5

Roots of the Second Indochina War

The Geneva conference that ended the First Indochina War (1946–1954) divided Vietnam at the 17th parallel. It created two zones to which the rival military forces could withdraw to regroup. The partition was to be temporary, for two years, at the end of which elections were to be held to reunify the country. The implementation of the Geneva agreements, including the elections, was to be supervised by an International Control Commission under Indian chairmanship, with pro-West Canada and Communist Poland as members.[1] The success of the commission's work depended on the cooperation of the governments of North and South Vietnam. Great Britain and the Soviet Union acted as cochairs of the Geneva conference to whom the International Control Commission reported periodically.

South Vietnam After the Geneva Conference

US Reaction to the Geneva Agreements

The United States and the new government of South Vietnam had refused to sign the Geneva agreements, though at Geneva the United States said that it would "not use force to disturb the Geneva settlement"; that instead it would seek "to achieve unity through free elections, supervised by the United Nations to ensure that they are conducted freely."[2] US actions in the subsequent two years completely contradicted these statements and were primarily responsible for the unfortunate events of the next two decades in Vietnam. The United States, in effect, encouraged the Diem government to turn the southern zone into an independent state and convert the provisional demarcation line at the 17th parallel into an international border. Further, the US government supported the Diem government's refusal to cooperate with the International Control Commission in the planning of the elections scheduled for 1956. Both the US and Diem governments feared that such elections would favor the Communist DRV. Therefore, those elections were never held, thereby denying Vietnamese the principal goal of their nationalist movement to unify the country. It was the single most important factor for the cataclysmic events of the next two decades in Vietnamese history.

Within days of the Geneva settlement, Secretary of State Dulles pursued the "united action" strategy in a new fashion by getting Britain and France, among others, to sign a pact that would in essence counter the spirit of the Geneva accords. Dulles's efforts resulted in the Manila Pact on September 8, 1954, creating the Southeast Asia Treaty Organization (SEATO). Its name belied its membership; it had only three Asian members—Pakistan, Thailand, and the Philippines—in addition to the United States, the United Kingdom, France, Australia, and New Zealand. Geographically, Pakistan did not even belong to Southeast Asia. The major nonaligned powers of South and Southeast Asia—India, Burma, Cambodia, and Indonesia—opposed the pact. SEATO did not include Laos, Cambodia, and South Vietnam, as this would have directly violated the Geneva agreements; SEATO's article 5, however, named these areas as "protocol" countries to be defended by SEATO powers, thereby legitimizing later US involvement in the Vietnam conflict.

SEATO represented a resumption of the cold war in Southeast Asia. It conflicted with the purposes and goals of the Geneva accords, which, in turn, reflected the five principles of peaceful coexistence contained in the April 1954 Sino-Indian agreement on Tibet signed just before the Geneva Conference began its deliberations on Indochina.[3] The non-aligned countries led by India regarded SEATO as an affront to the nationalist aspirations of the newly independent states, which had successfully sounded the death knell of a century-old French colonialism. The United States was seen as thoughtlessly taking over from where the French had left, inheriting from the latter the odium of a colonial or neocolonial power in Southeast Asia. The United States's global anticommunism and cold war rivalry did not have much appeal to a new generation of leaders riding the wave of a triumphant nationalism, emphasizing their "sovereign" right to determine the policies of the region and develop it in an atmosphere of peace and noninterference by the erstwhile, external, colonial powers. The Manila Pact and, specifically, US policy in Vietnam in the years following Geneva aggravated tensions and frustrated the Vietnamese people's yearning for a peaceful reunification of their country. Writing a decade after the Geneva agreements, a critic of US policy observed,

> In these two years can be found the roots of the critical political military situation as it has existed in Vietnam since 1960. In 1954 and 1955 the United States could still have charted a different course. But once it chose the direction it did in 1954 and proceeded in that direction through 1956, it became a captive of its policy and committed to its continuation.[4]

The Rise of Ngo Dinh Diem

While the Geneva conference was in session, on June 16, the French government, along with Emperor Bao Dai, announced appointment of Ngo Dinh Diem as premier of the "state" of Vietnam. Diem was a mixture of monk and mandarin who hailed from a prestigious Catholic family from Phu Cam in central Vietnam that had converted to Christianity in the seventeenth century. Members of his family had served as mandarins. Diem's father, Ngo Dinh Kha, was counselor to Emperor Than Thai, deposed by the French in 1907. Extremely bright in his studies, Diem, like his older brother, Khoi, had been promoted by the French in the 1920s to the high office of provincial governor. An anti-Communist nationalist, Diem was by no means a collaborator with the colonial regime. In 1933, the French showed readiness to restore some of the long-lost authority of the imperial council and advised the eighteen-year-old emperor Bao Dai to appoint Ngo Dinh Diem his minister of the interior. Diem sought and received assurances from the French that the council would have genuine authority to institute administrative reforms. Disillusioned because the council did not have the promised authority, he resigned his post within three months, much to the consternation of the French, who took reprisals against his family and threatened to arrest him. Bao Dai quickly lost, if he ever had any, interest in administration. He spent the next two decades largely ignoring his imperial obligations.

Diem remained in contact with the other non-Communist nationalists on an individual basis over the next decade but was not active in the nationalist movement. His reputation as a nationalist and a good administrator, however, was regarded important enough for Ho Chi Minh to invite him to join his government in 1945. Diem refused because of the Viet Minh's heinous acts toward his family and hundreds of other innocent people. In August 1950, Diem left Vietnam for the United States, where he lived until 1953, mostly at Maryknoll seminaries in Lakewood, New Jersey, and Ossining, New York.

During that period he acted as a spokesman for the Vietnamese nationalist movement, giving lectures and meeting a number of prominent politicians, including Senators John F. Kennedy and Mike Mansfield and Justice William O. Douglas. In May 1953, Diem stayed in the Benedictine monastery of Saint André les Bruges in Belgium. Around the time of the Geneva conference on Indochina, he and his brother Luyen were in Paris hobnobbing with French politicians. At that point the French government and Bao Dai, independently of the United States, chose Diem to head the South Vietnamese government.

With the partition of the country in July 1954, Diem faced numerous challenges to his authority. For the most part, South Vietnam was under the irregular control of the Cao Dai and Hoa Hao sects, each with private armies estimated at 50,000 men, and the Binh Xuyen sect, which held vice concessions in gambling houses, narcotic dens, nightclubs, and brothels and virtually controlled Saigon's police force. With admirable ability, Diem succeeded in crushing the sects and eliminating all extralegal challenges to his government within the first six months of his administration. His handling of the problem of rehabilitation of nearly 1 million refugees, most of them Catholics from North Vietnam, won Diem international acclaim, notably in the United States. In order to secure his position, Diem held a referendum on October 23, 1955; he received an embarrassing 99 percent of the vote, resulting in the removal of Bao Dai and making Diem president of the newly proclaimed Republic of Vietnam. Diem then announced his plans for election of a "national" assembly on March 4, 1956, which would draw up a constitution for the new republic. He repeatedly repudiated any obligations arising out of the Geneva agreements, including the crucial provision for Vietnam-wide elections for reunification of the country. Recognized by the United States and thirty-five other countries of the Western bloc, the Republic of Vietnam by late 1955 became, for all purposes, an independent member of the international community. From a situation of total collapse of governmental authority at the time of the country's partition in mid–1954, Diem had miraculously emerged as the central authority in South Vietnam.

US Support for Diem

In all these moves, the United States supported Diem to the hilt, parading him as an intense anti-French, anti-Communist, nationalist leader of spotless honesty and integrity. The Americans held Diem as a "nationalist alternative" to Communist Ho Chi Minh. But Diem had been out of Vietnam for so long before 1954 that he had no idea of his people's aspirations in a period of fast-paced political upheaval. His political style, moreover, was as paternalistic and aloof as that of the outdated mandarins, and he increasingly withdrew to the shelter of his "Forbidden Palace," depending for information and guidance on a close coterie of "court" sycophants and even more so on members of his extended family. Diem's popular base was slim, made up mainly of the refugee Catholics who constituted a minority of 10 percent. Most of the southern Buddhist population were hostile to the refugees because of both their religion and their northern origin.

With the advantage of historical hindsight, one can blame South Vietnam's many problems on the United States' unfortunate decision to give its full support to Diem. In 1954, despite the general misgivings about Diem's popularity, the influential senator Mike Mansfield recommended that if the Diem government collapsed, "the United States should consider an immediate suspension of all aid to Vietnam . . . except that of a humanitarian nature."[5] The US Department of State interpreted this to mean that all aid should be given to the Diem government to prevent its fall. On November 3, 1954, President Dwight Eisenhower sent General J. Lawton Collins as his special representative with the rank of ambassador in order to coordinate the work of all American agencies there. Immediately on arrival in Saigon, Collins announced that the United States would give "every possible aid to the Government of Diem and to his government only."[6] On February 19, 1955, Eisenhower formally offered the Diem government unconditional support against its Communist as well as non-Communist foes.[7] From the chaotic conditions of South Vietnamese politics, the United States resolved to stake its policy on the fortunes and whims of one person. That man of destiny or doom, it was not clear at the time, was Ngo Dinh Diem.

Under General Collins, the United States began, in earnest, to bolster the Diem government militarily. He worked the modalities for direct US financial assistance to the South Vietnamese government instead of the previous practice of funneling it through France. General John W. O'Daniel was assigned the task of training and reorganizing the South Vietnamese army, which was to consist of 150,000 regular and 45,000 civil guard. The DRV's complaints to the International Control Commission (ICC) and the cochairmen of the Geneva conference that General Collins's mission was "at variance with the Geneva Agreements" did not inhibit the US program. The United States held that its aid program began in 1950, much before the Geneva agreements came into force. As for training the South Vietnamese military personnel, the United States argued that it was only complementing the French Expeditionary Corps, which had been permitted to continue in South Vietnam under the Geneva agreements.

However esteemed his handling of the rehabilitation of nearly 1 million refugees from North Vietnam (who had felt apprehensive of their ability to pursue their faith under the atheist, Communist regime there), Diem's elevation of many Catholic refugees to high positions in the bureaucracy estranged the majority Buddhist population. At the same time, his aggressive policy against the sects—Hoa Hao and Cao Dai—were praised by many in South Vietnam, though these sects could have helped Diem in his anti-Communist policies. The casualty of all these well-intentioned yet highhanded measures was individual freedom. As Graham Greene reported from Saigon in April 1955,

> The South instead of confronting the totalitarian north with the evidences of freedom, has slipped into an inefficient dictatorship: newspapers suppressed, strict censorship, men exiled by administrative order and not by judgment of the courts. It is unfortunate that a government of this kind should be identified with one faith.[8]

A principal provision of the Geneva settlement that would meet with the aspirations of the Vietnamese who had participated in the nationalist movement against French colonial rule was the holding of elections in Vietnam—North and South—in July 1956 under the ICC's supervision to bring about the unification of the country. The Final Declaration of the Geneva conference required "consultation between the competent representative authorities of the two zones on the subject of elections" to begin a year after the Geneva agreements, on July 20, 1955. While the DRV announced on June 7, 1955, its readiness to hold such consultations with "competent representative authority" in South Vietnam beginning July 20, the Diem government declared on July 16 that it was "not bound in any way by these agreements, signed against the will of the Vietnamese people." Diem refused to talk to the DRV on any subject "if proof is not given us that they put the interests of the national community above those of Communism."[9] Moreover, he wondered how elections would be free in North Vietnam where the Communist government allowed very little freedom to the people. What he ignored was the fact that such freedoms were lacking in South Vietnam as well.

Diem was legally correct about the lack of obligation on the part of the South Vietnamese government to implement the Geneva agreements. He now argued it was the French high command in Vietnam that signed the Geneva agreements and the South Vietnamese government therefore was not responsible for their observance. Furthermore, since in terms of the Geneva agreements, the French high command transferred its authority in July 1955 to the South Vietnamese army, no party to the Geneva agreements was left in South Vietnam. Ignored here was the point that as a successor government to the French colonial regime that had signed the original agreements, the Diem government was bound under international law to accept responsibilities that a successor government has to assume. The United States supported Diem's stand.

Diem did not have the aura of prestige, sacrifice, and struggle against colonialism to match Ho Chi Minh's reputation. Despite his ruthlessness and atheism, Ho Chi Minh gave the impression of mildness and asceticism and was always dressed in simple fatigues and rubber sandals. A fervent Catholic with a monastic background, Diem seemed more a sectarian than a national leader and wore sharkskin and Irish linen suits. Both were bachelors. Having no family ties whatsoever, Ho Chi Minh stood above suspicion of nepotism. He had a reputation for honesty and sincerity and had gained the trust of the masses. Instead of living in the former governor-general's palace in Hanoi, Ho preferred to live in the guest house and keep his same, simple habits. For the avuncular Ho Chi Minh, the nation became his family.

In contrast, Diem had close ties to his extended family, almost equating it with the state by giving family members powerful positions: His brother Nhu and Nhu's wife became Diem's closest advisers. The megalomaniac Nhu was in a perpetual drugged fog (perhaps without Diem's knowledge) and espoused an obtuse philosophy of "personalism." Madame Nhu, who had recently converted from Buddhism to Catholicism, ardently championed her new faith and advocated puritanism in public life. Her extremist policies on religious and secular matters alike alienated large segments of the predominantly Buddhist population. Diem's elder brother, Thuc, was archbishop of Hué, the highest Catholic official in the land; another brother controlled central Vietnam as a virtual personal fiefdom; and yet another brother was ambassador to Great Britain. As the president's family became more and more entangled in governmental affairs, Diem became increasingly isolated from the Vietnamese people. Consequently, he became a prisoner of his family, with access only to such information as they (notably the Nhus) made available. Under their influence, Diem suppressed newspapers, enforced strict censorship, exiled men by administrative fiat, and suspended court judgments.

Communist Rule in North Vietnam

Initially, Hanoi also had to grapple with a host of problems that engendered considerable discontent among the people of North Vietnam. The Democratic Republic of Vietnam embarked upon its promised land redistribution in the already congested and overfragmented Red River Delta, where agriculture had suffered dismally in the final phase of the fighting immediately before the Geneva settlement. Famine could not be relieved by imports of grain because of lack of foreign exchange. The French had removed most of the machinery from the coal mines, which had been North Vietnam's principal earners of foreign exchange. Furthermore, the DRV launched a crash program of building roads and railroads leading to China by using forced labor on a massive scale. All these factors—combined with the most potent of them, religion—helped to swell the flood of refugees from the north to the south. The DRV's efforts to stem the migration had very little effect, particularly upon the Catholics, who had been told in their parishes that God had moved south, where the government was headed by one of their Catholic brethren. Although many Catholics migrated from North to South Vietnam from 1954 to 1955, more than 800,000 Catholics remained in North Vietnam.

In 1956, the land reform campaign, which had been given up in 1955, was resumed with dubious results. Many Communist Party cadres exploited the new land laws as weapons to settle scores with their old enemies or to secure material advantages for themselves. According to the critics of the DRV, land reform became a major terror campaign, taking hundreds of thousands, perhaps as many as half a million lives. The figures may have been exaggerated, though the fact of large-scale peasant discontent and repression was incontestable.

The DRV quickly adopted a socialist system on the Soviet model. In 1955, the State Planning Committee was established, but it was not before 1961 that the First Five-Year Development Plan was launched. The core of the new economic system in the DRV was to be the agrarian cooperative. The basic philosophy seemed to be that the society could move directly to socialism without any transitional capitalist stage. This was because there were few, if any, major Vietnamese-owned capitalist enterprises to be nationalized. Collectivization of agriculture proceeded by definite stages. By the early 1960s, thousands of cooperatives consolidated the traditionally fragmented, small units of land. Most of the cooperatives, however, were not large enough to generate adequate money or labor power for large-scale irrigation projects. In fact, in the initial years the government had to assist each cooperative with a substantial subsidy. By the late 1960s, the small cooperatives were combined into "high level" collectives, providing for common ownership of all means of production and distribution and giving a share to farmers in proportion to their contribution. The high-level collectives controlled far more land, money, and labor power than before, enabling substantial improvement in the irrigational infrastructure. The government established production targets as well as prices for purchase and sale of agricultural products.

Despite such far-reaching, intensive measures, the internal saving capacity of each collective remained very low. Later the government estimated such reinvestment funds to be capable of expanding the cultivable area in each collective by no more than about 2.5 acres. Nor were they enough to buy basic machinery to improve farming in each collective. Except for the half decade after the partition of the country in 1954, the extraordinary political and military situation in which the DRV was involved until 1975 inhibited any sustained effort to implement agricultural reforms in North Vietnam.

Paralleling the creation of agrarian collectives was the reorganization of business enterprises—large, medium, and small, in industry, forestry, fishing, construction, transport and communications, and the service sector. The DRV converted some private enterprises into state-private partnerships virtually controlled by the government. During the decade of the Second Indochina War (1964–1975), consumerism in North Vietnam declined to among the lowest levels in the world; the diplomatic staff in Hanoi reported mostly empty shelves in the capital's stores. Thus a whole generation of North Vietnamese, political and military leaders included, learned to live on bare necessities. No wonder that when the North Vietnamese troops and cadres marched into Saigon in April 1975, they went on a mad spree, wildly buying up—or more often looting—US-made consumer goods.

In terms of political stability, however, North Vietnam contrasted sharply with South Vietnam. The state was headed by a legendary hero, Ho Chi Minh, who was known for his qualities of determination, sacrifice, austerity, and wholehearted devotion to the cause of his country's liberation, reconstruction, and reunification. Ho had endeared himself to the masses through his simple habits. As an old Bolshevik, Ho also commanded respect in the Communist world. Ho's cabinet comrades followed his example, inspiring the common cadres to dedicate themselves to the achievement of socioeconomic goals. Their firm commitment to the reunification of the country gave them the support of the majority of the people, in both the North and South. As Eisenhower observed in his memoirs, "I have never talked or corresponded with a person knowledgeable in Indochinese affairs who did not agree that had elections been held at the time of fighting, 80 percent of the population would have voted for the communist Ho Chi Minh as their leader rather than Chief of State Bao Dai."[10] That was in 1954.

Unrest in South Vietnam

Diem's Oppressive Policies

The problem of "subversion" in South Vietnam was principally of Diem's making. After the suppression of the Cao Dai, Hoa Hao, and Binh Xuyen sects, Diem could have liberalized politics and turned to the much-needed alleviation of social and economic problems. Instead, in 1957 he unleashed a campaign to denounce and purge Communists, using emergency powers and vague definitions of espionage and treason to carry out arbitrary arrests of Communists and non-Communists alike. His brother Nhu's security apparatus included a secret police force trained by experts from Michigan State University. It terrorized all opponents and herded them into prison camps. Several thousand alleged Communists were placed into concentration camps like Phu Loi, where such atrocities as massive poisoning were reported. Dissident nationalists, whose numbers increased rapidly, were soon branded Communist traitors, and Diem clamped down on the press a censorship more severe than at the worst time of French colonial rule. As of May 1959, the repressive policies were based on the infamous 10–59 law (so called because it was the tenth law passed that year) creating special military tribunals that delivered summary judgments within three days after the accused were cited for "provoking economic disturbances" or "disrupting the security of the state" and gave out death sentences with no chance for appeal.

As for the rural areas, Diem did introduce some land reform. But his policies were ill conceived and ill implemented—and therefore disastrous in their effect. He sought to rehabilitate refugees and the landless poor by expropriating and redistributing landholdings beyond the high ceiling of 247 acres, which made very little land available for redistribution. Diem also abrogated a major land distribution program that had been undertaken during the First Indochina War, when more than 1.2 million acres of rice fields had been redistributed to the peasants. The Diem government confirmed only about 15 percent of such distributions. Because most of the requisitioned land, primarily in the Mekong Delta, was given to "foreign" landlords—supporters of Diem from central Vietnam and prominent Catholic refugees from North Vietnam—large numbers of peasants long established in the Mekong Delta became hostile to the government.

Diem's land reform program allowed for 20 percent of the rice land to pass from large to small farmers; in reality, only 10 percent of all tenant farmers benefited. As much as 47 percent of the land remained concentrated in the hands of 2 percent of the landowners; 15 percent of the landlords owned 75 percent of all land. The peasant discontent was further fueled by increased land rents and bribes to officials, together amounting to 45 to 50 percent of the crop. The few farmers who benefited from Diem's program were more often than not northern Catholic refugees, a situation that invited the charge of favoritism and thereby further deepened peasant alienation in South Vietnam. There were even widespread allegations that the Diem family had enriched itself by manipulating land transfers.

To add insult to injury, in June 1956, the Diem government replaced village notables with its own appointees, again northern Catholic "outsiders," summarily terminating the 2,000-year-old Vietnamese tradition of village autonomy. The new officials were unable to contain or resolve the discontent much less inspire confidence and trust among the peasantry.

By 1960, Diem, the all-knowing mandarin, had alienated all major sections of the South Vietnamese population. The intellectual elites were rendered politically mute, labor unions impotent, Buddhists distrustful, Montagnards suspicious. Loyal opposition in the form of organized parties was stifled out of existence, Diem's policies virtually assuring that political challenges to him would have to be extralegal and violent. Ultimately, these challenges emerged from diverse sources in South Vietnam: the armed forces, the religious sects, intellectuals, Communists, and even the peasantry.

Birth of the National Liberation Front

Against this backdrop of large-scale urban and rural discontent caused by the government's policies of alienation and repression, nepotism and corruption, family rule and religious insensitivity, the Mat Tran Dan Toc Giai Phong (National Liberation Front, or NLF) emerged in late 1960. The NLF was a grassroots organization that consisted of various elements within South Vietnamese society. For most of the NLF's fifteen-year existence, the common factor binding its components was not communism but nationalism, a determination to overthrow the regime in Saigon and to set up one that would end foreign intervention and guarantee a minimum of democratic liberties. Despite its considerable non-Communist membership and a non-Communist chairman (Nguyen Huu Tho, a Saigon lawyer), the real authority and leadership increasingly lay in its Communist constituents—the People's Revolutionary Party and the National Liberation Army, who took their direction (if not direct orders) from the Politburo in North Vietnam. The NLF's objectives did include reunification of the country but not necessarily under the hegemony of the north.

The origin of the National Liberation Front lay in the Saigon-Cholon Committee for Peace, formed in August 1954 to protest the Diem government's shooting at peaceful demonstrators asking for immediate release of political prisoners under terms of the Geneva agreements. The committee consisted of Saigon intellectuals and left-wing progressives (not necessarily Communists). Its ranks swelled as Diem refused to implement the provisions of the Geneva settlement in regard to the reunification of the country. Although its protests were peaceful and followed the proper legal channels, the Saigon-Cholon Committee suffered more than other groups after 1957, when

Nhu's security setup turned South Vietnam into a quasi police state. As the governmental repression became unbearably severe, particularly after the passage of the 10–59 law, the dissidents adopted violence to fight back. Eager to take part in armed attacks, the Communist (former Viet Minh) cadres left behind in 1954 in the south hoped to take advantage of the situation. They were discouraged by their comrades in the north on the grounds that the conditions were not yet ripe for that stage of the struggle. Hanoi warned the southern cadres, "To ignore the balance of forces and rashly call for a general uprising is to commit the error of speculative adventurism, leading to premature violence and driving us into a very dangerous position." Despite such inhibiting instructions, the southern Communists joined the militants in a series of attacks against government officials in the countryside.

A number of events during 1959–1960 culminated in the establishment of the NLF. In 1959, there were two significant revolts among tribal groups—the Kar in January and the Hre in July. In March 1960, Nguyen Huu Tho, president of the Saigon-Cholon Committee for Peace, urged his fellow compatriots in eastern Cochin China to resist. In May, some army units in coastal Quang Ngai Province revolted, and in November, three crack paratrooper battalions and a marine unit under Lieutenant Colonel Vuong Van Dong attempted a coup. It was at this point that various movements and political parties— Armed Propaganda Groups of the People's Self-Defense Forces, the Associates of Ex-Resistance Members, the Saigon-Cholon Committee, the Democratic Party, and others—coalesced into a national movement, creating the NLF as an organizational framework within which a general political military struggle could take place.

For quite some time, Hanoi had been under pressure from the southern Communist militants to support their movement. They criticized the north's weak protest of the nonobservance of the 1956 general elections and Hanoi's relatively passive reaction to Diem's repression during 1957–1959. In early 1959, Le Duan, secretary-general of the Lao Dong (Workers') Party—the name of the Vietnamese Communist Party since its resurrection by Ho Chi Minh in 1951—traveled to the south and later reported to the party that if the southern Communists did not join the other opponents of the Diem regime, they would lose credibility with the people.

Despite its misgivings regarding the timing of the insurrection, the northern leadership finally conceded. On May 13, 1959, the Fifteenth Plenum of the Lao Dong Party's central committee meeting in Hanoi decided that the time had come to initiate a struggle against the government of South Vietnam. The party leaders' goal was to create a unified Vietnam by any means. The following year, in September, the Third Congress of the party authorized support for an antigovernment revolutionary organization in the south. By December, the

NLF was established in South Vietnam. The creation on January 1, 1962, of the People's Revolutionary Party (PRP) within the NLF represented Hanoi's attempt to direct the southern insurgency via northern Communists, such as Nguyen Don, the director of Military Region Five (the northernmost third of South Vietnam) and alternate members of the Lao Dong central committee. The PRP only appeared to be independent; actually it was nothing but an extension of the Lao Dong Party.

Roots of the Insurrection

To what degree was South Vietnamese opposition to Diem's rule an indigenously inspired movement and to what degree was Hanoi involved in it? A few dates are significant though not conclusive in this respect. Until July 1956, Hanoi had hoped that the reunification of the country would be accomplished through elections. Thereafter, until early 1959, North Vietnam was compelled by considerations of Sino-Soviet global policies of peaceful coexistence to refrain from resorting to a violent alternative for achieving the country's reunification. During this period, the North Vietnamese hoped that the Diem regime would disintegrate in the south because of its own weakness. The first rumblings of the Sino-Soviet dispute leading to China's decision to oust Soviet technicians and reject Soviet aid in 1959 may have led to alterations in Hanoi's posture in regard to the south. Throughout the Second Indochina War, the Communists claimed that the war in the south was entirely a southern affair, the assistance from North Vietnam being no more than moral, ideological, and diplomatic. The South Vietnamese and US governments had a sharply different view of the "insurgency," as summarized by Douglas Pike.

> The National Liberation Front was not simply another indigenous covert group, or even a coalition of such groups. It was an organized effort, endowed with ample cadres and funds, crashing out of the jungle to flatten the [government of South Vietnam]. . . . A revolutionary organization must build; it begins with persons suffering genuine grievances, who are slowly organized and whose militancy gradually increases until a critical mass is reached and the revolution explodes. Exactly the reverse was the case with the NLF. It sprang full-blown into existence and then was fleshed out. The grievances were developed or manufactured almost as a necessary afterthought. The creation of the NLF was an accomplishment of such skill, precision, and refinement that when one thinks of who the master planner must have been, only one name comes: Vietnam's organizational genius, Ho Chi Minh.[11]

Even if the southern movement received organizational and material assistance from the north, its initial stimulus was undoubtedly southern. It is true that it had a core of Communist cadres. When the Viet Minh regrouped in terms of the Geneva accords between 1954 and 1955, a network of 5,000 to 10,000 cadres was left in the south, with instructions to blend into the new environment and agitate for elections. The Viet Minh also left behind large caches of weapons—but of these, 90 percent had been liquidated by the "extreme manhunt" Diem's government carried out between 1955 and 1957. The southern movement undoubtedly began as a response to Diem's mopping-up campaign of 1957 and basically involved southerners. As George Kahin and John Lewis observed,

> The insurrection is Southern rooted; it arose at Southern initiative in response to Southern demands. The Liberation Front gave political articulation and leadership to the widespread reaction against the harshness and heavy-handedness of Diem's government. It gained drive under the stimulus of Southern Vietminh veterans who felt betrayed by the Geneva conference and abandoned by Hanoi. . . . Contrary to U.S. policy assumptions, all available evidence shows that the revival of the civil war in the South in 1958 was undertaken by Southerners at their own—not Hanoi's—initiative.[12]

According to a Rand Corporation study, between 1956 and the launching of the NLF, approximately 30,000 northern agents, regroupees, were sent to South Vietnam. Although the regroupees did have an influence on the NLF, particularly in terms of military strategy and political goals, they could not have dictated their demands because of the local conditions and the NLF's heavy reliance on the grassroots structure. Geographically, the resistance forces were isolated from the north, making communication and transportation extremely difficult. In fact, the early NLF successes were without aid from North Vietnam. From the very beginning, the main military activity occurred in the deep south; the first "liberated" area was the Ca Mau Peninsula. Most weapons the NLF used were those captured from their enemy; approximately 80 percent of their weapons were of US manufacture. It was only after the massive infusion of US troops and weapons into South Vietnam from the mid–1960s that North Vietnam used the Ho Chi Minh Trail through Laos and Cambodia to supply the south with North Vietnamese manpower and materiel manufactured in Communist countries.

The NLF was originally intended to be a political rather than a military movement. Its initial doctrine was that of *khoi nghia*, or the general uprising. It would inspire the Vietnamese in the nation's 2,500 villages to such a pitch that at some precise moment there would come a spontaneous uprising, and the people, led of course by the NLF, would seize power. This was constantly drummed into the minds of the peasants by NLF cadres working in villages. The NLF's organizational structure therefore relied heavily on the participation of individuals, associations, and, in the countryside, entire villages. By 1963, the NLF became a gigantic organization composed of various departments such as the Farmers' Liberation Association, the Women's Liberation Association, and the Youth Liberation Association. The front's central committee in charge of political and military strategy consisted of representatives of such diverse elements as the political parties of South Vietnam, including the Democratic Party, the Radical Socialist Party, and indeed the People's Revolutionary Party.

As noted earlier, the NLF had given primacy to the political struggle, armed resistance being secondary. After mid–1963, however, the armed struggle gained precedence over the political aspect of the movement. Several factors were responsible for the shift in policy. First was the increasing use of sophisticated combat weaponry by the Army of the Republic of Vietnam (ARVN) against the NLF. The latter, therefore, augmented its guerrilla units and military capabilities. Their success against the ARVN supported the argument for larger, more numerous, and better-equipped guerrilla units that would bring a quicker ultimate victory. A second factor for the policy shift was that the northern cadres reinterpreted the revolutionary doctrine, placing greater stress on the armed struggle. Therefore, politically as well as militarily, the management of the NLF after 1963 passed on increasingly to the Hanoi-trained Communists of the People's Revolutionary Party, the arm of the Lao Dong Party in South Vietnam. The DRV's assistance to the NLF in the form of military training, arms supplies, and manpower were stepped up phenomenally after 1964 in direct correlation to the US commitment of troops, money, and materiel. The Americans, for their part, claimed that their increased involvement was a direct response to the level of insurgency in the south, which they alleged was entirely inspired, directed, manned, and supported by the north. The United States also believed that the Vietnam conflict was a test case of a theory of revolutionary warfare centrally directed from Moscow and Beijing. It was an attitude consistent with the policy of containment the United States followed in Indochina for a quarter of a century.

The Buddhist Crisis

Ironically, Diem's downfall was brought about by non-Communist elements in South Vietnam. Two military coup attempts in November 1960 and February

1962 had failed. The most serious challenge was posed in spring and summer 1963 by religious malcontents. The movement, led by Buddhist monks and nuns, drew its strength not from the abstractions of Communist ideology, which could only be antithetical to Buddhism, but from the wave of social discontent silently sweeping the population.

Traditionally, the Vietnamese had not perceived religion and politics as separate entities. Their religion was a blend of Confucianism, Taoism, Buddhism, and animism. As in most of Asia, religion provided "the authority for, and the confirmation of, an entire way of life—an agriculture, social structure, and a political system."[13] It is well said that the "Vietnamese are Confucians in peacetime, Buddhists in times of trouble."[14] Buddhism had always stressed morality that lay "beyond loyalty to existing authorities," and the Buddhist bonzes in the past had provided intellectual and moral leadership to oppose oppressive regimes.

During the French rule, the Buddhist monks had by and large remained apolitical. They had been allowed internal autonomy to run the monasteries and freedom to celebrate the numerous Buddhist holidays. Under the French, special permission was needed to build new pagodas, the existing ones starved of funds while the Catholic churches received large grants of land from colonial rulers. Unlike the Catholics, the Buddhists did not have a well-organized "church" hierarchy; each pagoda was, for most purposes, an independent entity.

During French rule, Buddhist monasteries and pagodas had enjoyed internal autonomy and the bonzes had, by and large, remained politically quiescent. Many of them had spent time in the 1930s abroad, notably in Japan and Thailand, acquainting themselves not only with the latest intellectual currents in Buddhism but also with the political movements in those countries. The centers they established on their return in Vietnam in Saigon, Hué, and Hanoi served as focal points of their contacts with Buddhist intellectuals in the country. While they did not actively participate in anti-French movements, they maintained ties with a variety of Buddhist activist groups, especially in major cities.

Under the French, Buddhism was recognized as a religion, to be pursued privately by its followers and requiring the government's permission for all public events, including processions to celebrate the Buddha's birthday. The Diem government had not seen fit to repeal such discriminatory laws, despite that an overwhelming majority were Buddhists and the Catholic colonial power had left the country.

With Diem's overtly pro-Catholic policies, the Buddhists felt threatened enough to organize themselves and form the General Buddhist Association in 1955. In a few years, the bonzes succeeded in building new (or enlarging existing) pagodas in many South Vietnamese cities and promoting discussion groups under the aegis of the newly formed Association for the Propagation of the Buddhist Faith. In 1963, in direct response to the religious crisis, the Unified Buddhist Church (UBC) was born. Its political arm, styled the Buddhist Institute for Secular Affairs, continued to operate even after Diem's downfall, until it was replaced by the Vietnam Buddhist Force in April 1966. The position of the Buddhist associations vis-à-vis communism and Communist regimes was one of absolute neutrality, neither praise nor condemnation. In fact, they did not take sides in the ongoing conflict in South Vietnam until the government blatantly acted against the Buddhists in 1963.

Even more than President Diem, one of his brothers, the Catholic archbishop Ngo Dinh Thuc, deliberately antagonized the Buddhists. Diem had lobbied with the Vatican for his brother to be appointed Archbishop of Saigon, but the Vatican had not obliged. Ngo Dinh Thuc spent most of his time at the presidential palace in Saigon exploiting his senior position in the first family and high spiritual position in the country to influence policy making at the highest levels as well as compelling the bureaucracy to help his large flock. Since the exodus of nearly 1 million Catholics from North to South Vietnam in 1954, the government had favored the Christian minority, not only through programs of rehabilitation of refugees but by giving preferred government positions to them. They certainly held more posts in civil as well as military services than their numbers—estimated at 2.2 million (10 percent of the population)—warranted. During French rule, Catholics had gotten used to receiving preferential treatment. A higher percentage of them spoke and read French than any other community; they were more sophisticated and better organized through their churches. They had shown inveterate hostility toward the Communists and the Viet Minh before 1954 and the Viet Cong (Diem's appellation for Vietnamese Communists) after 1960. As such, they were natural allies of the pro-West, anticommunist Diem regime. Because the Catholics were coreligionists of the family in power, even greater advantages flowed to them. A French Catholic publication, *Informations catholiques internationales,* averred in March 1963 that it was because of Archbishop Ngo Dinh Thuc's efforts that the missionaries had found it easy to baptize entire villages collectively. With official help the archbishop built a spectacular center called Our Lady of La Vang, twenty miles south of the 17th parallel. Government officials, irrespective of their faith, were compelled to donate funds to the center. For example, the police sold lottery tickets in support of the center, forcing drivers to buy them in lieu of payment for traffic offenses.

If the people in South Vietnam were looking for some divine indication that Diem had forfeited his mandate to rule the country, a clear sign appeared in spring 1963. On May 7, Archbishop Ngo Dinh Thuc forbade the display of

Buddhist flags in Hué to commemorate the 2,527th birth anniversary of the Buddha and banned the general festivities as well. In contrast, in the previous week, he had permitted Catholics of Hué to display white papal banners to mark the silver jubilee of his own ordination as a Catholic priest. On May 8, when several thousand Buddhists assembled in Hué to celebrate the Buddha's birth anniversary, the deputy chief of the province, Major Dang Xi, a Catholic, invoked the old governmental decree to prohibit flying the Buddhist flags without prior permission. The local radio station was to broadcast a speech by the much-respected bonze, Thich Quang Duc, as a part of the celebrations. A crowd of 3,000 congregated outside the radio station to listen to the bonze's speech. Suddenly, the radio station canceled the speech on grounds that it had not been submitted to the censors. In order to deal with the crowd, the station director called for help from Major Dang Xi, who promptly sent five armored cars. The commander ordered the crowd to disperse, but without giving adequate time, used tear gas and bullets; nine people lost their lives. Instead of holding the commander responsible, the Diem government blamed the whole incident—including the loss of lives—on the Viet Cong.

To protest the government's action, the Buddhists launched a series of self-immolations, beginning on June 11, 1963, with Thich Quang Duc sitting cross-legged in the middle of a busy intersection in the capital as his fellow monks and nuns doused him with gasoline and set him on fire in full view of the public and the media. Stanley Karnow witnessed the scene.

> He pressed his palms together in a prayer as a sheet of flame the color of his orange robe enveloped him. Pedestrians, amazed by the awesome sight, prostrated themselves in reverence, and even a nearby policeman threw himself to the ground. Trucks and automobiles stopped, snarling traffic. By the time an ambulance arrived, the old man had fallen over, still burning as the fire consumed his flesh.[15]

A few weeks later, the celebrated Vietnamese novelist Nhat Linh, who was to be tried for opposition to the Diem government, committed suicide by taking poison. Such acts of supreme sacrifice reflected the general frustration, bringing masses of people closer as equals against a common tyranny. The self-immolations continued as the government refused to negotiate. Madame Nhu publicly ridiculed the sacrifices as a "barbecue of bonzes"; her husband, Ngo Dinh Nhu, ordered the police to raid the pagodas. The press and television coverage brought the magnitude of the government's injustice and callousness as well as the sacrifices of the Buddhist bonzes to an international audience. The Confucians had theorized on a possible rebellion against those who had lost the mandate of heaven; the Buddhists now provided an emotional and spiritual platform to bring down an oppressive government. The bonzes and their lay followers made sure that the American media reporters and cameramen were present on the scene to record and later broadcast the self-immolation of the venerable Thich Quang Duc and self-immolations that followed. They also displayed Thich Quang Duc's heart preserved in a glass case for the people to pay homage to the martyr.

All through the summer of 1963, the Buddhist crisis persisted with the demonstrations increasing in intensity and numbers against a hardened government. On August 20, Diem and Nhu proclaimed martial law. In a bid to blame the action on the army, Nhu used his own loyal forces disguised as military to crush protesters. Then early in the morning on August 21, Nhu's forces attacked Buddhist temples in a dozen cities all over South Vietnam, arresting more than 4,000. They ransacked the capital's well-known Xa Loi pagoda and shot thirty monks—and more than 400 nuns and monks, including the eighty-year old Buddhist patriarch, were arrested. In Hué, where the crisis had originated, hundreds of nuns and monks had barricaded themselves in the Dieude temple. Nhu's forces battled for eight hours while 3,000 people rioted outside the temple in support of the monks under attack. The temple raids brought many middle-class citizens, including families that had thus far loyally served the bureaucracy and military, to join the antigovernment agitation. Among high government officials who quit in protest was the foreign minister, Vu Van Mau, who shaved his head like the monks and went on a pilgrimage to India. Madame Nhu's father, who was at the time ambassador to the United States, resigned his position and toured the country deploring the Diem regime's repressive measures against the Buddhist majority.

Among many who commented on the significance of the painful events of the spring and summer of 1963 was Paul Mus, the foremost French authority on Vietnamese tradition and symbolism. He characterized the Buddhist monks' action as "not a gesture of resignation, but rather one of protest—an advertisement of the intolerable gap between morality and the reality of the Diem regime."[16] In the words of the author Frances Fitzgerald, a distinguished student of Mus, "To the Vietnamese Buddhist majority, such immolations were a call first to reconciliation and then to rebellion."[17] Thousands congregated in pagodas throughout the country to offer prayers and join in processions to protest against a regime that appeared worse than the colonial rule of the past. The society broke out "from its untenable pyramid of superiors and inferiors to become a brotherhood of trust."[18] Those still under Confucian influence recalled that Vietnamese history had recorded the suicide of many conscientious mandarins who could not continue to give loyalty to emperors who had flouted the will of heaven. Throughout Chinese and Vietnamese history, Confucian scholars had warned of potential rebellions against rulers who had lost the mandate of heaven; the Buddhist rebellion of 1963 signified to Confucian minds a justifiable revolt against Diem's oppressive regime.

US Policy and Diem's Assassination

The Buddhist crisis exposed the excesses of Diem's rule to the world. It also changed the official US view of the merits of his administration. Thus far, the United States had been totally impervious to Vietnamese opposition to Diem, viewing the conflict exclusively as an extension of the clash between the forces of freedom and Communist totalitarianism. The United States had perceived the problem as being more military than political. In the Diem era, 75 percent of US economic aid to South Vietnam was used to bolster the country's military budget. The misplaced emphasis on military outlay is best illustrated in the construction of a twenty-mile highway between Bien Hoa and Saigon. Used mostly for military purposes, the highway absorbed more US funds than all the aid provided for social welfare and education programs in South Vietnam between 1954 and 1961. Not until 1961 did the United States try to pressure the Diem government to redress socioeconomic imbalances. Such a belated change in policy yielded no positive results; it only helped to estrange the United States from the Diem administration.

Even in late 1961, despite the evidence to the contrary generated by its own agencies, the United States perceived the conflict in South Vietnam mainly in terms of aggression by North Vietnam. A white paper entitled *A Threat to the Peace* bluntly stated,

> The determined and ruthless campaign of propaganda, infiltration, and subversion by the Communist regime in North Viet-Nam to destroy the Republic of Viet-Nam and subjugate its people is a threat to the peace. The independence and territorial integrity of that free country is of major and serious concern not only to the people of Viet-Nam and their immediate neighbors but also to all other free nations.[19]

Yet only a month before the publication of this document, a government report of October 5, 1961, had placed the Viet Cong strength at less than 17,000 men, adding that 80 to 90 percent of them were southerners. It affirmed as well that the Viet Cong were hardly dependent upon outside assistance.[20]

Policy Under the Kennedy Administration

When Kennedy assumed the presidency in January 1961, it was Laos and not Vietnam that loomed large as a critical issue in Southeast Asia. The Eisenhower administration stolidly supported the right-wing faction in Laos led by Prince Boun Oum, which had been, through 1960, reeling under attacks from the Communist Pathet Lao and the neutralists under Kong Le. Kennedy changed the US stand, withdrew support of the rightists, secured a cease-fire, and sought a compromise settlement at the fourteen-nation Geneva conference, which opened in mid–1961. Deliberations were based on the principle of a tripartite coalition government for Laos and neutralization of the country by resisting any interference by external powers. On July 23, 1962, formal signing of the agreements took place, following the defeat of the rightists by the Pathet Lao at Nam Tha on May 6. The defeat of the rightists and the neutralization of Laos were regarded as setbacks to the US position in Southeast Asia.

The strategic "loss" of Laos might have impelled the Kennedy administration to show its strength in Vietnam and assure America's allies in Asia of the continued US policy against the spread of communism. Washington considered it dangerous to give up ground in Vietnam because it would send the wrong message to the Soviets. On January 6, 1961, before Kennedy's inauguration, Soviet Premier Nikita Khrushchev declared that the Soviet Union would support the "wars of national liberation" around the world. The incoming US administration took the Soviet threat seriously. An elaborate memorandum of April 12, 1961, drawn up by W. W. Rostow—widely regarded as the author of the counterinsurgency doctrine—proposed that the ceiling of the Military Assistance Advisory Group (MAAG) in Vietnam be raised. In the alternative plan, a substantial number of "Special Forces types" would be sent there. On the day after the Bay of Pigs, not wanting to risk another setback at the hands of the Communists, Kennedy ordered the Pentagon to carry out a "quick review" of the Vietnam situation and "recommend a series of actions (military, political and/or economic, overt and/or covert) which . . . will prevent Communist domination" of the country.

The Pentagon's report stated that Kennedy transformed Eisenhower's "limited-risk gamble" into a "broad commitment" to prevent Communist domination of South Vietnam "giving priority to the military aspects of the war over political reforms." Within weeks of assuming the presidency, Kennedy had received an intelligence report that drew heavily on an elaborate telegram dated September 16, 1960, from the US Ambassador Elbridge Durbow to Secretary of State Christian Herter. It criticized Diem for his inability to rally public support, notably in his fight against the Communists, because of his "virtual one-man rule, his toleration of corruption extending even to his immediate entourage and his refusal to relax a rigid system of public controls." Durbow recommended that if Diem was unable to regain support of the people through political and social reforms, "it may become necessary" for the US government to begin consideration of "alternative courses of action and leaders"—in other words, to dump Diem and place bets on some other South Vietnamese leader. On May 11, the National Security Council with Kennedy in the chair outlined the US objective "to prevent Communist domination of South Vietnam, to create in that country a viable and increasingly democratic society, and to initiate, on an accelerated basis, a series of mutually supporting actions to achieve this objective."[21] Although Kennedy resisted pressures for putting American ground combat units into South Vietnam, he expanded the US political and military involvement there.

Following the NSC meeting, Kennedy directed the Defense Department to assess "the size and composition of forces which would be desirable in the case of a possible commitment of US forces in Vietnam." As an immediate measure, he authorized sending 400 Special Forces troops and 100 "other American military advisers" to South Vietnam. Yet he was reluctant to assume responsibility for ground action. This became evident in the instructions he issued to General Maxwell Taylor, whom he sent to South Vietnam in October 1961. "In your assessment you should bear in mind that the initial responsibility for the effective maintenance of the independence of South Vietnam rests with the people and government of that country. Our efforts must be evaluated, and your recommendation formulated, with that fact in mind."[22]

In General Taylor's view, the introduction of US military forces in South Vietnam was "essential in order to reverse the present downward trend of events." In prophetic words, however, he warned, "If the first contingent is not enough to accomplish the necessary results, it will be difficult to resist the pressure to reinforce. If the ultimate result sought is the closing of the frontiers and the clean-up of the insurgents within SVN, there is no limit to our possible commitment."[23] He recommended a force of not more than 8,000, of which a preponderant number would be "logistical-type" units. But the general proved wrong in his assessment of whether US commitment would lead to a larger conflict.

The risks of backing into a major war by way of SVN are present but not impressive. NVN is extremely vulnerable to conventional bombing, a weakness which should be exploited diplomatically in convincing Hanoi to lay off SVN. Both the DRV and the Chicoms [Chinese Communists] would face severe logistical difficulties in trying to maintain strong forces in the field in SEA [Southeast Asia], difficulties which we share but by no means to the same degree. There is no case for fearing a mass onslaught of Communist manpower into SVN and its neighboring states, particularly if our airpower is allowed a free hand against logistical targets. . . . I have reached the conclusion that the introduction of . . . a military Task Force without delay offers definitely more advantages than it creates risks and difficulties. In fact, I do not believe that our program to save SVN will succeed without it.[24]

Taylor's recommendation was endorsed by Secretary of Defense Robert McNamara and the Joint Chiefs of Staff who were, however, more apprehensive than Taylor that the conflict may be prolonged and might provoke North Vietnam and China to intervene. They differed sharply with Taylor on the numbers needed: They recommended sending six divisions, or about 205,000 troops. Kennedy rejected the latter view but stressed thereafter the military aspect of the problem to the detriment of political and socioeconomic reforms. That made for a wrong prescription and shortsighted policy. What was truly needed for the Vietnamese people was a democratic government that actively sought improvement in education, health, and living standards for the masses. This was, after all, the rationale of the anticolonial movement during which leaders had promised the people not just a change of masters from the French to the Vietnamese but a polity that would promote political, economic, and social freedoms. At the time of Kennedy's assassination in November 1963, there were 16,000 US "military advisers" in South Vietnam. In committing combat troops to South Vietnam without the condition that Diem must reform, Kennedy ignored his own dictum to General Maxwell Taylor in his letter of October 1961.

The events of the summer 1963 led to major changes in US policy toward the Diem government. On the day following Nhu's temple raids, Henry Cabot Lodge, Jr., arrived in Saigon as the new US ambassador replacing the pro-Diem Frederick Nolting. Lodge's report two days later to Washington formed the basis of a new policy that would culminate nine weeks later in the end of the Diem regime. The State Department, in what was to become one of the most controversial and crucial decisions of the Kennedy administration, authorized Lodge to proceed with a coup if his efforts to secure the removal of Nhu and his wife from the Diem administration failed. Lodge tried in long meetings with Diem to convince him of the political benefit of distancing himself from his controversial brother Nhu and his vitriolic-tongued wife, Madame Nhu. Diem would not agree. Through the local CIA operative, Lucien Conien, Lodge remained in contact with anti-Diem generals who were contemplating a coup.

Meanwhile, the Machiavellian Nhu indicated to Hanoi through the French ambassador and the Polish member of the International Control Commission his readiness to discuss a Franco-Polish proposal for the neutralization of

Vietnam—North and South. A beginning would be made by opening cultural and economic exchanges between Saigon and Hanoi. Nhu was certain the information would leak to the CIA, which would then force the United States to woo him and Diem again.

Should the United States have encouraged the two Vietnams toward neutralization, a proposal first propounded by India's Nehru and revived in mid–1963 by France's de Gaulle? Neutralization would have enabled an honorable withdrawal for the US before it was too late. Did the Ngo brothers really want neutralization? This is hard to say. They had always maintained contact with Hanoi through Buu Hoi, a North Vietnamese scientist and former advisor to Ho Chi Minh, who lived in Paris and had access to de Gaulle. Did the United States consider neutralization? According to the Pentagon Papers, Robert Kennedy argued before the National Security Council that if the war was unwinnable by any foreseeable South Vietnamese regime, it was time for the United States to get out.[25] There was no serious support to the idea then or anytime thereafter during the Kennedy and Johnson administrations.

On November 1, 1963, the generals succeeded in their coup. The regime ended ignobly. After seven hours of a siege, the Ngo brothers used a tunnel passage to flee from the presidential palace to some distance where they made it to Cholon, the Chinese suburb of Saigon. From his St. Francis Church hideout, Diem attempted to negotiate with the generals; in the process, he revealed his whereabouts. It appears that the officer sent by General Duong Van (Big) Minh to bring the brothers for negotiation instead killed them in cold blood.

The Diem regime ended unwept, unsung, and unlamented. It was a mark of the country's catharsis that no tears were shed for the Ngos. There was unrestrained rejoicing in the streets of Saigon. The generals' coup was regarded as a liberation, though the liberators had no record of being freedom fighters. There was no official inquiry into the assassinations. The two brothers were buried in unmarked graves; there have been no memorials to their work. In the death certificates, Diem was described not as "head of state" but as "Chief of Province" and Nhu as "Chief of Library Services," which were the last positions the two brothers had held, respectively, under the French.[26] It seemed as though people wanted to treat nine years of Ngo excesses as a bad dream, to obliterate this period from the country's history. As Fitzgerald observed, "the Vietnamese had committed the Ngo regime to that absolute death that comes to a family when it has no heirs, and that comes to a dynasty when the will of Heaven turns against it."[27]

What was the role of the United States in this operation? Was there partial or full complicity at the level of the State Department or the White House, or was Ambassador Lodge the lone actor? Lodge reiterated for years that he had used a language that had been approved by the president whereby he made it clear to Big Minh that the United States "will not attempt to thwart" a coup.

The liquidation of the Diem regime did not solve any of South Vietnam's basic problems. The political instability worsened, with several generals playing musical chairs for power. It was eighteen months before the steady team of Nguyen Van Thieu as president and Nguyen Cao Ky as vice president established some semblance of stability. All were pro-United States and dependent upon the United States to keep them in power. With the exception of General Minh, who was inclined to establish a "neutral" government with NLF participation, they were all thoroughly anti-Communist, believing that the conflict was first and last a Communist conspiracy hatched in Hanoi. Throughout the decade, from Diem's assassination to the withdrawal of US forces from Vietnam in 1973, the United States continued to give priority to the pursuit of the war effort. After 1966, believing that major socioeconomic reforms would have to await a successful conclusion of the war, the United States only halfheartedly insisted on democratic trappings such as elections.

Two weeks after the elimination of the Ngo brothers and one week before his own assassination, President Kennedy asked rhetorically at a news conference on November 14, "Are we going to give up South Vietnam?" His response was, "The most important program, of course, is our national security, but I don't want the United States to have to put troops there."[28] The situation posed a dilemma that would haunt Kennedy's successor, Lyndon Baines Johnson, for the next five years.

CHAPTER 6

The Indochina Imbroglio

The instability caused by coups and countercoups producing revolving-door governments led by politically incompetent generals—who were neither elected by the people nor represented their will—was most worrisome in early 1964 to President Lyndon Johnson, who was accustomed to unsullied successes in his long political career. The situation resulted in further alienation of the government from the people. That was part of the reason the war was going badly for South Vietnam. In April 1964, the US Department of Defense estimated that the South Vietnamese government controlled 34 percent of the villages as against the NLF's control of 42 percent, with the loyalties of the remaining villages still contested. The Strategic Hamlet Program had collapsed. The northern Communists were not long in taking advantage of the deteriorating situation in the south. In order to step up the level of guerrilla warfare to the stage of attacking towns and larger army units, Hanoi began to infiltrate large tactical units along the Ho Chi Minh Trail through Laos and Cambodia into South Vietnam. LBJ's dilemma in an election year was how to hold on to South Vietnam in the face of political deterioration there and stem the Communist gains without further augmenting the number of US troops. The answer seemed to be aerial attacks against North Vietnam and the Ho Chi Minh Trail to dissuade Hanoi from sending reinforcements to the South.

The initial suggestion to bomb the North came, predictably, from the Joint Chiefs of Staff in a memorandum of January 22, 1964, to Secretary of Defense Robert McNamara. In their unanimous opinion, the United States "must be prepared to put aside many of the self-imposed restrictions which now limit our efforts and to undertake bolder actions which may embody greater risks."

The war was so far being fought "on the enemy's terms." The restrictions had limited the war "within the boundaries of South Vietnam." The Joint Chiefs recommended that the war be broadened to include US air attacks on North Vietnam and to pursue the war in both South and North Vietnam with US combat forces.[1] In his 1995 memoir *In Retrospect*, McNamara said the recommendation represented a "revolutionary change" in US policy and "rested on an exposition of two and a half pages, with little analysis or supporting rationale."[2] McNamara's assistant secretary, William Bundy, a scholarly civilian, in a somewhat elaborate memo of March 1, 1964, proposed a blockade of Haiphong harbor "to hit at the sovereignty of North Vietnam" and to warn that "we would go further." He also recommended bombing strategic targets in the North such as railroads, highways, industrial plants, utilities, and military training camps, precisely those bombed after February 1965. By the end of March 1964, McNamara, on return from a trip to South Vietnam along with Maxwell Taylor, cautiously conceded that the bombing of the North would be an option to be considered, but only if "it is forced on us by the other side."[3] According to McNamara, the chief of the South Vietnamese junta at that time, General Nguyen Khanh, was opposed to bombing North Vietnam because he felt South Vietnamese forces would not be able to stand the North Vietnamese retaliation.[4]

The Gulf of Tonkin Incident

Meanwhile, LBJ had approved the Pentagon's proposal for a covert operation against North Vietnam on "an experimental basis" for four months beginning February 1, 1964, later expended for another four months. It was operative at the time of the controversial Gulf of Tonkin incident in August and included a snooping operation called the De Soto mission. Under its terms, in July, the commander of the Pacific, Ulysses Grant Sharp, Jr., ordered the Seventh Fleet to deploy the aircraft carrier *Ticonderoga* to the entrance of the gulf and the destroyer *Maddox*, under Captain J. Herrick, to enter the gulf for electronic espionage. Herrick was instructed to remain at least eight miles from the North Vietnamese coast and four miles from the islands in the Gulf of Tonkin.[5] He was also instructed to remain in contact with the US military command in Saigon for details of the South Vietnamese commando operations so that they could avoid "mutual interference."

On the night of July 30, two South Vietnamese swifts attacked Hon Me, an island seven miles from the coast where the North Vietnamese held a radar installation. Simultaneously, two other South Vietnamese naval craft attacked Hon Ngu, three miles from the North Vietnamese port of Vinh. The *Maddox*, which was by then in the vicinity, intercepted the North Vietnamese radar and radio to gather intelligence on Hanoi's response to South Vietnamese attacks. In the early hours of August 2, the *Maddox*, alarmed at the sight of hundreds of possibly armed North Vietnamese small naval craft, feared "possible hostile action." At that point Herrick contemplated aborting the mission but was overruled by his superiors in the Seventh Fleet.

At about 11 o'clock on the same day, the *Maddox*, then cruising about ten miles from the gulf, suddenly found three North Vietnamese patrol boats moving from behind the island of Hon Me toward the *Maddox* at twice its speed. Herrick ordered to open fire if the boats came within ten thousand yards and radioed the *Ticonderoga* for air support. The skirmish, lasting twenty minutes, resulted in the sinking of one North Vietnamese boat and the crippling of the remaining two. They had come within five thousand yards. The torpedoes they had launched failed to hit the *Maddox*; only one bullet did. There were no casualties. At that point, Herrick was ordered by the Seventh Fleet to end the encounter and withdraw. But President Johnson, who was immediately informed of the incident, directed that another destroyer and some protective aircraft accompany the *Maddox* back to the Gulf of Tonkin and attack any forces that would attack them. At the same time, he sent a personal message to Premier Khrushchev and a stern warning to North Vietnam that "grave action would inevitably result from any further unprovoked offensive military action" against American ships deployed on high seas. LBJ, indeed, wanted to project an image of a firm commander in chief in the face of a belligerent Barry Goldwater, the Arizona senator, who was the Republican presidential candidate.

At that point, the Joint Chiefs of Staff went overboard in their enthusiasm to meet any contingency. They ordered additional fighter-bombers to South Vietnam and Thailand and placed US combat troops on general alert. Admiral Sharp ordered the carrier *Constellation* to join the *Ticonderoga* and dispatched a destroyer, *C. Turner Joy*, to join the *Maddox* to "assert the right of the freedom of the seas" by moving within eight miles of the North Vietnamese coast and four miles off its islands. At the same time, the United States made sure that the South Vietnamese commando-manned coastal craft would be operating at Cape Vinhson and Cua Ron, about seventy-five miles above the demilitarized zone. Herrick was aware that the North Vietnamese radar and radio were monitoring the American and South Vietnamese naval movements. He asked Admiral Sharp for instructions to withdraw from the area. Instead, Sharp asked him to use the American ships as "decoys" to distract the North Vietnamese away from the South Vietnamese naval craft engaged in collecting coastal intelligence.

On August 3, at about eight o'clock, Herrick learned from intercepting North Vietnamese radio messages that their patrol boats were about to attack the *Maddox* and *C. Turner Joy*. He asked the *Ticonderoga* for air support. Eight jets soon circled overhead but saw nothing. Even so, an hour later, the *Maddox* and *C. Turner Joy* opened fire on all sides to prevent the North Vietnamese from firing torpedoes. The sonars of the US destroyers counted twenty-two torpedoes, none of which hit any of the American ships. In the hectic engagement, lasting a couple of hours, the destroyers sank two of the three North Vietnamese naval craft.

Herrick had his doubts about the engagement just concluded. He reported to his superiors and requested a thorough aerial reconnaissance during daytime. In the questioning carried out at his instance on board the two destroyers, it came to light that no one had seen or heard gunfire from any North Vietnamese craft; the pilots of the jets from the *Ticonderoga* also had failed to see any Communist craft during the forty-minute aerial sighting of the area. Herrick reported to Admiral Sharp that the *Maddox* had not made any "actual visual sightings" of North Vietnamese naval craft and that the radarscope blips could have been caused by "freak weather effects," and that an "over-eager" sonar operator may have misinterpreted them. By that time, President Johnson had briefed some key senators on the happenings in the Gulf of Tonkin and sought their help to pass a resolution of support, even though he was not aware of Herrick's doubts. So was Robert McNamara, who asked Admiral Sharp not to retaliate against North Vietnam "unless we are damned sure what happened." Thereupon, Sharp asked Herrick to "confirm absolutely that the second attack had taken place."

Before Herrick had the opportunity to investigate further, a Pentagon spokesman told the press at six o'clock on August 2 that a "second deliberate attack" on the *Maddox* and *C. Turner Joy* had taken place and that the first US attack on North Vietnam had been launched from the *Ticonderoga* and *Constellation* carriers.

In a dramatic nationwide television broadcast on August 2, 1964, at 11:30 PM, President Lyndon Johnson charged that the USS *Maddox* and *C. Turner Joy* had been wantonly attacked by North Vietnamese torpedo boats and that US aircraft had retaliated by bombing strategic North Vietnamese targets. He added, "Repeated acts of violence against the armed forces of the United States must be met not only with alert defense, but with a positive reply. That reply is being given as I speak to you tonight." As the Pentagon Papers revealed in 1968, Captain John Herrick, the local US commander in the South China Sea, had informed Washington that there was no direct, visual evidence of any North Vietnamese torpedo attack and that the sonar operators may have mistaken "freak atmospheric conditions" for torpedoes. Three days later, an emotionally charged US Congress (466–0 in the House of Representatives and 88–2 in the Senate) passed the much-heralded Gulf of Tonkin Resolution authorizing the president to take "all necessary measures to repel any armed attacks against the forces of the United States and to prevent further aggression."[6] The dissenting senators were Ernest Gruening of Alaska and Wayne Morse of Oregon. Morse's opposition was based on his information from "a high defense official" that the *Maddox* was, at the time of the incident, acting in concert with the covert South Vietnamese coastal intelligence-gathering operation in North Vietnam. In 1966, Senator Wayne Morse's proposal to rescind the Tonkin resolution failed because he could muster only five votes. Public opinion polls showed that 85 percent of the people supported President Johnson in his decision to retaliate against the alleged attacks on the US naval ships. War went on badly throughout the rest of 1964. The exigencies of the presidential election required Johnson and his aides to exercise restraint. In the ensuing six years, until its repeal in the face of mounting antiwar sentiment in the country, this blanket authority was to draw the United States far more deeply into the quagmire of war than the legislators had envisaged. Armed with that authority and without further reference to Congress, Johnson sent ultimately half a million Americans to Vietnam to fight in an undeclared war.

Did the so-called second attack occur at all? The documentation published on the incident leaves much doubt and inclines toward the conclusion that it never happened. As Stanley Karnow observes,

> It had not been deliberately faked, but Johnson and his staff desperately seeking a pretext to act vigorously, had seized upon a fuzzy set of circumstances to fulfill a contingency plan. Much of the truth was to trickle out in the years ahead—yet some relevant evidence has remained confidential, presumably to spare prominent U.S. bureaucrats who concealed or twisted the facts, either intentionally or inadvertently then and later.[7]

A crucial actor in the episode was, indeed, the defense secretary, Robert Strange McNamara. Testifying before the Senate Foreign Relations Committee three and a half years later, McNamara averred that he had seen "unimpeachable" proof in the four intercepted North Vietnamese radio messages of Hanoi's intentions to attack the US destroyers. He would not make the messages public because they might compromise US intelligence-gathering methods. Contrary to his previous statement of 1964, he conceded that Captain Herrick knew about the clandestine South Vietnamese operations, though not fully. And because he had some doubts about the second attack, he had asked Admiral Sharp to reverify the details of the incident and only then conduct retaliatory bombing of the North.

The Pleiku Incident and Bombing of the North

With such sweeping congressional authorization and a national consensus behind him, Johnson exercised no restraint in escalating the war. The NLF's attacks on the US air base at Pleiku on February 7, 1965, provided the provocation for US bombing of North Vietnamese military installations and staging areas. Pleiku was a market town used by the Montagnards of the central highlands, strategically exploited by the Army of the Republic of Vietnam (ARVN) to make forays against the North Vietnamese infiltrating along the Ho Chi Minh Trail running through southeastern Laos and northeastern Cambodia. Three miles away, US troops were located at Camp Holloway with a number of aircraft and helicopters parked on the airstrip. Units of US and ARVN heavily guarded it. The dastardly attacks by the Communists on the US air base in the early hours of February 7, 1965, resulted in the loss of eight American lives with more than 100 badly wounded; ten US aircraft were destroyed.

The US responded to the Pleiku losses with Operation Flaming Dart. Jets took off from the carrier *Ranger* to bomb a North Vietnamese camp near Dong Hoi, sixty miles north of the dividing line between the two Vietnams at the 17th parallel. Two weeks later, General Westmoreland asked for two marine battalions to protect the American airfield at Danang. On April 1, the president authorized two more marine battalions comprised of 18,000 or so "logistical" troops to be sent to South Vietnam ostensibly for management of supplies but in reality to undertake offensive operations.

Operation Rolling Thunder

On March 2, 1965, the United States launched the more intensive and long-lasting Operation Rolling Thunder (ORT). The operation's objectives were to cripple the DRV's economy, reduce the flow of troops and supplies to the south, and force the North Vietnamese to agree to a negotiated settlement. Originally planned to last eight weeks, ORT continued on a daily basis (with few pauses) from March 1965 to November 1968, using a million tons of bombs, rockets, and missiles—roughly 800 tons a day for three and a half years. Successive commanders as well as chiefs of staff, including generals Wheeler and Westmoreland, were to report to successive secretaries of defense—Robert

McNamara and Clark Clifford—that the bombing strikes had not, in any major way, reduced North Vietnam's or the NLF's military capacity or gravely damaged the DRV's economy.

North Vietnam offered few strategic targets because its economy was principally agrarian and most of its military equipment was not manufactured in the country but came from China and the Soviet Union. Moreover, effective bombing of targets was hampered by unfriendly weather—monsoons and typhoons—for three to four months a year. Furthermore, while supplies from the north did make a difference in the Viet Cong's ability to fight in the south, North Vietnam was as completely dependent on those supplies as the US generals thought. Most of the Viet Cong's guns and ammunition—the mainstay of their weaponry—came from captured South Vietnamese and American military warehouses and war casualties. Although the US generals were aware of the relative futility of bombing, they continued to plead for more troops, deployment of more B-52s, greater intensification of the bombing, and to add new weapons such as napalm bombs to their raiding arsenal. This was the pattern that established itself for the duration of LBJ's administration, leading rapidly to the United States sinking hopelessly into the Vietnam "quagmire."

The War Escalates

The spring of 1965 witnessed a major debate in Washington on the desirability, feasibility, and quantum of US troops to be deployed in South Vietnam. In addition to the administration's conviction that only deployment of US combat troops could prevent South Vietnam from falling to the Communists, the president and his national security advisor, McGeorge Bundy, saw bombing of the north and increased American military presence and participation as bargaining chips in eventual negotiations with the enemy. In his Johns Hopkins University speech of April 6, 1965, Johnson urged North Vietnam to agree to unconditional negotiations offering financial assistance toward a large part of the Mekong Development Project, a "stick and carrot" approach he would follow for the next three years. Supporting the decision was the defense establishment, including Robert McNamara, William Bundy, chiefs of staff General Wheeler and General Westmoreland, who recommended doubling the number of US troops in Vietnam to 40,000 by June.

Now emerging, however, were significant new voices opposing further US involvement—particularly of ground troops. Leading the "doves" in the US Senate were Frank Church (Idaho), Jacob Javits (New York), George Aiken (Vermont), and most influential of all, the chairman of the Foreign Relations Committee, William Fulbright. He strongly opposed further US commitment on grounds that it was certain to drag the country into a "bloody and pro-tracted jungle war in which the strategic advantage would be with the other side." They urged negotiations wherein the Communists should be offered "a reasonable and attractive alternative" to military victory. Clark Clifford (later to become secretary of defense), an influential Washington attorney and close friend of LBJ, privately warned the president that a greater military commit-ment to South Vietnam may land the United States into a "quagmire" without any "realistic hope of ultimate victory." Alone in the State Department, George Ball outlined prophetically a scenario of how heavy US losses in early stages caused by a lack of preparedness to fight in a "hostile countryside" would ne-cessitate reinforcements, and how the whole effort was likely to end with hu-miliation at a "terrible cost." He advocated an expeditious compromise settlement of the conflict before the "investment trap" mired the United States beyond retrieval. Everything Ball had predicted came to pass.[8]

In early 1965, when the commitment of US troops was not substantial and containment of that involvement was still possible, such voices of reason and restraint struck a discordant tone in a confident and defiant Washington. The US involvement grew rapidly thereafter as the ARVN suffered heavy losses, in-cluding the vicinity of the capital. Communist attacks of May–June 1965 on the provincial capital of Song Be, barely fifty miles west of Saigon, on Quang Ngai in central Vietnam, and on the regional military headquarters in Dong Xoai in Phuoc Long Province destroyed some of the ARVN's best battalions, leading to the collapse of the government in Saigon. These setbacks triggered frantic requests from Westmoreland pleading how the South Vietnamese forces would not be able to withstand the Communist pressure any longer without a substantial addition of US ground troops, along with even more in-tensified bombing of North Vietnamese strategic targets. Westmoreland urged that the number of US troops be raised to 180,000, with an additional 100,000 during fiscal 1966 "to seize the initiative from the enemy." His chief, Robert McNamara, went beyond endorsing Westmoreland's request by asking the president to call up reserves. On July 28, 1965, LBJ announced that he was meeting Westmoreland's need for troops and that he was determined not to let the United States be defeated. "We will stand in Vietnam," he declared.

McNamara's War

Thus began "McNamara's War"—a gargantuan struggle between a super-power and a small third-world country. As Stanley Karnow observed,

So American soldiers went into action in Vietnam with the gigantic weight of an industry behind them. Never before in history was so much strength amassed in such a small corner of the globe against an opponent apparently so inconsequential. If Ho Chi Minh had described his war with France as a struggle between "grasshoppers and elephants," he was now a microbe facing a leviathan.[9]

The logistical chief of this massive mobilization—Robert McNamara—brought his superb assembly-line management skills he had honed at the Ford Motor Company, where he had risen to be the first non-Ford chairman of the board. The US fighting force had everything in the American armory except nuclear and missile weapons: jet bombers, helicopters, bombing arsenal, tanks, automatic rifles, chemicals, defoliants, medical equipment, and supplies, with the widest variety of PX goods, including all kinds of beer and cigarette brands. Karnow provides an eyewitness account of South Vietnam's "convulsive transformation" under McNamara's organizational magic wand.

American army engineers and private contractors labored around the clock, often accomplishing stupendous tasks in a matter of months. Their giant tractors and bulldozers and cranes carved out roads and put up bridges, and at one place in the Mekong delta they dredged the river to create a six-hundred-acre island as a secure campsite. They erected mammoth fuel depots and warehouses, some refrigerated. They constructed hundreds of helicopter pads and scores of airfields, including huge jet strips at Danang and Bienhoa . . . almost overnight, they built six new deep-raft harbors, among them a gigantic complex at Camranh Bay, which they completed at break-neck speed by towing prefabricated floating piers across the Pacific. They connected remote parts of the country with an intricate communications grid, and they linked Saigon to Washington with submarine cables and radio networks so efficient that US embassy officials could dial the White House in seconds and President Johnson could, as he did frequently, call to check on progress.[10]

What McNamara could not supply was superior motivation to that of the Viet Cong to fight a guerrilla war in the Mekong swamps or a political will to match Hanoi's determination. The Vietnamese, whether Communist cadres or nondescript recruits, were fighting for their country's reunification; the American troops, against an alleged Moscow–Beijing-sponsored Communist international conspiracy to take over all of Southeast Asia.

By the end of 1965, even while supervising every detail of the war, "the first real Secretary of Defense" as Secretary of State Dean Rusk described him and "a dull, narrow technocrat, who questioned nothing" as Professor Noam Chomsky—arguably the most vitriolic critic of the war—said about him,

McNamara developed serious doubts about the United States's role in Vietnam. Back from a visit to South Vietnam on December 17, 1965, he told members of a two-day special meeting on Vietnam at the White House that "our military action approach is an unacceptable way to a successful conclusion" and that it would be advisable to "explore other means." A fourteen-point major "peace offensive" was launched by Vice President Hubert H. Humphrey, McGeorge Bundy, and Averell Harriman to forty countries inviting North Vietnam to enter "negotiations without pre-conditions." To enable its success, a bombing pause was ordered that lasted thirty-seven days beginning Christmas day. On January 12, 1966, President Johnson ruefully expressed his frustration to the US Congress. "The days may become months and the months become years, but we will stay as long as aggression commands us to battle." The peace offensive stalled because Hanoi demanded an indefinite termination of bombing as a precondition to opening negotiations. The United States resumed bombing on the last day of January; no approaches were made to Hanoi for the next eleven months.

Impact of War on North and South Vietnam

Bombing, however, had very little affect on the progress of the war and soon became almost an end in itself. North Vietnam offered few bombing targets of real strategic value because its economy was largely agrarian, most of its sophisticated military equipment coming from Soviet and Chinese sources. For one-third of the year, during the monsoon season, poor weather obscured the landscape and inhibited the efficacy of strategic bombing. Moreover, the NLF's dependence on North Vietnamese supplies was not absolute; most of the NLF's ammunition was, in fact, obtained by capturing South Vietnamese and US arms depots. The bombing in the north united the people there and made them even more determined to fight.

Between 1965 and 1966, the South Vietnamese government became relatively stable. Or at least the premiership of Nguyen Cao Ky, the flamboyant air force marshal, and the presidency of General Nguyen Van Thieu lent the semblance of stability. Ky remained in the government as vice president and a real power at least until the Communist Tet offensive of 1968, when a number of his powerful allies in the armed forces were killed off. Thereafter, until 1975, the US government's policy was to strengthen the Thieu regime. During the Ky-Thieu and later Thieu regimes, the people continued to distrust the government, criticizing it in private for its acts of crass corruption and nepotism.

By spring 1965, US forces in South Vietnam numbered 45,500; in the next twenty-four months, the numbers would rise to a staggering half a million.

Corresponding US estimates of Viet Cong were 160,000 in spring 1965 and 250,000 two years later. The US military strategy was to search for and destroy the enemy in the south through a variety of means, including bombing, chemical defoliation, psychological warfare, and counterinsurgency operations. The criterion of success was not how much territory was conquered or brought under control but how many Viet Cong were killed. Unit commanders were consequently compelled to justify previous requests for aerial support by altering figures of enemy casualties, even if these were not matched by actual counts of bodies or captured weapons. Discrepancies in the body count were explained away by the Viet Cong "practice" of not leaving the dead behind. Weapon counts were manipulated by adding caches previously captured but not reported.

The United States gave massive economic and military aid to the Saigon government, whose armed forces numbered nearly 1 million by the end of the 1960s. The inevitable consequence of such a policy coupled with growing US military presence was the militarization of South Vietnamese society. The dominance of the armed forces was evident everywhere. Opportunities for graft and corruption available to military officials in a US-funded war were unlimited and debilitating to the larger society. Black marketing of basic necessities, smuggling of foreign goods, pilferage from US and South Vietnamese military bases, foreign exchange racketeering, and substandard performance in military construction jobs became rampant. A class of nouveau riche emerged that completely undermined the old social system in which bureaucrat intellectuals and monks had commanded general respect.

The war's effects on the common people were disastrous. Millions of desperate refugees from the countryside flocked to the cities. Many youths either volunteered or were forced by the NLF to join its military forces. Others were drafted by the ARVN. Still others escaped NLF recruitment or deserted the ARVN by dissolving into the burgeoning population of Saigon-Cholon. United States aid to South Vietnam did not improve the lot of the people there. A substantial portion of the funds went not into agricultural or industrial development but into the creation of services for the Americans. Some of the aid did go to bolstering the fighting efficiency of the South Vietnamese troops, but much simply lined the pockets of the generals. A large part of the economy consisted of a support population of secretaries, translators, interpreters, maids, shoeshine boys, and prostitutes, none of whom contributed to the economic production of goods. Agriculture suffered because of bombing raids, defoliation, the paucity of labor power, and the general lack of incentive. Many of the unfortunate migrants in cities remained unemployed, found themselves in the army, or became beggars, pimps, mafia underlings, or members of street gangs. Much of the population came to depend on the continued presence of US troops and the money they spent. Tempted by the lures of city life and fast money or simply out of economic necessity, young girls migrated to Saigon or to the periphery of US military bases to become prostitutes. According to a 1975 World Health Organization estimate, Saigon alone had about 400,000 prostitutes, making that city, as Senator William Fulbright described it, a huge brothel. The city's population expanded from the prewar 2 million to more than 7 million, placing an unbearable strain on the city's infrastructure.

By August 1971, there were 335,000 civilian dead, 740,000 wounded, 5 million refugees in Vietnam, and 1 million refugees in Laos. By 1975, there were an additional 4 to 5 million refugees (two-thirds of the country's total population) in Cambodia alone. As of December 31, 1971, the US armed forces reported 45,627 killed and 302,896 wounded; the South Vietnamese army had lost 137,000, with three times that number wounded. By 1971, the United States had spent over $150 billion, averaging more than $190,000 per NLF member killed. An MIT study pointed out that the costs of the war, including future payments to veterans, equaled the entire gross national product (GNP) of the United States in 1971—more than $750 billion.

US Disengagement

As early as 1967, a number of high US government officials were aware of the futility of the war in Vietnam, though they were then in a minority. The US mentality refused to accept defeat or acknowledge that the sophisticated weaponry that gave the United States tremendous land, water, and air superiority was ineffective in the face of the poorly clad, poorly fed, and poorly equipped Viet Cong, who were determined to sweep their land clean of foreign intruders once and for all regardless of the costs. It took a long time for the US generals trained in conventional warfare to understand the sociopolitical implications of guerrilla warfare and the frustrating inability to crush what might be called a people's war.

Such discordant voices in the US administration had been preceded by nationwide student protest. The national consensus that existed in favor of LBJ's policy in the wake of the Tonkin incident diminished substantially, particularly among the youth opposed to the draft. In November 1965, two students immolated themselves in front of the Pentagon and the United Nations; 20,000 people, mostly young, marched on the White House protesting US participation in the war and urging negotiations for peace. The American people were becoming increasingly divided toward the "unwanted and undeclared war." Although the majority did not favor a precipitate withdrawal, they wanted a cease-fire and negotiations toward a durable peace. The media became overwhelmingly critical. The doyen among journalists, Walter Lippman, who had previously supported US policy in Vietnam, cautioned on February 3, 1966, that LBJ would eventually find himself "in a dead-end street" unless he changed course. As the "attainment of our aims and the end of the fighting continues to elude us," Lippman said, there would be an unacceptable level of domestic turmoil. Equally, opposition in the US Senate increased as potential presidential hopefuls—notably Eugene McCarthy and Robert Kennedy—openly parted company with fellow Democrat Lyndon Baines Johnson. Kennedy complained the resumption of bombing as the "first in a series of steps on a road from which there is no turning back—a road that leads to catastrophe for all mankind."[11] Senator Fulbright accused the administration of "arrogance of power" and "loss of perspective."

By that time, the war had become LBJ's primary preoccupation, an obsession that woke him at nights (daytime in Vietnam) and brought him to the Situation Room in the White House for checking on the "progress." Any opposition to the war effort was regarded by LBJ as a personal affront deliberately directed to denigrating his presidency in history and importantly, destroying his chances of re-election. He ridiculed Fulbright as being "half bright" and accused opponents of the war, including draft dodgers, of sympathizing with the Communists and being traitors to the national cause.

Among US officials who began questioning the purposes of the war and America's role in it was defense secretary McNamara, whose attitude toward the conflict underwent radical changes. His visit to South Vietnam in December 1965 had been responsible for first doubts, reinforced not only by continuing reports of daily and weekly losses of men and aircraft but by memos from his civilian aides, notably John McNaughton and Adam Yarmolinsky, and by consultation with academics, particularly Jerome Weisner (MIT) and George Kistiakowsky (Harvard), and the Jason Study—the result of deliberations of a group of forty-seven academicians convened by these two professors in Wellesley, Massachusetts, in summer 1966. McNaughton, an original hard-liner much as McNamara himself, had morphed into a pragmatist owing to a widespread feeling in the country that the "establishment is out of its mind."[12] Notably, this was not the first time a McNamara aide had fundamentally differed from his boss's view (or for that matter, the administration's) of the Vietnam conflict. Alain Enthoven, a senior aide to McNamara, strayed from his chosen specialty (Europe) to write a memo on Vietnam. Enthoven plainly stated that the main issue in Vietnam was not communism but nationalism, which had "welded" the North Vietnamese together through more

than twenty years of almost uninterrupted fighting, and he predicted that nationalism would "continue to inspire them to endure greater hardships."
Bombing was not likely to destroy their society or determination and hope for
reunification of their country. The real task for the United States would be, if
possible, to create a similar nationalist spirit in South Vietnam, failing which
"we will have lost everything we have invested . . . no matter what military
success we may achieve."[13]

Back from yet another visit to South Vietnam in October 1966, McNamara
for the first time publicly admitted that the war was going badly for the
United States and that it would continue to worsen. He added that South
Vietnamese leadership was incapable of victory as long as they could not inspire the people to support the war effort. He still did not propose unconditional withdrawal from Vietnam. He wanted the troop strength and bombing
raids to be maintained at the same level, but now emphasized a more vigorous
pursuit of socioeconomic projects in South Vietnam to ameliorate the material conditions of the people. McNamara suggested some "credible gestures"
to induce the Communists to negotiate, such as a total bombing halt and the
possibility of giving the Viet Cong representation in the South Vietnamese
government. The generals remonstrated vociferously and went over the head
of their defense chief to their commander in chief. LBJ sided with them and
reaffirmed in his State of the Union Address at the start of 1967 his resolve to
"stand firm" in Vietnam.

McNamara's new position served as a catalyst for policy makers to identify
themselves as hawks or doves in official Washington. Perceived as hawks were
Dean Rusk, Walter Rostow, General Westmoreland, Admiral Sharp, Ambassador Ellsworth Bunker, and senators Stuart Symington, Henry Jackson, and
Strom Thurmond. Counted among the doves were Senator William Fulbright
and most members of the Senate Foreign Relations Committee. So were Mc-
George Bundy, George Ball, and Bill Moyers, all of whom resigned their official positions in the administration. In early 1967, skeptics included
McNamara, Averell Harriman, John McNaughton, and Alain Enthoven.

In the twenty-four months since mid–1965, the number of US troops in-
ducted in South Vietnam rose sharply from 45,000 to 500,000, a nearly twelve-
fold increase.[14] The corresponding US estimates of Viet Cong or NLF forces
moved up from 160,000 to 250,000, an increase of 56 percent. Yet the US and
ARVN troops were losing ground to their foes. Despite extensive "search and
destroy" operations—that included saturated bombing of suspected Viet Cong
strongholds, aerial chemical spraying of defoliants on vast jungle canopies,
psychological warfare, and counterinsurgency operations behind enemy
lines—there was no demonstrable progress for the US–South Vietnamese

forces. Confounding the evaluation of success were the criteria of success: US and South Vietnamese troops reported not how much territory was wrested from Viet Cong control but how many Viet Cong were killed each day of combat. These figures were monitored by the US command headquarters in Saigon and Pacific region headquarters in Honolulu and transmitted to the Pentagon and White House. Unit commanders routinely justified their requests for aerial support in the field by augmenting figures of Viet Cong casualties, even though they did not match the actual body count or number of captured weapons—the latter manipulated by producing weapons from caches captured elsewhere and not reported. As for the lower count of Viet Cong corpses, unit commanders ascribed it to the alleged Viet Cong practice of not leaving behind their dead comrades' bodies. Such vitiated statistics of Viet Cong casualties were reported to the US public on the evening television broadcasts. As critics of the war noted sarcastically, the number of reported Viet Cong casualties soon surpassed the CIA's estimate of total Viet Cong troops.

As the months rolled on in 1967, a frustrated McNamara veered more toward negotiation than military escalation as a means of bringing the conflict to a solution. Realizing that the Communists would not make significant concessions until after the US presidential elections in November 1968, McNamara presented a plan to the president that essentially recommended a holding operation. This would include continuation of bombing raids on North Vietnamese staging areas and the Ho Chi Minh Trail as well as energetic planning and implementation of socioeconomic programs in South Vietnam. By October, he was more forthright in the internal administration debates, recommending a halt to bombing at some early point to encourage the Communists to come to the table. McNamara also wanted to reduce the number of US troops in South Vietnam and study ways by which to reduce casualties and give the ARVN greater responsibility for the security of their own country. Those were the essentials of what later would be called "Vietnamization" during the Nixon administration. The Joint Chiefs of Staff criticized the McNamara plan for its "defeatism" and urged upon the president the need for more intensified bombing of the North and further escalating US troop commitment, even if it needed calling army reserves.

Public Opinion and Resignations of Policy Makers

A poll in October 1967 showed 46 percent of the public regarded the commitment to Vietnam was a "mistake" while 44 percent supported it. An overwhelming majority, however, were opposed to a complete withdrawal and favored stronger attacks against North Vietnam. The strongest support came from the college-educated, upper-income middle classes whose sons were least likely to be drafted for combat duty under the prevailing deferment system. By 1967, a number of high US officials became aware of the futility of pursuing an undeclared, unconventional war in Vietnam. Although they were in a minority, they were aware of the increasing frustration among the US public over the lack of progress in the war. Baffling to the skeptics in the government and to critics of the war among the wider public was the fact that the United States, despite its tremendous military superiority over land, water, and air, had proved ineffective against the poorly clad and poorly equipped Viet Cong, who seemed to regard no price too high to cleanse Vietnamese soil of American aliens—a continuation in their perspective of their nationalist, anticolonial struggle against the French. Yet it was hard for the US public and policy makers, accustomed as they were to the historical streak of US successes and its status of a superpower, to accept military reverses or defeat at the hands of a third-world country.

The end of 1967 saw a spate of resignations of important officials who could no longer stand the gulf between their personal opinion of the course of the war and their public posture of support to LBJ. Among the first was the national security advisor, McGeorge Bundy, who outlined the reasons for his resignation in a memorandum of November 10, 1967, to the president. Bundy held that Vietnam had become a political issue with the American voting public, who could not quite appreciate why General Westmoreland's strategy of "search and destroy" operations had failed to make any appreciable progress on the ground in South Vietnam.

McNamara resigned in March 1968. There has been considerable controversy regarding McNamara's role in what was nicknamed "McNamara's War." In his memoirs published nearly three decades later, he wrote of his conviction dating as early as the Gulf of Tonkin incident in mid–1964 that the primary problem in South Vietnam was not a military issue but a political and economic one, concluding that "unless we can introduce political and economic stability in that country, there is not any possibility of a military solution."[15] McNamara regretted that "under pressure of events and without clearly recognizing where our actions might lead, we had begun to change course."[16] In the award-winning documentary *Fog and War*, he saw his role for seven years as secretary of defense essentially as assisting the president in his policy, the kind of defense his critics said the Nazis had advanced for their crimes against humanity.

McNamara's successor, Clark Clifford, soon had similar reservations about the US role in Vietnam.

I was convinced that the military course we were pursuing was not only endless, but hopeless. A further substantial increase in US forces would only increase the devastation and the Americanization of the war and thus leave us even further from our goal of peace that would permit the people of South Vietnam to fashion their own political and economic institutions.[17]

Government and Politics in South Vietnam

A positive point in favor of relative stability in South Vietnam, at least at the central government level, was marked by the emergence of a new political duo, Nguyen Cao Ky and Nguyen Van Thieu, in June 1965. At thirty-four, Ky, a northerner, had risen to become air vice-marshal and commander of the South Vietnamese air force. He had worked with the CIA for some time. Ky was capable but impetuous and showed directness in dealing with those above him, including Americans. Often dressed in a flamboyant purple jumpsuit or some other colorful outfit, Ky had a striking presence. The forty-two-year-old Thieu, in contrast—a Catholic born in central Vietnam and chief of staff of the armed forces—was tactful to the point of being intriguing and deceitful. Ky became prime minister and Thieu chief of state in mid–1965.

A freshly convened constituent assembly gave the Republic of Vietnam (South Vietnam) a new constitution in early 1967. It provided for a presidential form of government with two houses of legislature on the pattern of the US Constitution, giving the president enormous powers. The first elections held under the new dispensation were "observed" by a US delegation of congressmen, governors, high officials, and business executives. By that time, both Thieu and Ky wanted to be president. A compromise under which Thieu would run for president and Ky for vice president was eventually agreed upon by both. Ky would also be chairman of a military cabal that would formulate official policy on all key matters. The uneasy alliance lasted through the four-year term, during which Thieu employed his guile to the utmost to win personal loyalty of key generals and accumulate almost all power in his hands, reducing Vice President Ky to the nominal authority that the US Constitution allowed to its vice president. When Ky filed for candidacy challenging Thieu in the October 1971 elections, Thieu managed to have him disqualified on a flimsy pretext and got himself elected president without a contest. Thereafter, Thieu remained head of state and of government until ten days before the final debacle of April 30, 1975, when South Vietnam was taken over by the North Vietnamese and NLF forces. Thieu was helped out by the CIA to Taiwan for some time, after which he settled down in Britain. Around the same time, Ky made it to California's Orange County, where later he wrote his memoirs.

The Tet Offensive

An event that conclusively changed the course of the war and adversely affected US will to continue the fighting occurred in early 1968. This was the Tet offensive, so called because it was launched on the Vietnamese national holiday of Tet. The Communist documentation currently available indicates that the Vietnamese Communist Party (VCP)'s Politburo and the Central Office of South Vietnam (COSVN) ordered in mid–1967 the preparation of a contingency plan for large-scale attacks on Saigon and other main cities, which would compel the United States to deploy troops in their defense and deescalate the general war and also importantly, stop the bombing of the North. Such a widespread, synchronized offensive would convince the United States that the Vietnam war was unwinnable and that it would be prudent to negotiate a political settlement of the problem and withdraw its troops. A series of conferences ensued, at which representatives of the Politburo, the DRV's Ministry of Defense, the COSVN, and the Communist military commanders in the South discussed details of the proposed offensive, culminating in the VCP's Central Committee's resolution of October 25, 1967, ordering a general offensive in the south, with attacks mainly on Saigon and upper Mekong Delta provinces. The resolution—dubbed the Quang Trung Resolution after the Vietnamese emperor of that name, who had defeated Chinese invaders during the Tet festival in 1789—envisaged neither a total nor an immediate Communist victory. Three scenarios were outlined: a complete victory that would compel the United States to enter negotiations; partial success that would include US-ARVN troops retaking cities and continuing the war; or complete Communist failure that might encourage the United States to augment its combat strength and even extend the war into Laos and Cambodia. The planned offensive would extend in three phases from January to October 1968. The first phase, from January to March, would aim at major strikes on urban centers; the second phase would consolidate gains in the newly occupied areas; the third would provide leadership for a general uprising against the South Vietnamese government in a final attempt to bring it down.

For several months before the Tet offensive, the war was going badly for both sides. The US-ARVN were frustrated that the war was dragging on with hardly any territorial gains. The US bombing, however, was inflicting losses on North Vietnam on a scale the latter had not anticipated. Since 1965, the north had been sending a large number of their regulars in response to the dramatic augmentation of US combat troops in the south. By 1967, North Vietnam was finding it increasingly difficult to make up for the heavy NLF casualties or to maintain the flow of supplies along the Ho Chi Minh Trail to the south. Moreover, the NLF was finding it difficult to get fresh recruits in the countryside, which was being increasingly deserted by young men heading for the cities as refugees or fleeing to the relative security of the central highlands. Giap, the master strategist and defense minister of the DRV, admitted in the 1980s that the US bombing had resulted in heavy losses both in the north and the south, and that it was an important factor in the Politburo's decision to launch the Tet offensive. Giap also admitted that such a major departure from their strategy of a war of attrition was undertaken for its likely impact on public opinion in the United States and on LBJ's prospects in the presidential elections in 1968.

On January 31, 1968, the Vietnamese Lunar Year, or Tet, the Viet Cong attacked the US embassy in Saigon and occupied its compound for a day. On the same day and during that week, the Viet Cong–North Vietnamese Army (NVA) units attacked and occupied almost all the major cities and towns in South Vietnam, including the ancient imperial capital of Hué. General Westmoreland reported to McNamara that as of February 11, the Communists had attacked 34 of 44 provincial towns, 64 of 242 district towns, and all of the autonomous cities. He added that the Viet Cong were helped in this massive effort to the extent of 20 percent to 35 percent by the NVA, "employed as gap filler," where Viet Cong strength "was apparently not adequate." Except for Hué, which was held by the Viet Cong–NVA for more than six weeks until February 24, all the other urban centers were retaken by the US-ARVN forces within a week of their occupation by the Viet Cong.

The suddenness and enormity of the Tet offensive shocked the US and South Vietnamese governments alike. Its timing during the Tet holidays, noted in previous years for truce on both sides in the conflict (much like the US Christmas pause in bombing), was unexpected. While on the one hand, the US forces were put on maximum alert, a large number of South Vietnamese troops were granted leave to enjoy the national holiday. President Thieu was away on a two-week vacation. Such complacency was based on the NLF's inability thus far to hold any urban facility in South Vietnam for more than a week. Their attacking commandos, always a handful, had failed on most occasions to get reinforcements before the US-ARVN gained the upper hand and retook the facility.

This time, however, was different. A mere 1,000 NLF troops kept more than 11,000 US-ARVN troops engaged in Saigon for three weeks. The Communists had been able to hold several cities and towns for a week and Hué, the former imperial capital, for the longest period of all—more than six weeks. The losses on all sides in that short period were staggering.

The US military was shocked by the enormity of the NLF–NVA strength demonstrated by the Tet offensive. In their view, however, the Communists had launched the offensive not from a position of strength but out of "desperation."

Therefore, General Westmoreland as well as the Joint Chiefs of Staff recommended more of the same remedy as before: more ground troops, enlargement of the zone around Hanoi and Haiphong for bombing, and "blanket authority" to air commanders to bomb strategic targets so as to interdict the flow of supplies to the south. And the president went along, at least for the time being, with the army's request because, as he made clear, the United States "was not prepared to accept the defeat in Vietnam." At his instance, McNamara authorized an additional deployment of ground troops going beyond the previously approved ceiling of 525,000—and sending to South Vietnam the 82nd Airborne Division and about one-half of a Marine Corps division, both of them consisting largely of Vietnam veterans. By the end of February, however, the situation on the ground had worsened so much that following a visit to South Vietnam, General Wheeler reported that the NVA–NLF still held the initiative and were operating with "relative freedom" in the countryside. Far from being crushed or decimated, he added that the NLF's recovery was likely to be rapid because their supplies were adequate enough to maintain the momentum of the winter-spring offensive, concluding that the NLF's determination was "unshaken" and had "the will and the capability to continue." He joined Westmoreland in requesting an additional 206,756 troops (including fifteen tactical fighter squadrons).

The Tet offensive produced a military stalemate, though it did have a tremendous impact on US politics. The NLF was not successful in holding any of the cities and towns except Hué, and that for only a short period. The NLF's expectation that the Tet offensive would inspire major popular uprisings in its favor all over urban Vietnam did not materialize. Its losses were heavy—about 40,000 killed and many more wounded. The effect on US and South Vietnamese forces was disastrous. In Washington, a major debate on the potential costs of continuing the war took place based on the assumption that only a quarter of North Vietnam's forces were involved in the Tet offensive. It was feared that a larger commitment of NVA troops might escalate the costs of the war beyond the threshold of tolerance of the American public. From that point on, the United States seemed resolved to disengage from Vietnam "with honor." Bombing and other forms of warfare would be continued to secure the best terms in the ensuing negotiations. McNamara resigned on February 28. On March 31, LBJ in a nationwide broadcast told of his resolve not to run for re-election in November. According to Dean Rusk, LBJ's decision was prompted by his belief that "if he took himself out of the political process, it would enhance his position in bringing the war in Vietnam to an end."[18] In tune with the president's altered strategy of depending on negotiations to end the conflict, he turned down the March 1968 request of generals Wheeler and Westmoreland for an additional 206,000 troops. By the end of the year, Richard Nixon was elected to the presidency on a platform of "ending the war and winning the peace" in Vietnam.

Nixon, Kissinger, and the International Situation

Nixon's presidency began with his stated goal of an "era of negotiations" with the Soviet Union, a détente in the same manner as the Soviet Union had done with Western Europe. The Soviet Union sought accommodation with its former archrival, the United States, in order to strengthen itself against its perceived threat from China. The Soviets desperately needed an infusion of Western, especially US, technology and it needed to divert from the disastrously expensive and unneeded strategic arms race with the United States to modernize its economy. While a US–Soviet détente may be desirable in itself, Nixon's principal preoccupation was how to secure honorable withdrawal from Vietnam with minimum military losses to the United States and by retaining the political integrity of the Republic of Vietnam. As a senior official in the State Department, Raymond Garthoff, observed, "The dominant foreign policy preoccupation of Nixon and Kissinger in 1969, and indeed, for the entire period through 1972 was not a détente summit meeting with Moscow but finding an honorable exit from Vietnam."[19] Kissinger himself has noted in *The White House Years* that his aim was "to enlist the Soviet Union in a rapid settlement of the Vietnam war. In all my conversations with Dobrynin, I had stressed that a fundamental improvement in U.S.–Soviet relations presupposed Soviet cooperation in settling the war."[20]

As the Nixon–Kissinger duo built bridges of détente with the Soviet Union, it simultaneously made diplomatic overtures to China as a counterweight to the Soviet Union and as a likely mediator with the DRV, urging Hanoi to compromise in the same manner as did China during the Geneva conference in 1954. The Sino-Soviet relations, mildly strained since 1959, had worsened in the mid–1960s, with each rivaling to be leader of world communism and influencing the Communist parties in other countries—most importantly in Vietnam. Until the late 1960s, the DRV had managed adroitly to secure military and economic assistance from both Communist giants, depending on China for small and less sophisticated weapons while receiving from the Soviet Union technologically advanced equipment such as radar, surface-to-air missiles, and antiaircraft guns. With China embroiled in the unsettling Cultural Revolution, the Soviet Union's assistance—military, economic, and diplomatic—was crucial to the DRV. Until his death in 1969, Ho Chi Minh managed not to allow pro-China and pro-Soviet factions within the VCP to affect the pursuit of war in the south. He had also balanced his government's relations with the rival Communist giants, refusing Chinese pressure to condemn Soviet "hegemonism"—pleading that tiny Vietnam, involved in a life-and-death struggle with the United States, could not afford the luxury of alienating either the Soviet Union or China. China's relations with the Soviet Union deteriorated in the late 1960s, bringing the two to major border clashes and deployment of several divisions of rival forces along the Ussuri River. China perceived the Soviet Union under Leonid Brezhnev as entering into pacts and alliances with several countries in a bid to "encircle" China. China suddenly felt the need as never before of befriending the United States at the same time as the Soviet Union, too, desired a détente with its rival in the cold war.

The complicated world situation, particularly the state of Sino-Soviet relations, suited Nixon and Kissinger, whose finesse in keeping several balls in the air at the same time helped the United States in its bid to get the best terms possible during the tortuous negotiations on Vietnam in Paris. For some years, the United States and China had maintained secret contacts in Warsaw, their respective ambassadors to Poland periodically meeting to apprise each other of their countries' position on matters of mutual interest. These ties were immeasurably strengthened by Kissinger's furtive visit to Beijing in early 1972, which was followed by Nixon's visit to China even though the United States had not yet recognized the People's Republic of China. The American détente with the Soviet Union and China played a crucial, almost determining role in the eventual signing of the Paris Accords on Vietnam in January 1973.

From 1969 to the signing of the Paris accords in January 1973, the United States followed, albeit with some modifications, the "two tracks plan" of Henry Kissinger, Nixon's national security adviser and, later, US secretary of state.[21] According to Kissinger's plan, the United States and the DRV would negotiate a military settlement of the war whereas the Saigon government would seek a political accommodation with the NLF. Although US forces would gradually be withdrawn, a greatly expanded ARVN—armed and supplied by the United States—would bear the brunt of the fighting. The process was dubbed "Vietnamization." This would also save US honor and bring the American boys home. The ARVN soon had more than 1 million troops, including eighteen- and nineteen-year-old draftees taken from the poor peasant population; large numbers of city dwellers avoided the draft through bribery or influence. The greater flow of US monetary aid only worsened the social situation.

On the larger plane, Nixon promulgated a new doctrine in May 1969 to limit the US role in subsequent Vietnam-type situations. In the face of future aggression that did not involve one of the nuclear powers, the United States would "provide elements of military strength and economic resources approximate to our size and our interests" and would consider the "defense and progress of other countries" as "first, their responsibility and second, a regional responsibility."[22] The new policy was also based on rapprochement with China, which seemed eager to use its newfound friendship with the United States against the Soviet Union. During Nixon's visit to Beijing in February 1972, the Chinese, in secret agreements, allegedly promised not to attack Taiwan precipitately and to tolerate a US presence in Vietnam on the same reduced level as in South Korea. As mentioned earlier, Beijing's interest in leaving Vietnam divided fit into the traditional Chinese policy of weakening its neighbors, whether Communist or not. The Nixon Doctrine would promote Vietnamization with peace and honor for the United States. It would also shore up the strength of the declining dollar worldwide. The US policy was, in the words of Whittle Johnston, who had worked for McGeorge Bundy and Kissinger, "a measured effort to preserve the solvency under the conditions of eroding domestic support."[23]

The "gradual" withdrawal of US troops did not occur without further bloodshed. Efforts to make the operation compatible with the achievement of peace with honor involved resumption of more saturation bombing of North Vietnam (which had been halted by President Johnson) and of the countryside in South Vietnam and the mining of Haiphong Harbor to prevent Soviet supplies from reaching North Vietnam. From 1970 to 1973, the Vietnamese conflict truly became an Indochinese war. Its implications were grave. The bombing of Laos and Cambodia was undertaken to strike at Communist bases and supply routes from North to South Vietnam passing through those countries. The large-scale invasion of Cambodia in 1970 was aimed at capturing the alleged underground headquarters of the Central Office of South Vietnam. (It was not found.) A large number of peasants were killed in these operations, and millions of refugees from the countryside flocked into Cambodia's capital of Phnom Penh, contributing to the swelling of its population from half a million to 4 million—half the country's entire population. The bombing during Nixon's first two years in office surpassed the total tonnage the United States dropped in Europe and the Pacific during World War II. In May 1972, the daily costs of bombing were estimated at $20 million.

Cambodia Since Geneva

Cambodia was the most successful of the three Indochinese states in achieving a national integration and preserving its independence despite the wars raging around it. Its success could, in large measure, be attributed to the magnetic, complex personality of Norodom Sihanouk, who was the country's king at the time of the French withdrawal in July 1954. In March 1955, he abdicated the throne and the position of head of state in favor of his father so as to free himself actively to participate in the country's politics and lead its government until his sudden overthrow in 1970. Immensely powerful and popular, Sihanouk kept his small country from becoming seriously enmeshed in the neighboring conflict.

Cambodia's foreign policy during the Sihanouk era amounted to a struggle to survive as an independent state hemmed in between two potentially hostile neighbors, Thailand and Vietnam. At the Afro-Asian Conference at Bandung in April 1955, thanks to Nehru's mediation, Sihanouk received from China and the DRV adequate assurances of noninterference in the affairs of his country. Thereafter, Sihanouk adopted neutrality in foreign affairs as a "dictate of necessity."[24] Until the early 1960s, he alternated between pro-West and pro-Communist policies. By the middle of the decade, however, he became convinced that the future lay with China as the regional power, the United States's interest in the region and ability to control it being limited and transient. Sihanouk also decided that the North Vietnamese and the NLF represented the winning side in the Vietnam conflict and were therefore potential neighbors of Cambodia. Consequently, friendship with the Chinese and the Vietnamese Communists became the anchors of Cambodia's foreign policy, though the Cambodian leadership trusted neither side. Sihanouk was suspicious of the Vietnamese for their traditional expansionism at Cambodia's expense. Further, he distrusted Communists in general, as they might well see a feudal prince as a logical candidate for political liquidation. Yet Sihanouk knew that friendship with China could be used as a lever against the Vietnamese, who were historically suspicious of their northern neighbors. Sihanouk thus befriended his enemy's enemy.

Cambodia's Neutrality

Intent upon safeguarding its national integrity, Cambodia nervously watched its borders. In 1964–1965, exasperated by frequent frontier incursions by US and South Vietnamese forces in pursuit of guerrillas, Sihanouk severed diplomatic relations with the United States. In the following years, however, the Communist use of Cambodian territory increased. The US bombing of North Vietnam and of the Ho Chi Minh Trail passing through southeast Laos had made it necessary for North Vietnam to seek alternate routes of supply. The Ho Chi Minh Trail was extended to northeast Cambodia, which lay beyond the bombing zone. More significant, the Communists used the facilities of the new port of Sihanoukville to bring in supplies and materiel from North Vietnam and China. These would be transported by profit-seeking Chinese entrepreneurs in Phnom Penh to the eastern provinces, where the Communists had built underground storage facilities. As the war expanded, the Communists occupied larger chunks of Cambodian territory, allegedly using them as sanctuaries for about 20 percent of their forces.

There is no doubt that the Communists badly needed the sanctuaries and would hold them with or without Sihanouk's consent. Recognizing the inevitable, the Cambodian prince strove to keep Communist occupation to a limited area by obtaining Communist promises of self-restraint. To maintain some degree of control over the Vietnamese Communists, Sihanouk allowed the NLF to maintain a legation in Phnom Penh.

The Communists abandoned such restraints toward the end of 1968. The area of the sanctuaries under Communist use and control increased. Well-staffed hospitals, extensive training camps, and ammunition-manufacturing facilities replaced the rudimentary structures of the earlier days. The Communists established an almost complete administration in the area, even collecting taxes and growing crops. By the beginning of 1969, varied accounts, Cambodian and American, placed the estimates of Communist troops in the sanctuaries at 40,000 to 50,000. United States intelligence further claimed that the headquarters of the guerrilla movement, COSVN, was itself based well within Cambodia's borders.

The Khmer Rouge

Of immediate concern for Sihanouk's government was the increase in the activities of the Khmer Rouge, the Cambodian Communists. In 1954, because of Sino-Soviet pressures at Geneva, the Viet Minh had abandoned the cause of the Khmer Rouge, agreeing that it be disbanded and that its cadres retreat to Hanoi. Consequently, about 5,000 Khmer Rouge, later labeled the Hanoi Khmers, withdrew to North Vietnam. A few radicals, known as the Khmer Viet Minh, were decimated by Sihanouk's government. The radical ranks were later reinforced by younger and newer leaders such as Ieng Sary, Khieu Samphan, Hou Yuon, and Saloth Sar (later known as Pol Pot), most of them trained in law or economics.[25] In contrast to the Hanoi-based Khmer Rouge, many of whose members were married to Vietnamese women, the new breed of Cambodian Communists (also known as Khmer Rouge) were nationalist Communists, fiercely anti-Hanoi and independent of the Indochina Communist Party. The new Khmer Rouge never forgot nor did they forgive the Vietnamese Communists for their "betrayal" in 1954.[26] In the late 1960s, contrary to Hanoi's wishes, the new Khmer Rouge conducted maquis-type operations against Sihanouk's government.

Sihanouk was not privy to the internal dispute between the Khmer Rouge and the Vietnamese Communists. In January 1970, he went abroad, ostensibly for medical treatment of chronic obesity but really to try to bring diplomatic pressure on Hanoi to restrain the Khmer Rouge. During his absence in March 1970, his prime minister, General Lon Nol (who was pro-US and anti-Khmer Rouge), staged a coup deposing him. Sihanouk learned of the coup while he was on his way home via Moscow. Accepting asylum in China, he headed the Cambodian government-in-exile. In a book written from exile, he blamed the CIA for his ouster.[27] Some time between 1970 and 1975, the Khmer Rouge made Sihanouk (in Beijing, but still popular in Cambodia) the nominal head of the Khmer Rouge; the prince seemed to have no choice but to accept the role.

Meanwhile, the United States withheld support from the Lon Nol regime for a "respectable" period of five weeks. Thereafter, the Nixon administration stood solidly behind the Lon Nol government with plenty of military assistance to fight the Khmer Rouge, who had, by April 27, 1970, blocked five out of the seven approach roads to the capital. Washington used its new leverage with Phnom Penh for enlarging the Vietnam conflict. In a gross reversal of his policy of withdrawal from Vietnam, Nixon decided on April 30 to invade Cambodia and capture the COSVN, which the United States believed to be the headquarters of the Communist military operations in South Vietnam. The official explanation was that one such decisive victory would tilt the balance and compel Hanoi and the NLF to agree to a political settlement at the Paris talks.

The US action did indeed fuel a civil war in Cambodia, a land that had so far been an oasis of peace in the midst of the holocaust in Laos and Vietnam. As for the military value of the adventure, it was very limited; large caches of ammunition were found but not the COSVN itself.

The Paris Accords of 1973

On January 27, 1973, the DRV, the Provisional Revolutionary Government (PRG) of South Vietnam, the Republic of Vietnam, and the United States finally signed the Paris Accords, bringing about a cease-fire in Vietnam, Cambodia, and Laos. The agreement provided for withdrawal of all US troops, the return of prisoners of war to the parties concerned, and a cease-fire without demarcation lines. For South Vietnam, there was to be a democratic solution: The PRG and the Thieu government were to resolve their conflicts through mutual consultation. A Council of Reconciliation and Concord was to be set up to organize elections in the south, after which a tripartite coalition government of Thieu, the PRG, and neutralists would be created. Reunification of Vietnam could be considered through subsequent consultations between the north and the south. With regard to Laos and Cambodia, the Paris Accords confirmed the provisions of the Geneva agreements of 1954 and 1962.

Among the unstated provisions of the Paris settlement was an "understanding" that North Vietnam would continue to station about 140,000 troops in South Vietnam until such a coalition government was established in Saigon. This made the Vietnamese parties to the accords view the truce as a temporary one, because none was really sure that the proposed political arrangement would be implemented to the satisfaction of all parties. As it happened two years later, the DRV used its troops in the south as the vanguard of its march into Saigon in April 1975 and takeover of South Vietnam. Underlying the accords was an exchange of letters between the United States and the DRV whereby the US agreed to pay $3.2 billion toward the reconstruction of North Vietnam, ravaged by US bombing. The sum was never paid. The North Vietnamese march into Saigon in April 1975 had, in Washington's view, absolved the United States of that promise. The DRV, however, made the release of POWs and information about US troops missing in action (MIA) dependent on the United States paying the "promised" reconstruction assistance—a condition Hanoi finally gave up in the early 1990s.

Communist Victory in Vietnam and Cambodia

Not long after signing the peace accords, the three Vietnamese parties—the PRG, DRV, and Thieu—again took up their conflict. Thieu demanded immediate withdrawal of DRV troops as a prerequisite to elections, though neither the DRV nor the PRG had ever acknowledged the presence of North Vietnamese troops in the south. Thieu also hampered the PRG candidates' freedom of movement to campaign. With Thieu mounting a new offensive against the PRG-held areas, war was resumed by the end of the year. The level of military operations was on the whole low-key on all sides, however, because of the reduced levels of external support from the United States, China, and the Soviet Union.

The eagerness with which the US forces had pulled out and the congressional prohibition of any recommitment of US combat troops made it most unlikely that the United States would return to South Vietnam if the latter were attacked by the north with overwhelming strength. The Paris Accords had left the balance of forces decidedly in favor of North Vietnam, leaving to Hanoi the choice of the opportune moment for attacking the south. In March 1975, the DRV suddenly launched a major offensive that ended in the capture of Saigon on April 30.

The DRV's gamble was perhaps predicated on the military weakness of the Thieu government caused by reduced US aid and the perception that the administration of Gerald Ford would be incapable of any retaliation owing to the post-Watergate US political environment and dwindling US commitment to the conflict. The gamble paid off. Thieu's order to his army in the central highlands to make a "tactical retreat" led to their resounding defeat. Thieu resigned on April 21 and left the country. A government established under the neutralist General Duong Van Minh surrendered to the Communist forces on April 30. It was a victory for the bulk of the Vietnamese people, who had fought long for this moment. In recognition of Ho Chi Minh's contribution to the movement, Saigon was renamed Ho Chi Minh City.

Meanwhile, in Cambodia, the Khmer Rouge had continued its guerrilla operations against the Lon Nol regime. The Khmer Rouge ranks were not, however, united. In the early 1970s, Hanoi had sent to Cambodia about 5,000 Khmer Rouge who had lived in North Vietnam since 1954. These Hanoi Khmers, as they were disparagingly called by the indigenous Khmer Rouge under Pol Pot's leadership, were expected to control the latter, inhibiting their independence and frustrating the Cambodian goal of thwarting long-term North Vietnamese ambitions to dominate all of Indochina. After the Paris accords of January 1973, open conflict developed, the Pol Pot group purging or killing large numbers of the Hanoi Khmers. The Khmer Rouge did not comply with Hanoi's urging to lay down arms as stipulated in the Paris peace accords. Although Hanoi cut off all further military assistance, the Khmer Rouge continued with the offensive, toppling the Lon Nol regime a fortnight before the North Vietnamese capture of Saigon.

Reasons for the US Failure in Vietnam

The US debacle in Vietnam can be attributed primarily to the incorrect diagnosis of the reasons for the insurrection. The conflict was not as much pro-Communist as it was anti-Diem and later anti-Ky and anti-Thieu, all of whom failed to initiate and implement the much-needed political and socioeconomic reforms. Beginning as it did with the southern initiative, the movement was manned and supported mainly by southerners and not by Hanoi, as Washington had wrongly perceived. The conflict called for a political rather than a military solution, possibly to satisfy a widespread urge to reunify the country.

The infusion of massive US military aid fueled inflation. The economic aid was not substantial. Moreover, as much as 40 percent of the economic aid, according to a *New York Times* estimate, was swallowed by corrupt contractors, high administrators, generals, business intermediaries, and government officials. US supplies meant for the war effort were pilfered on a gigantic scale. As former premier Nguyen Cao Ky wrote in 1976, "In Qui Nhon market, you could buy anything from army rations and clothing to washing machines and grenades . . . and if you wanted to buy a tank or a helicopter it would be arranged."[28]

The infusion of US military forces had an even worse effect. The specter of alien forces on Vietnamese soil revived anticolonial, nationalist sentiment. The Second Indochina War was as much directed against the US presence as was the first against the French colonial rule. The Vietnamese rightly perceived that it was because of US support that several corrupt, self-serving military dictatorships had survived in Saigon for a decade and in Cambodia for half a decade, contributing to social and moral decay, spiraling inflation, and devastation of the countryside. After 1964, large numbers of non-Communist university students and faculty and professionals joined the NLF because, like their predecessors at the turn of the previous century, they seemed to feel they were on the verge of losing their country. In the early years after the Geneva settlement of 1954, the United States failed to insist on socioeconomic reforms or liberalization of the political process—and thus failed to create among the South Vietnamese people either a feeling that they had some stake in the country's independence or a desire to support the central government. The shortcomings of the Diem regime were basic; the momentum lost was never regained. The postponement of sociopolitical reforms until the end of the military conflict and the characterization of that conflict as one between Communists and anti-Communists contributed to US ineffectiveness and to South Vietnam's ruin.

CHAPTER 7

The New Vietnam

Vietnam suffered immensely in the period following World War II, undergoing continual conflict from 1940 to 1975, with only a brief respite of peace following the Geneva agreements of 1954. Millions of Vietnamese children grew up in that period carrying memories of bloodshed, terror, bombing, and dislocation. Vietnam occupied the front page of newspapers and figured prominently in other media consistently for years, probably more than any other single country or event during that time. The Vietnamese conflict divided public opinion all over the globe, particularly in the United States, whose social, political, and economic fabric was torn by the long, undeclared war. That a small country with only low-grade weaponry could hold back a large and well-armed nation put in doubt the very basis of strategic defense in the modern world.

The loss in human lives was staggering. Eight million tons of bombs, four times the tonnage used in World War II, had been rained on a tiny country. Ten million gallons of a chemical, Agent Orange, had been sprayed in order to destroy the canopy of its lush forests. The United States spent nearly $150 billion and lost about 58,000 lives (with several times that number maimed or disabled for life); the figures for the Vietnamese on both sides of the conflict were unavailable, but casualties were roughly estimated at more than 2 million. The disruption of normal life was spread over many years for some but lasted at least a decade for the nearly 5 million refugees from the countryside who flocked to major cities for protection.[1] Saigon became a cesspool of vice where a large segment of the noncombatant population busied itself in corruption of diverse sorts. Human morality and values seemed to lay in irreparable ruin all over South Vietnam. It was, therefore, a great relief for millions of people to see the end of the Vietnamese conflict in 1975. The end of the war and the reunification of Vietnam a year later were hoped to usher in an era of peace and reconstruction to a war-ravaged country.

In at least the first decade after the war ended, the Communist leadership in Vietnam did not show itself as adept at peace and reconstruction as it was at war and revolution. The bleak economic situation in Vietnam in the decade following the end of the war in 1975 may, in some substantial measure, be attributable to the particular conditions in the previous decade. The continued failure of the Vietnamese government to improve the economic condition of the common citizen is related to several other factors, including leadership. The socioeconomic legacy of a long and devastating war; the special character of the US-subsidized, war-oriented economy of South Vietnam; a succession of natural disasters such as droughts and floods between 1976 and 1978; wars with China and occupation of Cambodia; and the absence of expected foreign assistance all may be responsible for the failure to stabilize the economy and fulfill the wants of a people whose primary consumer needs had been denied for decades.

In the short run, the leadership was divided between those who stood for ideological purity and insisted upon the immediate transformation of the South Vietnamese economy to socialism and those pragmatists and moderates who saw no alternative to making concessions and offering capitalist incentives, especially to encourage agricultural production in the south. Economic policies therefore vacillated from liberalism in 1975–1976 to rigidity during 1976–1979, to make way again for limited private trade and manufacturing and practical incentives to farmers. For the morale of revolutionary cadres, the impact of such a policy of postponing the creation of a Communist society was indeed grave.

The war's adverse effect on the economy of North Vietnam and on the society and economy of South Vietnam were incalculable. The war in the countryside had turned South Vietnam, formerly a leading exporter of rice, into an importer of grain to feed a large population that could not attend to agriculture, had been conscripted into the army, or had simply fled to urban centers. Nevertheless, the war had created a false sense of prosperous economy, particularly in Saigon and around the US military bases. The vast array of imported consumer goods, including shiny automobiles, stereo systems, and electrical appliances, was subsidized by the United States. The large amounts of external funds pumped into the economy resulted in galloping inflation, impoverishing the middle class and people with fixed incomes. The only people who seemed to prosper in the US-sponsored "free enterprise" system were smugglers, black marketers, building contractors, and intermediaries of all sorts, not to mention pimps and prostitutes.

During the Second Indochina War (1964–1975), the southern economy had thus become almost parasitical, dependent on external financing and on purchases by the US armed forces of South Vietnamese goods and services. More than 50 percent of the gross national product was generated by a service sector almost completely dependent upon a US-funded war and in which imports (equal to 25 percent of the GNP in 1971) were twelve times the exports. The industry accounting for 8 percent of the GNP was 85 percent dependent upon foreign countries for raw materials and absolutely dependent on foreign machines and fuel. Consequently, with the beginning of the withdrawal of US forces in 1971, the service sector suffered grievously, bringing the rate of growth of the GNP in the following four years to about 1 percent per annum, while the population increased by about 3 percent. The subsequent debacle of the Saigon government burst the economic bubble completely.

The economic situation in North Vietnam, too, was critical. The losses there due to US "strategic" bombing from 1965 to 1972 were staggering. A United Nations' mission visiting Vietnam in 1976 reported that the entire North Vietnamese economic infrastructure had been blasted out of existence during those seven years. Railroads had been thrown out of commission for long stretches on various lines, most of the bridges on the Hanoi-Langson and Hanoi-Vinh lines having been blown up. Tongking's dike system, built over two millennia, suffered grievously, with 183 dams and canals and 884 water installations in need of major repairs. Twenty-nine of the thirty provincial capitals were damaged and nine of them completely destroyed. Thousands of villages were damaged, dozens obliterated.

Hanoi had, however, taken advantage of the time—about twenty-eight months—that elapsed between the cessation of US bombing of North Vietnam and the Communist takeover of Saigon to restore its infrastructure, including Tongking's intricate and vital dike system. By mid–1975, the government had repaired or rebuilt the numerous cement and glass enterprises as well as dockyards in the Haiphong industrial sector, the chemical enterprises in Viet Tri, and the steel complex in the Thai Nguyen industrial center. Roads and bridges had also become serviceable again.

The ecological balance in the south had been damaged the most. The report of the UN Commission to Vietnam pointed out that chemical warfare had created a large number of "blank zones" in the countryside. The US armed forces had engaged in large-scale defoliation because the thick foliage helped the guerrillas to hide and also obstructed the landing of US aircraft. The defoliation operations were undertaken, however, in the name of a "food denial program" against the guerrillas. By 1969, more than 5 million acres of land had been sprayed with herbicides, mostly Agent Orange against forest vegetation and Agent Blue (which had arsenic in its composition) against rice and other food crops. The ruinous impact of these chemicals on the productive abilities of the soil was immeasurable. The removal of the jungle canopy increased the exposure of the soil to sunlight, which altered the soil's properties. The rate of soil erosion increased with rapid exhaustion of humus. It was estimated that an equivalent of three decades of South Vietnam's timber supply had been destroyed and that it would take anywhere from five years for the fruit trees to a century or so for the rare timber trees to become productive again.[2]

Postwar Economic Measures

After the Communist victory in 1975, the new government took up the task of reconstruction at all levels: economic, social, political, ideological. Huynh Kim Khanh summarized the gamut of socioeconomic woes of the new Vietnam thus:

> The legacy of the US-Thieu regime was an economic and social malaise of unknown proportions: an economy that was on the verge of bankruptcy; a threatening famine in the northern provinces of Central Vietnam; more than three million unemployed people, excluding an army of a half-million prostitutes about to be out of work; six to seven million refugees who had been forced by wartime activities to flee their native villages into the cities, etc.[3]

The new government also had to do something about the former employees of the deposed government of South Vietnam, which included 1.1 million regular troops in addition to the half million paramilitary forces, 125,000 police, and 350,000 civil service officials, only some of whom could be relied upon for their loyalties to the Communist regime. Given the ideological context, reconstruction in the south meant not only rehabilitation of urban refugees but relocation and "reeducation" of several million individuals, practically one-third to one-half the population of South Vietnam. Also to be relocated were a large number of handicapped persons from an estimated 2.2 million war casualties, some of whom could not be expected to contribute to the rebuilding of the economy at full strength and who, in fact, might need state assistance of some kind.

The new government's short-term strategy was twofold: to convert the economy from "free enterprise" to socialist and to integrate the South Vietnamese economy with its northern counterpart. Its immediate tasks included efforts to restore the industrial capacity of the Saigon-Cholon area and to dispatch a large number of people to the countryside to take up agriculture again. The government planned an immediate additional employment for more than 1 million people in agriculture and allied occupations by bringing more than 1.2 million acres of fallow land in the Mekong Delta under cultivation. The new slogan in mid–1975 was "Break with the past: return to the countryside to work for production." As in post-revolutionary China, the new program had its sadistic overtones in compelling the city-bred, soft-lived intellectuals, civil servants, and vast numbers of army officials of the former government to work with their hands in a "reeducation" program.

Other short-term measures announced by the government were largely in the area of banking and currency reform. Thus private banks and other financial and lending institutions were abolished in August 1975. A month later, all individuals and organizations were required to exchange old dong notes at the rate of 500 to 1 for new notes issued by the National Bank of Vietnam. Limits were announced for categories of individuals and organizations in terms of how much of the old money could be exchanged; the surplus funds were to be deposited in savings accounts. Any large withdrawals had to be sanctioned by the government. The new government thus created at one stroke a large amount of surplus capital for reinvestment. The sectors of the society most affected by the new measures were the so-called comprador-bourgeois class, mostly merchants, importers, and intermediaries who had become wealthy by dealing solely with governments—whether South Vietnamese or American.

Since the new government was socialist and revolutionary, it predictably announced a number of anticapitalist, anti-Western measures. Immediately after the takeover of Saigon, the government declared a policy of nationalization of foreign enterprises. It refused to honor the fallen South Vietnamese government's debt obligations. The government nationalized all manufacturing and industrial activity even though the prospects of success were dim due to lack of raw materials, fuel, and above all, spare parts for machinery that typically was of US origin. Only retail trading remained in private hands.

After the initial demonstration of revolutionary zeal, the government bowed to the tactical needs of foreign exchange and capital. In 1977, Vietnam announced a number of measures calculated to woo foreign capital. In a reversal of its previous policy, it accepted responsibility for the South Vietnamese government's debt obligations to Japan and France. Ideological purity was clearly abandoned in favor of pragmatism. The government welcomed outside investment of finance and technology on a joint-venture or production-sharing basis, with Vietnam supplying the labor. The government allowed remission of profits overseas by foreign investors, further assuring that the new joint enterprises would not be expropriated. A little earlier, Vietnam had joined the International Monetary Fund (IMF), unlike most Communist countries (with the significant exceptions of Yugoslavia and Romania), which had either refused to join the international body or withdrawn from it. Vietnam also joined the World Bank and the Asian Development Bank while retaining the status of an observer of the Moscow-dominated Council for Mutual Economic Assistance (COMECON, the Communist equivalent of the European Common Market) International Investment Bank. All these steps softened the attitude of some countries, particularly members of the European Economic Community, Sweden, and Japan, who signed economic assistance agreements with Vietnam. Vietnam also made specific efforts to attract capital from noncommunist countries for oil exploration and the mining of tin, tungsten, apatite, phosphate, and anthracite coal.

Five-Year Plans and Economic Policy

Economic planning in Communist Vietnam has been the responsibility of the Vietnamese Communist Party, whereas implementation of the plans is left to the government. Crucial to understanding the Vietnamese economic policies are the deliberations of the Fourth National Party Congress (December 1976), the Fifth Congress (March 1982), and the Sixth Congress (December 1986). The party's goal has been to take the country through a period of transition to socialism. This would be achieved in three stages. The first would conclude with the Second Five-Year Plan in 1980; the second would cover "socialist industrialization" through five successive five-year plans till 2005; the third would extend till 2010 and would be devoted to "perfecting" the transition to socialism.

Second Five-Year Plan

At the Fourth National Party Congress in December 1976, the VCP adopted an ambitious Second Five-Year Plan (1976–1980). The DRV's First Five-Year Plan (1961–1966) had been abandoned in 1965 due to the exigencies of the war. The Second Five-Year Plan constituted a hurried revision of a plan originally formulated only for North Vietnam in 1974 and then expanded to include projects for South Vietnam. The formulation of an integrated plan for all of Vietnam took some time. Hence the late announcement of the plan, in December 1976, allowing only four instead of five years to meet its targets.

The objectives of the Second Five-Year Plan were twofold: to build a material and technological base for the new socialist state and to raise the standard of living of the population. To this end, the plan proposed a threefold program: reorganization of production in the south along the lines of collectives in North Vietnam, reallocation of labor, and implementation of a "correct investment" policy through better economic management.

Of the projected outlay of 30 billion dongs (about $10 to $12 billion), more than half the sum was to come from outside donors. The Soviet Union promised $2.7 billion and East European countries $700 million. China was expected to contribute $600 million. Vietnam also continued to hope that some US assistance would be forthcoming, particularly after the advent of the administration of Jimmy Carter and as a reward for Vietnamese efforts to investigate the whereabouts of US soldiers missing in action. The US aid never materialized. Assistance from socialist countries also dropped below expectations or, as in China's case, dried up altogether, making Vietnam's foreign exchange problems acute and the prospects of implementing the Second Five-Year Plan bleak.

The plan combined major agricultural and industrial projects involving large-scale demographic changes. Out of the total planned expenditure, $3.5 billion was marked for agriculture, $3.5 billion for industry, and an equal amount for transportation and services.[4] The plan stressed the primary sector of the economy, though it also aimed at laying the groundwork for heavy industry. Thus 30 percent of the total outlay was earmarked for agriculture in the expectation by 1980 of a food production of 21 million tons (including 1 million tons each of meat and saltwater fish and 450,000 tons of other fish and fishmeal), with an annual surplus of 3 million tons of rice for export.

Most of this agricultural development was to take place in the south by reclaiming 6.4 million acres of land, mainly in the Mekong Delta. The government envisaged large-scale collectivization of agriculture through the creation of 250 giant agrofarm collectives, each employing about 100,000 persons. By 1978, before the march into Cambodia, the Hanoi government, which claimed to have established 137 such collectives in South Vietnam, "released" some 4 million people, who were then settled in the new economic zones (NEZs) in both parts of the country. Additionally, half the population of the Saigon-Cholon and Gia Dinh areas and people from the densely populated Red River Delta were relocated in the NEZs, particularly on the country's border with hostile Cambodia. Urban people moving into the NEZs were given the necessary tools and a six-month grain supply with the expectation that they would bring new land under cultivation and grow enough grain for their sustenance.

Vietnam's economic plan thus involved demographic relocation on a gigantic scale not unlike that in the Soviet Union and China after their respective revolutions. The Vietnamese government also announced plans to remove about 10 million people from the country's overcrowded areas to the mountainous zones in the north and west bordering all three of the country's neighbors. In the following two decades, from the Red River Delta and the central coast alone, about 4 million people would be resettled in the mountainous zone, Mekong Delta, eastern coast, and offshore islands, especially the Spratlys. As economic units, the NEZs would develop centers of light industry, helping to produce articles of consumption not only for the domestic population but also for export. In previously sparsely populated areas, the NEZs would be used to bring new lands under cultivation.

The concept of organizing territory into NEZs was not new; in 1970, North Vietnam had created twenty-three NEZs in fourteen provinces. In the south, however, the motives for the establishment of the NEZs were not purely economic: They were primarily aimed at population control. They facilitated the work of the internal security police and the strategic purpose of peopling the underpopulated regions along the country's borders.

The plans for industry and commerce in South Vietnam matched the pattern earlier implemented in North Vietnam during the First Five-Year Plan. The plan aimed at denuding the south of all Western—specifically, US— influence and transforming its economy into a socialist one. Despite this proclaimed goal, the government in effect allowed private enterprises to continue in a new form: All were newly designated as state-private partnerships. The previous owners, except those who had flagrantly sided with the former South Vietnamese government, were compensated with government bonds and reemployed by the government to manage the new partnerships. Although some of the richest smugglers and black marketers were apprehended and holdings of large landowners confiscated, most small businesses continued under private ownership. In March 1978, the government took over the retail trade partly by compensating the owners and rehiring many of them as managers of what became government-owned consumer goods stores. Another major economic measure integrated the currencies of North and South Vietnam in May 1978 with the issue of a new currency that became legal tender throughout the country.

The plan accorded investment in transport and communications the same high priority as investment in industry. This was necessary because the transportation systems had been severely damaged by bombing during the war in both parts of the country, north and south. Repairs were undertaken to arterial highways, bridges, and ports, particularly Haiphong, which had been the north's principal port for international trade and had been badly damaged by US bombing in late 1972. The wartime road network was to be adapted to peacetime activities and new major roads were to be built connecting the north and south to supplement the old coastal highway.

Failure of the Second Five-Year Plan

Vietnam's wars with Cambodia and China in 1978–1979 cost Vietnam dearly. The occupation of Cambodia by Vietnamese forces and maintaining a state of preparedness on the Sino-Vietnamese border limited the funds available for developmental programs. In 1979, the party decided to decentralize industry as part of the national defense strategy, and the following year the government formally increased the defense expenditure to absorb almost half of the nation's budget. Consequently, the government had to abandon a number of development programs, in particular the NEZs and population resettlement schemes.

There were other reasons for the failure of the Second Five-Year Plan. The plan had run into major problems almost from the start. Paucity of funds, internal and external, was one factor. The government's lack of appreciation of the socioeconomic structure of pre–1975 South Vietnam and the forced pace of changes was another. Many loyalists of the former anti-Communist regimes were accused of sabotaging the state's plans. Moreover, there was widespread corruption among the party cadre and officials, who lined their pockets at the cost of the state. Finally, three successive years of bad weather, floods, and drought severely affected the targeted production in agriculture.

In terms of funds, no more than two-thirds of the total planned investment actually became available; loans and grants from abroad fell far below expectations. China made only loans, not grants, beginning in 1976, and cut off even those by 1978. The United States did not contribute to reconstruction; the US embargo on trade with Vietnam continued. Even Soviet economic aid was reduced, presumably because after 1978 it was contributing heavily toward defense expenditures—an estimated $3 million a day toward Vietnam's military commitments in Cambodia. As for aid from Western countries, three-fourths of the promised amount was held back after early 1979 because of resentment over Vietnam's march into Cambodia.

Economic assistance from the Soviet Union nevertheless played a major role in Vietnamese planned expenditure. Soviet technical assistance was crucial in agriculture, public health, transport and communications, geological explorations, and energy. The treaty of friendship and cooperation signed in November 1978 called for economic cooperation between the Soviet Union and Vietnam for ten years. Another agreement signed in July 1980 provided for offshore drilling for oil. Due to successive crop failures, some of the Soviet economic aid had to be diverted to finance about 10 percent to 15 percent of Vietnam's food grain requirements. On the fifth anniversary of the Soviet-Vietnamese friendship treaty, Tran Quynh, vice chairman of the Vietnamese

Council of State, wrote in *Nhan Dan* that Soviet aid had been further stepped up "to counter attempts by Vietnam's enemies to paralyze the nation's economy."[5] He indicated that the Soviet Union was supplying 100 percent of Vietnam's fuel and lubricant imports, 100 percent of its communications systems and military equipment and weaponry, and more than 90 percent of its fertilizers and metallurgical products. In partial repayment of loans and grants, Vietnam had to supply the Soviet Union with natural resources and labor, sending more than 100,000 workers to the Soviet Union for several years.

Vietnam's foreign exchange predicament was further compounded by its export trade, which lagged far behind the plan's projections of an annual increase of 10 percent. Vietnam's exports in 1980 were only about 15 percent of its imports. Vietnam's principal export was coal, responsible for 95 percent of the total; major imports included wheat, wheat flour, fertilizers, machinery, and oil. Most of its trade was with the Soviet Union and East European countries. Owing to its trade deficit, Vietnam had to send several thousand workers to the Eastern European countries (in addition to those to the Soviet Union) to earn Soviet bloc currency to repay the loans and to offset the unfavorable balance of trade.

The State Planning Committee report submitted by Vice Premier Nguyen Lam in December 1980 revealed that food production had not kept pace with the increase in population, that severe shortages of raw materials and energy had crippled industry to about half its capacity, and that per capita income had actually declined since the Second Five-Year Plan was announced. National income had increased by 9 percent in 1976 but only by 2 percent in 1977. In the remaining years of the plan, national income actually declined because of inclement weather that reduced agricultural output and costly wars with Cambodia and China during 1978–1979, which had necessitated diversion of 50 percent of the national budget to military expenditures. The report stated that during the plan period, agricultural output increased by only 18.7 percent and industrial production by 17.3 percent against a projected growth of 50 percent in agriculture and industry. Total area under cultivation increased by 4.4 million acres, that under irrigation by 1.5 million acres. Mechanized plowing through use of tractors increased by 37 percent. There was all-around progress in the production of coal, construction materials, and industries. In no area, however, were the targets reached. Thus in 1980, the harvest amounted to about 12 million tons against a target of 21 million. Due to severe food shortages between 1977 and 1980, rice was rationed to a level matching the lowest point of supply in North Vietnam during the war. About 3 million tons of rice had to be imported annually between 1977 and 1980. In 1980, Vietnam's real gross domestic product (GDP) declined by 3.7 percent, whereas gross industrial output decreased by 9.6 percent over the previous year.

Another reason for the plan's failure was the government's inordinate hurry to unite the two halves of the country and transform it into a socialist state. North Vietnam, which did not have enough qualified management personnel and technicians, took upon itself to administer a country suddenly doubled in size, refusing to put trained South Vietnamese into administrative positions of trust, technical know-how, and responsibility. By not fully integrating the south, the government undermined the Second Five-Year Plan. As stated earlier, the Second Five-Year Plan, originally devised for North Vietnam, had been extended to the south without adequate consideration of South Vietnam's special problems, particularly the difficulty of the transition from a US-subsidized capitalistic economy to a socialist economy.

Economic Liberalization and the Third Five-Year Plan

Aware of the reasons for the failure of the second plan, the Central Committee's Sixth Plenum decided in September 1979 to decelerate the process of turning family farms into collectives and cooperatives in South Vietnam both because of social resistance and, more important, because it had failed to yield results. After 1979, the government decided that family farms that were run efficiently should be left alone. Others that had been converted into cooperatives were not to be hastily taken over by state enterprises. All control stations established to check the movement of goods between rural areas and urban centers—which had become virtual bureaucratic bottlenecks and hunting grounds for pilferers, profiteers, bribe takers, and black marketers—were abolished. The VCP agreed that in some fields of industry and trade private management would be more capable than government control in meeting consumer needs. It acknowledged that there were severe problems in the public-sector undertakings: poor management skills, inadequate technological know-how, and insufficient worker enthusiasm. The party therefore resolved to rescind the government orders nationalizing private business and trade and to restore small-scale enterprises and retail trade to the private sector. Additionally, the party unhesitatingly adopted the capitalist practice of increasing productivity through manipulation of economic incentives.

Despite such clear directives, by its last year, 1980, the plan had failed to move the country forward economically. As the Ninth Plenum observed in December 1980, the failure came about because of bureaucratic reluctance to implement "capitalist" directives, for fear that the creation of a socialist state would thereby be jeopardized. The Ninth Plenum endorsed the Sixth Plenum's resolutions on flexible application of policies. Moreover, it resolved to decentralize management, clearly defining the rights of major industrial and economic establishments to take their own decisions at the local level in most matters, including wage schemes, bonuses, and worker welfare. A directive of the party's Central Committee forbade interference by party members in the self-management of cooperatives, allowing the latter a greater sense of autonomy.

In yet another liberal move, the government tax on foreign gifts was repealed, permitting such gifts to be sold or exchanged for profit. The People's Committee in Ho Chi Minh City fully exploited the opportunity, organizing its own import-export facility by promoting a mail-order service to help the movement of incoming "gifts" from overseas. Thus trade with foreign markets was indirectly established by circumventing the punitive international trade limitations. The pragmatic liberalization implicit in the decisions of the two plenums countered the overly rigid and dogmatic tenor of the Fourth Congress in 1976, thereby providing a better base for the Third Five-Year Plan.

Though the government formally approved the Third Five-Year Plan (1981–1985), it was not publicized much. Emphasis was instead placed on annual socioeconomic plans. In 1981, the first steps toward decentralization and privatization (to be dramatically augmented after the Sixth Congress in 1986) were taken. The new plan did not officially abandon the goal of transforming the economy of the south along socialist lines. It did, however, urge slowing down the pace of such a transformation by the temporary retention of nongovernmental economic activities. The VCP's Central Committee issued two significant directives in January 1981. The first directive approved development of a "family economy" by allowing the peasants to utilize such economic resources, including land, as were not being used by the agricultural cooperatives. Additionally, peasant families were encouraged to sign contracts with the collectives whereby they could farm land owned by the latter and agree to deliver to the state certain assigned quotas of grain or produce. The peasant families were allowed to sell any surplus on the open market or to the state for a price to be mutually settled. The government officially recognized the private sector in various other economic fields, including small industry, forestry, fisheries, as well as retail trading. With all these measures, a free market flourished alongside the government's rationing system. The second directive asked the state-owned enterprises to function on the basis of self-accounting and self-financing.

By the middle year of the plan, the government reported that at least half of the peasants' total income and one-third to half of the food supplies came from the "family economy." The new policy brought into the economy large numbers of peasants in the south who had thus far refused to cooperate with the government and boycotted the agricultural cooperatives. It is important to note that unlike the peasants in North Vietnam, most of whom were tenants, most South Vietnamese peasants were freeholders who cherished their property rights and refused to join the cooperatives.

As a result of such "capitalistic" initiatives, Vietnam turned an economic corner in 1983, when agricultural production reached 17 million tons, enough to meet domestic needs and leave a small surplus for export. The industrial production marked a 25 percent increase over that of 1978, though the increase in exports still fell short of the plan's target. A substantial part of the growth during the Third Five-Year Plan occurred in small industries and handicrafts, which were now run along commercial profit-making lines.

The reactions of the party hierarchy to these economic achievements were mixed. Some of the party leaders regretted the large-scale corruption among officials and cadres, whose excuse seemed to be that their work did not give them the benefits others received from the system of incentives and bonuses. The leaders were apprehensive of the "creeping capitalism" and its cultural manifestations. They warned of losing the struggle to capitalism in Ho Chi Minh City by delaying the socialist transformation of Nan Bo (South Vietnam) in trade, industry, and agriculture. They wanted the "capitalist" economic policies to be reversed and put back on the socialist track.

Turning the Battlefield into a Marketplace: Doi Moi (Renovation)

The economic situation in Vietnam worsened in the mid–1980s with large-scale levels of unemployment and miserable living conditions for the middle class. The continuing occupation of Cambodia and the ongoing conflict with the Khmer Rouge there had sapped Vietnam's economic strength. A new major international factor affecting the Vietnamese economy in the mid–1980s was the stoppage of economic and military assistance by the Soviet Union, which had financed Vietnam's misadventure in Cambodia since 1978. The new wave of political and economic reform in the Soviet Union under Mikhail Gorbachev influenced all Communist states, including Vietnam. Yet it was not easy for Vietnam to diversify sources of foreign economic aid. A major impediment to doing so was the United States, which had first imposed an economic embargo on North Vietnam in 1964 and then extended it to a unified Vietnam in 1975. Later the United States linked the embargo to Vietnam's assistance in providing information on American MIAs. Until the United States lifted that embargo, Vietnam would not be able to receive financial credits from the IMF, the World Bank, and the Asian Development Bank, where the decisions were dependent on US support. The US embargo also inhibited other Western countries and Japan from extending economic assistance to Vietnam as long as the Vietnamese military occupation of Cambodia continued.

Under such circumstances, it was no wonder that the reformers in the VCP hierarchy held the upper hand at the Sixth Party Congress, which met in December 1986. In hindsight, that conclave could be termed a historical turning point in recent Vietnamese history for a number of reasons. Vo Van Kiet, leader of the reformist group, appealed to the assembled delegates to turn Indochina from a battlefield into a marketplace. The Sixth Congress approved *doi moi* (renovation) with a succession of steps toward economic modification and administrative decentralization. Since that momentous decision, the pace of economic reform may have faltered at times, but there has been no change in the general direction the VCP charted for the country. The Seventh Congress, held in 1991, enthusiastically voted for the continuation of *doi moi*. With the exception of the Eighth Congress, which gave a qualified endorsement to liberalization policies, all Congress meetings have strongly supported *doi moi*.

At the Sixth Congress, Vo Van Kiet had advocated application of the liberal measures of the south to the north, where the living conditions had been miserable for decades. Two years earlier, in 1984, the IMF had estimated that despite all the socialist policies the Hanoi government tried to impose on the south, 80 percent of the south's economy remained in private hands. In the more liberal atmosphere after 1986, the ruling north made a greater effort to draw economic lessons from the defeated south.

The *doi moi* reforms were directed at developing a multisectoral market, introducing revolutionary changes in the country's legal, banking, and monetary systems, containing inflation and reducing budget deficits, and in general creating an economic environment conducive to foreign direct investment (FDI). To avoid control by any single foreign state or integrated group of foreign states, Vietnam diversified its international economic relations. For the domestic economy's development, in April 1987 the VCP's Central Committee adopted a package of reforms that increased cash incentives to peasants and workers. Rice farmers were allowed to earn up to 40 percent of profits over production costs, and the more productive among the industrial workers were rewarded with bonuses at piece-rate wages. The government granted tax exemptions to new and expanded industries and handicraft industries that produced goods solely for export. To relieve hardship among the middle class, the government legalized moonlighting by government employees. It abolished subsidies to government-run economic units. In November 1987, the government authorized decision making by factory managers on the use of equipment, production targets, and sources of finance.

New directives approved by the party's Central Committee in April 1988 laid down specific policies on management in agriculture. Farmers were permitted to hold up to 40 percent of the contracted output, thus encouraging them to invest more labor and capital. In industry, the government gave autonomy in production and business to state-owned enterprises, allowing them to operate on the basis of their self-generated finances without expecting compensation for losses from the state. In mid–1989, the government dramatically announced that it would discard the centralized planning and controlled economic management in favor of a market-oriented economy.

In addition to these measures aimed at boosting domestic production, the government showed a keen desire to attract foreign investment. Even before the Sixth Congress, the government had in 1984 appointed a group of economists in Ho Chi Minh City to look into the possibility of foreign investment. It also requested the Economic and Social Commission for Asia and the Pacific (ESCAP) to send some senior experts to Vietnam to assist it in drafting legislation on foreign investment and to establish export processing zones (EPZs). As the columnist Hoang Ngoc Nguyen observed, the government "lacked everything from a legal framework to give foreign investors confidence in operating in a strange and socialist land, to an institutional framework to facilitate business activities, and to competent government executives and experienced local businessmen who could make foreigners feel at home."[6] Finally, in December 1987, the National Assembly adopted a law allowing the establishment of companies that were wholly foreign owned in all sectors except defense. It offered guarantees against nationalization of foreign property for twenty years and later introduced further regulations to help the actual implementation of the law. The government was, however, aware of the reluctance of foreign investors—particularly from the West and Japan—to invest in Vietnam because of the latter's military occupation of Cambodia and the US economic embargo on Vietnam. The Vietnamese government therefore took major initiatives in foreign policy to improve its relations with the United States and other Western nations, the Association of Southeast Asian Nations (ASEAN), and Japan.

The Economic Impact of *Doi Moi*

The results of these liberal measures over the last nearly two decades have been dramatic. The inflation rate, which had touched 700 percent in the mid–1980s, came down to 13 percent in 1995 and to 6 percent in 2000. The rate of economic growth doubled from 3 percent in 1986 to 6 percent in 1990. It averaged 7.4 percent in the decade from 1994 to 2004, bringing praise for Vietnam from *The Economist* (London) as "Asia's best-performing economy in 2004."[7] This was achieved despite the short-term setback experienced in 1998–1999 in the aftermath of the Asian currency crisis, which plunged most of the ASEAN states into recession. The World Bank reported that the

Vietnamese economic development had lifted substantial numbers out of poverty, from 58 percent in 1993 to 29 percent in 2002. The Ninth Congress in 2001 noted that the poverty rate had declined from 30 percent in 1992 to 20 percent in 1995 to 11 percent in 2000. It placed the country's food production at 35.6 million tonnes, increasing the per capita food from 748 pounds in 1995 to 976 pounds in 2000. The Congress also stated that the employment in the previous decade had increased by 10 million new jobs. The international trade, which had hovered around $1 billion before 1986 and was for the most part restricted to Eastern Europe and the Soviet Union, became more diversified and doubled to about $2 billion by 1990. After the United States partially lifted restrictions on trade and investment—signaling its allies to take similar action—Vietnam's export-import trade soared to more than $23 billion in 1999, a year in which Vietnam attained the distinction of being the second largest exporter of rice in the world, exporting 4.5 million tons. The trade deficit decreased from 49.6 percent in 1995 to just a few percentage points by 2000.[8]

The direction of international trade through the years has significantly changed in favor of the ASEAN countries, Japan, Western Europe, and the United States after signing the Bilateral Trade Agreement (BTA) with Vietnam. Principal exports currently include rice, coffee, tea, rubber, fish, oil, garments, and textiles. A number of industrial centers and zones has been established all over the country, reducing unemployment in cities and underemployment in rural areas. The export growth, largely financed by foreign direct investment (FDI), has grown exponentially thanks to cheap and efficient labor. Trade tariffs have been drastically reduced through treaties with ASEAN, the United States, Japan, Australia, and New Zealand.

The cataclysmic changes in the late 1980s in the Communist world brought about by the collapse of doctrinaire Marxism-Leninism in the Soviet Union and Eastern European countries as well as the political breakup of the Soviet Union and the end of its leadership of the Communist world had tremendous impact on all Communist states, including Vietnam. Most socialist states felt compelled to examine the flaws in their unproductive centralized economic systems and to consider experiments with market economies, such as China had begun. With powerful winds of change blowing across the former Soviet Union, Eastern Europe, and China, furious debates took place in the higher echelons of the government and the VCP over the pace of political and economic reform in Vietnam. The discussions came to a head at the Seventh Congress of the VCP in June 1991. The liberals, led by Vo Van Kiet, favored turning state enterprises into shareholding companies; the conservative diehards in the party hierarchy fiercely opposed both political pluralism and dilution of socialism. The liberal position was hamstrung by financial stringency caused by massive reduction of aid and concessional trade from Russia. The situation was not helped by the continuing US trade embargo. The United States had also successfully pressured the IMF into denying credit to Vietnam. Though in the end an overwhelming majority of the Congress delegates enthusiastically endorsed the *doi moi*, the pace of privatization of the State-Owned Enterprises (SOEs) was affected. At the same time, following China's example, the Congress resolved not to allow political pluralism or democratization, which would challenge the VCP's monopoly of power.

The ODA and FDI

Following an improvement in relations with the United States and the US government's decision of July 2, 1993, to clear Vietnamese debts, foreign aid and soft loans from the IMF, the World Bank, and Western nations flowed in. France and Japan had resumed the aid in November 1992 before the US action. In November 1993, the first donors' meeting of twenty-three donor states and international agencies held in Paris pledged $1.86 billion in loans for 1994. Individual governments pledged three-fifths of the amount; the IMF, World Bank, and Asian Development Bank pledged the remaining two-fifths. Of the governments, Japan, Australia, France, Great Britain, and South Korea provided more than 50 percent of the aid; in 1992, Japan offered the largest amount of all donors—$555 million—90 percent of it in soft loans and the balance in grants and technical aid. Subsequent donors' meetings have offered Vietnam official development assistance (ODA) totaling $20 billion by 2002, which has been used besides direct economic development for improvement of infrastructure, environment protection, and human resource development. The three largest donors contributing a total of 70 percent of this amount are Japan, the World Bank, and the Asian Development Bank.

Before the first donors' meeting, the Vietnamese government prepared a list of 121 projects for which it would need external financial assistance totaling $9.6 billion. Thirty-eight were economic infrastructure projects to be completed in four to seven years and needing $7.55 billion; seventeen were social infrastructure projects that would take $1.83 billion. The government's bias in favor of rapid industrialization was reflected in the focus on transport and energy, on which it hoped to spend 70 percent of the total for infrastructure, nearly $5.22 billion. In contrast, agriculture, which was responsible for 36 percent of the GDP and employed 80 percent of the population, was to receive external assistance of only $2 billion, or 21 percent of the total. The government's wish list also included a number of airports and seaports on a build-operate-transfer (BOT) basis. A 1994 World Bank study estimated Vietnam's external financing needs for a targeted annual growth of 8 percent of GDP at a somewhat lower figure of about $1.26 billion in 1994, rising to a little more than $2 billion in 1999. The World Bank further estimated that FDI would account for one-third to two-fifths of these amounts, leaving the rest to ODA long-term loans and grants of about $100 million a year.

To facilitate the FDI, Vietnam promulgated a series of economic laws streamlining procedures and licenses, relaxing regulations for imports of goods, and reducing tariffs. Significant incentives for promoting exports and for repatriation of profits on FDI were announced. Tax exemptions were given to new and expanded industries and to handicraft industries that produced goods solely for export. An official floating exchange rate was introduced, and in July 2000, the first stock market was established in Ho Chi Minh City, facilitating infusion of external capital directly into domestic enterprises. By the end of June 2002, Vietnam had 3,348 FDI projects with total capital of $38.58 billion, accounting for 13 percent of the GDP. Of these, 2,100 projects were in the industrial sector with investment of more than $20 billion, responsible for 36 percent of the gross industrial production employing more than 450,000 persons.

The State-Owned Enterprises

A major area of *doi moi* reform was the public sector and the plethora of State-Owned Enterprises (SOEs), which together comprised the largest employer and a source of tremendous influence, power, and patronage for the party bosses at all levels. Most of the SOEs showed little profit, if any. They received liberal, unsecured loans from state-owned banks; they bought and sold to each other without regard to commercial considerations and in general had little accountability.

The SOEs, which occupied a place of pride in the socialist economy before the *doi moi*, came increasingly under pressure to perform well. In order to get approval for their economic liberalization measures, the reformers had to concede the retention of state control over such strategic parts of the economy as electricity and gas, coal and petroleum, minerals and forestry, transport and communications. A series of government decrees in 1987–1988 were directed toward reducing or removing bureaucratic controls over the management of the SOEs, which were to be run on strictly commercial practices and show profits. State subsidies were reduced or abolished. The SOE managers would be responsible thereafter not only for the better management of production and marketing but also to obtain financing in competition with the private sector. All transactions between SOEs were to follow accounting procedures prevalent in the private sector. In making loans to the SOEs, the state-controlled banks were asked to examine their profitability, though political pressures continued to make this impossible in many cases. Many of the influential SOEs successfully obtain loans and cash advances from other financial sources, such as the Social Security Fund.

Although technically the VCP resolved to "modernize" the SOEs, the underlying message was to privatize the unprofitable ones. In 1992, the government established the Central Steering Committee for Enterprise Reform, which was to receive proposals for privatization for a particular SOE from People's Committees at the provincial level.

A major step that helped consolidation of hundreds of SOEs was taken through a governmental decree in 1994 that created during the next two years eighteen General Corporations. The new entities operated strategic industries, utilities, and communications. Under pressure from VCP reformers as well as international lending agencies, privatization was sped up in 1997 by creating a Financial Investment Company and a National Debt and Asset Management Company under the aegis of the Ministry of Finance. In the next half decade, some 636 SOEs were privatized.

The total number of SOEs was halved from 12,000 in 1986 to 6,000 in 1994. The reduction was achieved partly through closure of unprofitable units at the local level and merger of smaller SOEs with larger ones. The total number of industrial SOEs declined from 3,000 at the beginning of the *doi moi* in 1986 to a little more than 1,800 in 1998. The contribution of the SOEs to the GDP and industrial output steadily declined from 1986 (when it was 100 percent) to about 40 percent in 1999. In March 2001, in anticipation of the review at the Ninth Congress, a Five-Year Plan for the reform and privatization of SOEs was drawn up, setting triennial targets. The goals for 2001–2003 were to subject 1,499 SOEs to privatization, 140 to divestiture, and 220 to outright liquidation. In order to make the remaining SOEs more accountable and profitable, new specific measures were laid down for auditing and efficient management of resources.

Critics of *Doi Moi*

The social, cultural, and political consequences of *doi moi* caused considerable disquiet among the conservatives, especially older revolutionaries among the party hierarchy who feared losing control over society, in particular the younger population. Since the Sixth Congress of 1986, they had been faced with the hard question of reconciling party ideology with an increasingly capitalist economy. Having fought for decades for the establishment of an equitable socialist state, they could not stomach what they regarded as the growing cultural degeneration of the people under the impact of foreign capitalism. By mid–1995, they were demanding that the previous target for output of state enterprises and cooperatives—fixed at 40 percent of the GDP by the year 2020—be increased by 6 percent, thereby reducing the share of the private sector, including FDI.

Both party and military leaders were concerned that FDI brought a large number of foreigners to Vietnam, a reminder of colonial French and, later, American presence in the country. The leaders warned the public of the dangers foreigners posed, in that they might corrupt youth and stir up support for political pluralism, besides exploiting the country's natural resources. The media observed that since the time the government welcomed foreign direct investment, drug use, gambling, juvenile delinquency, and prostitution had increased alarmingly. Moreover, as onetime reformer and VCP secretary-general Nguyen Van Linh said, foreign investors were exploiting Vietnam's natural resources not for the development of Vietnam but for the benefit of the investing countries. Conservative critics of the liberal economic policies also lamented the growing income gap between urban and rural areas in the country, particularly in northern and central coastal Vietnam. They argued that the West's game was to continue to exploit countries such as Vietnam in order to keep them perpetually underdeveloped. In the process, the gap between rich and poor nations would be widened. They also maintained that the West's attempts to promote privatization and economic competition were designed to weaken the authority of the state.

The Eighth Congress held in June 1996 was the scene of a confrontation between progressives advocating continuation of economic reform and conservatives who criticized the damage these changes were causing to the fabric of Vietnamese society. The more important questions were whether the economic changes would compel political changes and how long the VCP would be able to block political pluralism and democratization. Most alarming to the reformist group was the conservative demand that the output share of the state enterprises and cooperatives be raised to 60 percent by 2020. Prime Minister Vo Van Kiet found it necessary to make concessions to the conservatives so that they would agree to retract their controversial demand. The concessions included encouragement of import substitution, a freeze on further privatization, and recognition of the importance of the state enterprises to domestic tax revenues. In effect, the Eighth Congress voted to continue with *doi moi* but to discourage any new initiatives that would favor private enterprise, including FDI.

Opposition to economic reform mounted during the last years of the century when the Vietnamese economy suffered a devastating blow with the Southeast Asian currency crisis of 1997. Foreign direct investment, never too happy with Vietnam's rampant corruption and bureaucratic deadlocks, fled the country: Seventy percent of it came from ASEAN states, which received 60 percent of Vietnamese exports. The FDI plummeted by 60 percent in 1998 and by 64 percent the following year. By the end of 1999, Vietnamese operations of three-quarters of foreign companies were in the red. Exports dwindled and the Vietnamese dong became overvalued. By 2000, the trade deficit exceeded US$1 billion; 45 percent of the 6,000 SOEs were losing money. To add to the government's woes, the IMF and the World Bank withheld loans of about US$500 million in 1999 and US$700 million in 2000, demanding that Vietnam adopt a "more comprehensive approach" to economic reform.[9]

The growing economic crisis strengthened the conservatives' opposition to policies that would promote cooperation with the capitalist world, facilitate the FDI, and encourage Vietnam's becoming part of the global marketplace. The consequence was the rejection by the Politburo of a draft bilateral trade agreement with the United States whereby the Vietnamese trade tariff would be reduced drastically from 40 percent to 3 percent that, according to a World Bank study, would increase exports to the United States by $800 million in the first year of the agreement itself.[10] In the end, however, the conservative general secretary Le Kha Phieu had to give in to the potential benefits of the Bilateral Trade Agreement and sign the agreement with the United States in July 2000.

Government and Politics in the New Vietnam

Reunification

After the Communist takeover of South Vietnam, it was expected that some decent interval would be allowed before the political, economic, and administrative integration of the two halves of the country would begin because of traditional southern fears of the north's domination. Indeed, during the protracted war in the south, the DRV had assured the NLF that it would not overpower the south. In the wake of its victory, however, the northern leadership was overwhelmed by the counterargument that reunification of the country and integration of the south would be difficult if they were delayed. They feared that the south's economic and political interests would become well grounded if given the time, and the corrupt, capitalist way of life to which the southerners were accustomed during the war would have a deleterious effect on the north. Therefore, within a few months of the fall of Saigon, the Communist leaders decided on political and administrative integration within a year.

On April 26, 1976, the first anniversary of the Communist victory, elections were held for the National Assembly for all of Vietnam. By July 1976, the two Vietnams were formally unified, the DRV dissolved, and the Socialist Republic of Vietnam (SRV) proclaimed, with Hanoi as the capital of the entire country. The NLF was also disbanded, its numerous mass associations absorbed by its counterparts in North Vietnam. The Lao Dong Party was also disbanded, as was the People's Revolutionary Party of the south. The two were combined into the Vietnamese Communist Party in December 1976. Thus the year 1976 represented the culmination of the decades-long dream of the Vietnamese to end the artificial divisions of their country under both the French and the Geneva agreements and to unite under a common political banner.

The Leadership of the Party and the Government

The party and governmental structure of the DRV was extended to the SRV. As in all Communist countries, two parallel hierarchies exist in Vietnam from the highest to the lowest levels of the party and government, with the party's Politburo having primacy over the government. The party itself had grown from about 1,000 members in 1941 to 5,000 in 1945 to a massive 500,000 in 1953. After the establishment of a Communist government in North Vietnam in 1954, the party's membership was relatively stable until the 1960s, when it was extended to senior cadres who led the movement in the south aimed at reunification of the country. By 1975, the party's ranks had swollen to nearly 1.5 million. The link between the party and the general public involved in the "people's war" was provided by numerous associations organized mostly on a functional basis: for workers, peasants, students, artists, women, and so on. Among them were the Vietnam Fatherland Front, the Vietnam General Confederation of Trade Unions, the Red Scarf Teenagers' Organization, and the Ho Chi Minh Communist Youth League. These organizations also served as recruiting grounds for the party cadres.

The Vietnamese Communist Party and its precursor, the Indochina Communist Party, record only eight congress meetings in their combined history of six decades. Following the founding of the ICP in 1930, the First National Party Congress met secretly in Macao in 1935; the second met in Tuyen Quang in the North Vietnamese highlands in 1951; the third met in Hanoi in 1960 to launch the movement in South Vietnam. Since the establishment of the SRV, the party has held five congresses: in 1976, 1982, 1986, 1991, and 1996. These infrequent congresses have arrived at some of the most momentous decisions at crucial points in the party's or country's history. They constitute large conclaves of more than a thousand delegates, which makes them too unwieldy for any articulate deliberations. At the Eighth Congress in 1996, 1,198 delegates represented national-, provincial-, and district-level party committees and organizations. Twenty-five to thirty delegations from fraternal parties in other countries usually attend the congresses as well, sometimes using the occasions to present medals and honors from their countries to Vietnamese leaders.

The VCP has functioned at four levels: central, provincial, district, and village. At the apex is the Politburo (political bureau) elected by the party's Central Committee. The Politburo had twelve or thirteen full members and one or two alternate members until 1991, when it was expanded to sixteen; it was expanded still further to nineteen in 1996. The Politburo possesses authority and responsibility for implementing policies approved by the Central Committee from time to time. The Central Committee, a much larger body than the Politburo, is elected at the national congress and has about 120 members and fifty alternates. Serving the Politburo are the Party Secretariat, a Central Control Commission, and a Central Military Party Committee. Between 1986 and 1996, the Secretariat had thirteen members, five of them—including the most powerful of them all, the secretary-general—holding concurrent membership in the Politburo. The Central Control Commission and the Central Military Party Committee were appointed by the Central Committee but worked under the direction of the Politburo. Numerous departments, more or less corresponding to the governmental agencies and overshadowing them, worked under the control of the Secretariat.

The Eighth Congress introduced a new five-member Politburo Standing Board to replace the Secretariat as a bridge between the Central Committee and the Politburo, with wide powers to implement the Politburo's decisions on a day-to-day basis. The new Standing Board included the top three leaders—party secretary-general Do Muoi, President Le Duc Anh, and Prime Minister Vo Van Kiet—and two others roughly representing the former Central Control Commission and the Central Military Party Committee. It is too early to say whether the new Standing Board will be more powerful than the larger Secretariat it replaced.

Constitutions of 1980 and 1992

The SRV gave itself two constitutions: the first in December 1980 and the second in 1992. The first was patterned on the 1977 constitution of the Soviet Union. Under both constitutions the National Assembly, with an elected membership (about 500 under the 1980 constitution, reduced to 400 in 1992), was the supreme representative body endowed with legislative powers, including the power to amend the constitution.

Under the 1980 constitution, the National Assembly members elected a new body, the Council of State. A presidium or collective presidency, the council held both legislative and executive functions and acted as a standing committee of the National Assembly. The Council of State consisted of a chair, several vice chairs, a secretary-general, and seven members. Its term, like that of the National Assembly, ran for five years. It had wide planning and policy-making functions, such as the power to declare war, proclaim mobilization or a state of siege, ratify treaties, supervise the work of the Council of Ministers and the Supreme People's Court, and make laws in certain fields when the National Assembly itself was not in session.

Parallel to the Council of State but subordinate in powers was the Council of Ministers, the highest administrative body, elected by the National Assembly or, when the latter was not in session, by the Council of State. The Council of Ministers elected its own standing committee of ten to thirteen members, a close body coordinating all administrative activities. Each minister was to be assisted by two or more vice ministers depending on the volume of work.

A National Assembly was elected under the 1980 constitution in April 1981. It in turn elected a Council of State with Truong Chinh as chairman. Its four vice chairmen included Nguyen Huu Tho, former chairman of the NLF, and Xuan Thuy, former foreign minister of the DRV. Pham Van Dong, the DRV's prime minister since 1955, became the chairman of the Council of Ministers.

Although legally supreme, the National Assembly and its "committees"—namely, the Council of State and the Council of Ministers—acted at the direction of the VCP's Politburo. Thus the elected national legislature and its elected bodies (the Council of State and Council of Ministers) were no more than agencies for the implementation of the party's policies, thereby acknowledging the party's supremacy over the legislative and executive branches of the government.

The 1992 constitution retained the leadership role of the party, leaving the routine administration to an executive branch headed by the prime minister. The Council of State, or collective presidency, of the previous constitution was abolished. Instead, the office of the president was revived, giving it a largely ceremonial role as head of state and chief commander of the armed forces.

The strength of the National Assembly was reduced from 500 to 400 to make it a more efficient deliberative body. With its standing committee and numerous committees, it exercised the functions of the now-defunct Council of State, including planning and budget. The president was empowered to ask the National Assembly to review policies and high-level governmental appointments.

In order to emphasize the country's priorities, the 1992 constitution institutionalized the market-oriented policies adopted by the government since the party's Sixth Congress in 1986. The new constitution also demonstrated the country's resolve to live peacefully with the rest of the world by deleting references to the country's wars against its old enemies: France, the United States, and China. Instead, it emphasized a policy favoring good relations with all nations, irrespective of their political beliefs.

The Leadership of the VCP

The Vietnamese Communist Party leadership has been a remarkable and relatively stable gerontocracy. The average age of the members of the Politburo in 1992 was a little over seventy. All were educated in the 1920s or 1930s in Vietnam or in South China and spent their youth in the mountainous jungles of North Vietnam during World War II and the First Indochina War, and some of them in the Vietnam war. All belong to the generation of veteran revolutionaries but have little knowledge of modern economy, technology, or methods of management. Barring a few purges and deaths, the leadership remained the same for four or five decades. Ho Chi Minh, Pham Van Dong, Vo Nguyen Giap, and Truong Chinh officiated at the birth of the Viet Minh in 1941; in 1946, the Central Committee of the Viet Minh was expanded to include Le Duan, Pham Hung, and Nguyen Chi Thanh. Differences, ideological or otherwise, were not allowed to reach perilous levels that could lead to massive purges. In 1956, the party took note of the failure of the land reform movement and removed Truong Chinh from his position as secretary-general, though he was allowed to remain a member of the Politburo. The post of secretary-general remained vacant until 1960, when Le Duan, considered a southerner, was appointed to emphasize the party's decision to launch the movement in the south. In the 1960s, the leadership was influenced by the Sino-Soviet rivalry and was divided among pro-Chinese and pro-Soviet factions. The conditions of war, however, compelled the party leadership to hold the middle position. Ho Chi Minh (until his death in 1969) and Le Duan (until 1976) served as arbiters during these critical times, successfully closing the ranks in the name of the movement for the country's reunification.

In the aftermath of the war, the party's solidarity suffered. Between 1975 and 1985, the pro-Soviet faction marked its ascendancy. During that decade, Le Duan, the party's secretary-general, and Le Duc Tho, who had at the Paris talks negotiated the withdrawal of the United States from Vietnam, emerged as the main leaders. In 1976, under immense pressure from China to choose sides in the Sino-Soviet rivalry, Le Duan opted in favor of the Soviet Union. The decision led to a purge of several pro-Chinese members of the party. The duo ruthlessly removed members of the old guard opposed to their authority, particularly if they were pro-China. At the party's Fourth Congress in 1976, four members of the Central Committee and Politburo member Hoang Van Hoan, who was a former ambassador to China, were purged. Three years later, Hoang defected to China and openly condemned the Le Duan clique. Some pro-China leaders, including hard-liners such as Truong Chinh, moderated their stand in order to retain their positions of power. Truong Chinh was made chair of the newly established Council of State. Until 1985, four categories of indiscretion or disloyalty could invite dismissal from the party: advocacy of a softer approach toward China and the Khmer Rouge; criticism of the management of the economy, particularly the collectivization program in South Vietnam; corruption or inefficiency; and finally, opposition to Le Duan and Le Duc Tho's leadership.

In February 1980, a major cabinet shake-up involved nineteen changes. The most important of these was the removal of Vo Nguyen Giap, architect of the Vietnamese Red Army, legendary hero of Dien Bien Phu, and defense minister. He was "retired" for his failure to modernize the armed forces and for his faulty assessment of China's capabilities in its invasion of Vietnam in February 1979. Giap continued, however, to be a member of the Politburo and was later put in charge of the less powerful portfolio of family planning.

Those who were promoted included the heroes of the 1975 offensive against South Vietnam, the march into Cambodia in late 1978, and the 1979 war with China. Thus Giap was replaced as defense minister by Van Tien Dung, the mastermind of the Saigon offensive of 1975. Pham Hung, one of the principal leaders of the long conflict in South Vietnam, was made minister of the interior in 1980. Le Trong Tran, a general trained in the Soviet Union and East Germany and crucial to the South Vietnam offensive, took over as chief of the general staff. Le Duc Anh, military commander of the Vietnamese forces in Cambodia, was elected a member of the Politburo in 1982. He later became the country's defense minister, a position he held until the party's Seventh Congress in 1991.

At the time of the Fifth Congress of the VCP in 1982, about 500,000 members were purged. In order to replace their ranks and at the same time to rejuvenate the party, a recruitment drive enlisted as many as 350,000 new members, 90 percent of them under thirty years old, 70 percent of them war veterans. The soldiers of the revolution were now expected as party cadres and leaders to direct peacetime reconstruction. Despite the policy of infusing fresh blood into the party, of the top bodies only the Central Committee was changed, as one-third of its members were replaced by young people drawn from the armed forces. The Politburo membership was still a gerontocracy.

Political Pluralism and Democratization

Alongside the controversy over economic liberalization, the major debate in the late 1980s was whether *doi moi* should be accompanied by political pluralism. Tran Xuan Bach, a member of the Politburo, was expelled from the VCP in March 1990 for openly championing political pluralism. The party's action clearly demonstrated that its leadership would follow the Communist Chinese example in actively advocating economic reform without brooking any democratization of polity. The Seventh Party Congress in June 1991 reendorsed *doi moi*. The congress elected as chairman of the party Do Muoi, a conservative reformer who cautiously supported the economic reform movement but did not favor political liberalization. Reflective of this balance between economic and political reform was the composition of the new Politburo, in which a strong group of dogmatists provided a counterweight to the pronounced reformists. Vo Van Kiet, an avowed liberal, was made prime minister, enabling active pursuit of further economic liberalism. He was also enjoined by the chairman to follow for the same reason an active ASEAN-centered foreign policy.

The VCP leadership did, however, undertake constitutional reform in the hopes of inhibiting demands for political pluralism but pacifying domestic dissenters as well as international investors. In April 1992, the National Assembly thus approved a revised constitution through a so-called amendment to the 1980 constitution. It introduced a stricter separation of powers between the legislature and the executive. Although the VCP's monopoly of power was left undisturbed, the National Assembly was accorded an enhanced participatory role. Also, as mentioned before, the Council of State was abolished, again augmenting the importance of the National Assembly as a legislative body. Moreover, because the new constitution revived the office of the president and empowered him to request the National Assembly to review governmental policies and senior appointments, the National Assembly became central to the political process.

The 1992 constitution allows the VCP to introduce a greater measure of democratization through the National Assembly. In revising that body's position and power, the VCP's intention seems to have been gradually to bring about political renovation from within by giving a more meaningful role to greater numbers of party members in the National Assembly and then broadening the participatory base of the public when circumstances would permit.

Some optimists among political reformers believed this policy could lead to a constitutional state and the rule of law in Vietnam. This might encourage the rise of a legitimate political opposition to the dominant Communist political system in the country. If the provisions of the 1992 constitution were truly honored in letter and spirit, the National Assembly's decisions would be binding on all, preventing even the VCP leadership from questioning them.

If the phenomenal economic liberalization of the decade since 1988 and the implementation of the 1992 constitution raised hopes that some measure of political pluralism would be allowed, they were dashed by the Eighth Congress in June 1996. The VCP unequivocally reasserted its authority over all aspects of the country's life, particularly the political and social spheres. A party document drafted in April 1996 in advance of the Eighth Congress signaled the party's mood—"Leadership without control is tantamount to no leadership."[11] Many among the party hierarchy were infected with "Gorbachev phobia," believing that communism had collapsed in the former Soviet Union not because anything was ideologically wrong with Marxism-Leninism but because of political mismanagement under Gorbachev's leadership. Like its Chinese counterpart, the VCP clearly demonstrated its resolve to retain its monopoly of political power and callously to disregard demands (especially in the south) for political pluralism.

Indicative of this resolve was the re-election at the Eighth Congress of the same aged and ideologically balanced triumvirate: seventy-nine-year-old Do Muoi as the VCP's secretary-general, seventy-five-year-old Le Duc Anh as president, and seventy-three-year-old Vo Van Kiet as prime minister. And although as noted earlier, the congress voted to continue the *doi moi* approach, it called for a halt to any further economic liberalization. The Politburo's new membership reflected a similar setback for the reformists. Only four of the eighteen were ardent reformers: Prime Minister Vo Van Kiet and three deputy prime ministers, Pham Van Khai, Tran Duc Luong, and Truong Tan Sang.

Pressure to hand over authority to a younger set of leaders continued after the Eighth Congress. In response to such demands or perhaps because of continued illness, in mid–1997 the party's Central Committee secretly chose their successors, who were then confirmed by the National Assembly in late September 1997. Vo Van Kiet was replaced as premier by Phan Van Khai, aged sixty-three, a southerner and former deputy premier widely regarded as a pragmatic reformer. President Le Duc Anh was replaced by Tran Duc Luong, aged sixty, a former deputy premier from the central Vietnamese province of Quang Ngai. Tran was relatively less known, a mining engineer who was elected to the Politburo in 1996. His election as president came as a surprise because it was generally expected that a prominent military leader, General Doan Khue, would succeed Le Duc Anh. On December 29, 1997, Do Muoi was replaced as secretary-general of the party by Le Kha Phieu, an army political commissar in his mid-sixties known to be a conservative Marxist. (Traditionally, one of the three top positions in Vietnam's political apparatus is held by a military man.) The advent of a "younger" leadership loosened the gerontocracy's longtime grip on Vietnam's government and the Communist Party.

At the Ninth Congress held in April 2001, the gerontocracy finally and formally gave way to a younger leadership—the average age of the new Central Committee being fifty-five. It was a conscious decision to infuse fresh blood into the party. Attended by 1,168 delegates representing some 2.5 million members, with eighty guest delegates and thirty-four international delegations, the basic tasks of the Ninth Congress were to review the achievements and shortcomings of the fifteen-year-old *doi moi* and to decide the orientation for Vietnam's economic development in the twenty-first century. In the documentation preparatory to the congress, it was observed that the economic development was marked by instability and low efficiency. The party listed corruption and "lifestyle degradation" as cancers affecting its cadre and the administration. In fact, in the four years before the Ninth Congress, the party purged many senior officials for corruption and other economic crimes.

Notable changes at the Ninth Congress included Nong Duc Manh—former speaker of the National Assembly—becoming secretary-general of the party, replacing Le Kha Phieu, who was not popular with the party's rank and file and who had spoken during the visit of President Clinton in 2000 about the need to put an end to US hegemony and restore a multipolar world. As speaker, Manh had enhanced the role of the National Assembly as envisaged by the 1992 constitution. Urbane and widely traveled, favorably regarded by the United States, Manh belongs to the Tay ethnic minority and holds a reputation for "getting things done." It was rumored that he was a "biological son" of Ho Chi Minh. Questioned about it, Manh demonstrated his political sense and humor by saying that "every Vietnamese is a son or daughter of the legendary Uncle Ho."[12]

On the economic front, the Ninth Congress noted that the Vietnamese economy was not very competitive and that the purchasing power of the average Vietnamese was very low. It noted the slowdown in FDI and reiterated the need to remove bureaucratic obstacles in the investment and business environment by abolishing many administrative regulations that were "troublesome and harassing to enterprises and were suppressing the productive forces" in the country. On the whole, the Congress was far more supportive of the *doi moi* than the Eighth Congress in 1996. While the Ninth Congress endorsed the enhancement of the "leading role" of the state economic sector, it reemphasized the "establishment of a socialist-oriented market economy" and its efficient and unhindered operation.

CHAPTER 8

Vietnam and Its Immediate Neighbors

It is ironic that in the post-unification period Vietnam's principal problems in external relations lay with its Communist neighbors. Vietnam's march into Cambodia in late 1978 and its occupation of that country for slightly more than a decade created one focal point. Another was the Sino-Soviet feud. The long war with the United States had given North Vietnam an excuse not to take sides in the conflict between the two Communist giants. In 1976, however, China compelled Vietnam to choose between the two, and Vietnam did so in favor of the Soviet Union. It is hard to say whether during the decade and a half after Vietnam's unification, considerations of regional leadership or partisanship in the global Sino-Soviet rivalry dominated its policies toward its neighbors, Cambodia and Laos. An additional factor determining Vietnam's relations with Communist countries was its reaction to the liberal policies of *glasnost* and *perestroika* adopted by the Soviet Union and enthusiastically embraced by Eastern European states. The Vietnamese leadership was divided on the question whether to follow the East European example and liberalize the administration both economically and politically or to adopt the Chinese model and accept only economic liberalization, suppressing citizens' demands for democratic rights (as did China in Tiananmen Square in 1989).

With the dramatic Communist victories in South Vietnam and Cambodia in spring 1975 and the "silent Communist revolution" in Laos in December, it was widely believed that the Communists would regard the three triumphs as the culmination of the "liberation" movements in the Indochinese Peninsula and devote themselves to the tasks of domestic reconstruction. Even those anti-Communists who believed in the domino theory and saw its practical fulfillment in the "fall" of the three capitals in rapid succession regarded the phenomenon as applicable only to the states of the Indochinese Peninsula because of their common history of French rule. The initial feeling of panic and grave apprehension among the states in the Association of Southeast Asian Nations gave way to the reassurance that there would be more than a breathing spell before the new Communist states would be ready or willing to actively assist the fraternal Communist movements in the other states of Southeast Asia. Even in the non-Communist world, hardly anyone expected such fissures to develop among the new Communist states as would provoke large-scale interstate warfare ending in the Vietnamese blitzkrieg in Cambodia at the turn of 1978 and the "punitive" Chinese march across the southern border into Vietnam in February and March 1979. Nor did anyone predict that the new government of Vietnam would create an atmosphere in which an estimated 1 million of its people, most of Chinese ethnic origin, would prefer to take the risk of a clandestine, financially costly departure by unsafe boats to indeterminate destinations than to remain in the country. The question of the boat people, as they were called, aroused global concerns and helped revive tensions in Southeast Asia.

The post–1975 events also brought to the fore the political interdependence of the three Indochinese states—Vietnam, Laos, and Cambodia. The emergence of Communist regimes in all three countries in the same year, 1975, was no coincidence. The Communist organization of Laos, the Pathet Lao, and a segment of the Khmer Rouge had both received assistance from Hanoi, perhaps with Hanoi's expectation that they would seek Vietnamese guidance and direction after coming to power. Events in Vietnam in the previous two decades had partly shaped and overshadowed the political developments in the two other Indochinese states.

Vietnam and Cambodia

Historical Hatred

Vietnam's Southeast Asian neighbors, notably Cambodia, have reason to suspect Hanoi's expansionism. The Khmers, proud inheritors of a glorious legacy of empire once extending over the southern belt of mainland Southeast Asia, have historically hated the Vietnamese, who deprived them of the rich Mekong Basin in the eighteenth century and then shared with Thailand the suzerainty over what was left of the Khmer empire. The French conquest of Vietnam and Cambodia did not obliterate the memories or fears of Vietnamese aggressiveness. The prospect of withdrawal of the French in 1954 revived Cambodian apprehensions. At the Geneva conference that year, the Cambodian delegation openly expressed its suspicions of domination by the Viet Minh, which had already occupied portions of Cambodia in April 1954. Cambodian diplomacy during 1954–1955 was geared toward enhancing the country's security against the Vietnamese through a military alliance with the United States. Such moves were aborted quickly after Prince Norodom Sihanouk received assurances of noninterference from North Vietnamese premier Pham Van Dong. Tensions between Phnom Penh and Saigon continued even after a pro-US government was established in Cambodia in 1970 under General Lon Nol. Thus in the wake of the "friendly" US-Vietnamese invasion of their country in 1970, Cambodian officials turned their eyes away from the Cambodian massacre of thousands of Vietnamese civilians on the pretext that they were all Viet Cong. The hostility was mutual. The South Vietnamese forces treated Cambodia as a "military playground, with any Kampuchean fair game." According to William Shawcross, South Vietnamese air force pilots were, "until then very lazy, [and] actually paid bribes for the privilege" of flying bombing missions seven days a week over Cambodia.[1]

Cambodian suspicions of the Vietnamese were not limited to non-Communists or anti-Communists. As early as 1930, the Vietnamese Communists had betrayed their "imperialistic" ambitions. In January of that year, Ho Chi Minh succeeded in uniting the three Communist parties of Vietnam. In October, the party was renamed the Indochina Communist Party to include Cambodia and Laos, probably for the Comintern's convenience in treating all of Indochina as a national section of the Communist International. Until 1951, when the ICP technically divided into three national parties for the practical reason of organizing better resistance against the French, there was no separate Cambodian Communist Party. The ICP early advocated a federation of Vietnam, Cambodia, and Laos after the liquidation of French rule, although subsequently the ICP did pass resolutions leaving it to each nation to decide whether or not to join such a federation. Nevertheless, the Cambodian Communists did not abandon their fear that Vietnam would—by virtue of its geographic size, population, educated workforce, economic strength, and military prowess—some day compel Cambodia and Laos into a composite polity under Vietnamese domination.

The Khmer Rouge

Differences between the Khmer Rouge and Vietnamese Communists originated in 1954 at the Geneva conference on Indochina. Presumably under the pressure of Moscow and Beijing, which were eager to arrive at a settlement as part of their global policy of peaceful coexistence, the North Vietnamese did not press the cause of the Khmer Rouge but instead agreed that it be disbanded and that its cadres retreat to Hanoi. The Khmer Rouge never forgave the Vietnamese Communists for what they perceived as betrayal. Retreating to North Vietnam, several thousand of them fought in the maquis against Sihanouk's government in the 1960s. The North Vietnamese were quite content with Sihanouk's cooperation in allowing the flow of men and materiel along the Ho Chi Minh Trail across eastern Cambodia and from the port of Sihanoukville (Kompong Som) into South Vietnam and, most importantly, in permitting the establishment of extensive secret base camps inside the Cambodian border for the Vietnamese NLF. By 1969, there were an estimated 40,000 to 50,000 North Vietnamese and NLF troops in the Cambodian sanctuaries.

It was certainly not the first time that a Communist state had, for tactical reasons and out of its own national interest, sought and received assistance from a non-Communist government at the expense of a "fraternal" Communist Party. It was, therefore, only natural that the Khmer Rouge's distrust of the North Vietnamese would continue even after a tactical alliance among the four regional Communist groupings of Pathet Lao, Lao Dong, NLF, and Khmer Rouge was established soon after Sihanouk's overthrow in early 1970. At this point, Hanoi needed the Khmer Rouge's cooperation in keeping the supply lines to the NLF open by harassing the troops of Lon Nol, the United States, and South Vietnam in eastern Cambodia. The tension between the Khmer Rouge and Vietnamese Communists was such that the former insisted on having an upper hand in the operations without Vietnamese assistance.[2] Even though the North Vietnamese were contributing substantially to the growth and training of the Khmer Rouge during the early 1970s, they did not want the latter to develop independence and the ability to frustrate long-term North Vietnamese ambitions to dominate all of Indochina. In order to ensure a pro-Vietnamese position, the North Vietnamese sent into Cambodia about 5,000 Khmer Rouge who had been held in reserve in Hanoi ever since their withdrawal from Cambodia in 1954. These Hanoi Khmers, as they came to be called, clashed with the homegrown Khmer Rouge under the leadership of Pol Pot and Khieu Samphan. In 1973, many Hanoi Khmers were purged or killed by the Pol Pot group.

By 1972, the Khmer Rouge numbered well over 50,000, most of them young people, not necessarily communist, with varying grievances against the US-backed Lon Nol regime. The evidence of their superior training, discipline, fighting power, and ability to handle Chinese, Soviet, and US weapons supplied to them by the North Vietnamese was noted in skirmishes with Lon Nol's troops as well as in the successful maintenance of the supply lines to the

NLF. In early 1973, the Khmer Rouge was confirmed in its suspicion of the North Vietnamese when the latter repeatedly pressured them to accept a cease-fire that was presumably the precondition for a US grant of reconstruction aid to Hanoi. Despite Hanoi's end to its military aid and the US saturation bombing, the Khmer Rouge continued the offensive that brought the downfall of the Lon Nol regime a full fortnight before the North Vietnamese marched into Saigon.[3]

The Khmer Rouge would not easily forget the North Vietnamese subordination of Khmer interests to their own in 1973 and 1954. Nor would they forget the timely, massive military assistance they received from Beijing starting in mid–1974. The Chinese leaders had attempted unsuccessfully to encourage a US dialogue with Sihanouk, who since his ouster in 1970 had been in exile in Beijing. Finally, the Chinese threw in their lot with the Khmer Rouge, replacing the North Vietnamese as the principal suppliers to the Khmer Rouge of automatic weapons, ammunition, and mines. Chinese equipment was used in the final siege of Phnom Penh and its capitulation, achieved partly through mining the waterways and cutting off the capital's food supply.

Tension between the Khmer Rouge and the Vietnamese Communists continued after the overthrow of the Lon Nol regime in March 1975. Moreover, at least one of the four factions into which the Cambodian government was divided was clandestinely linked with Hanoi, whereas another advocated rapprochement with Vietnam on pragmatic grounds. The Phnom Penh government was a coalition, the core of which consisted of the Khmer Viet Minh and the student groups that had produced leaders such as Pol Pot, Ieng Sary, and Khieu Samphan. They allied with moderates led by Sihanouk and other non-Communists who were intensely nationalist, wary of Vietnamese expansionism, and pro-Beijing, favoring rapprochement with the United States. Foremost in their links with Vietnamese Communists were obviously the Hanoi Khmers led by Chea Sim, the minister of the interior. Last was a smaller group of "constructionists" who advocated accommodation with Vietnam for pragmatic reasons. Its leader, Heng Samrin, became the clandestine conduit of top secret decisions of the Phnom Penh government to Heng Samrin's allies in Hanoi.

Pol Pot's Regime: The Crisis Deepens

Through Premier Pol Pot's five-hour speech in September 1977, the Khmer Rouge told the world that Hanoi had all along harbored plans to compel Cambodia into an Indochinese federation as the first step toward its annexation. The Pol Pot regime was certainly justified in attempting every means to avert Cambodia's conversion to a Vietnamese satellite. But it should have been realistic enough to appreciate the immensely superior Vietnamese military machine and should therefore have acted in such a way as not to give an excuse for the alleged Vietnamese expansionism to succeed. As soon as the Khmer Rouge assumed power in March 1975, the government led by Pol Pot embarked on an action that perhaps had no precedent in human history. The government emptied the cities and towns, compelling all "intellectuals"— teachers, former civil service officials, monks, and everyone wearing glasses— to work with their hands in agriculture. The regime demonetized the currency; shut down all academic institutions and businesses, including banks; and closed the country to the world. These programs (rather, pogroms) carried out in the most brutal, insensate manner dislocated, decimated, and alienated the bulk of the Cambodian population to the shock and dismay of the entire civilized world. Estimates of those killed vary, but probably more than a million people lost their lives. The horrors of the Pol Pot regime made any aggression by an external power to terminate the horrible conditions in Cambodia look relatively benign in comparison. Further, it created a large exodus of Khmer people into Vietnamese sanctuaries in eastern Cambodia that spilled into Vietnam, where the Vietnamese could organize the Khmer refugees into an alternative rallying point for overthrowing the anti-Hanoi Pol Pot regime.

Instead of playing the Vietnamese against the Chinese so as to maximize their own diplomatic maneuverability, the Khmer Rouge chose to adopt adventurist policies that were certain to provoke Vietnam to an eventual showdown. First, beginning in April 1977, they took the initiative to attack the border provinces, particularly the NEZ in Tay Ninh, with a view to bringing pressure on the Vietnamese to vacate the sanctuaries inside Cambodia. Second, they allied themselves with Vietnam's enemy, China, and invited several thousand Chinese military and technical personnel to Cambodia in what Vietnam called a bid to encircle it. Such policies, internal and international, could neither ensure Cambodia's domestic stability nor reduce its vulnerability to Vietnamese aggression. The Vietnamese march into Cambodia, at the back of the newly born Kampuchean United Front for National Salvation (KUFNS), occurred at a time when Vietnam's hand was forced by the Pol Pot government's ill-conceived tactics.

The new Cambodian leadership believed that its fears of Vietnamese expansionism had been confirmed by the Vietnamese refusal to quit the sanctuaries on Cambodian soil that Prince Sihanouk had allowed them since the late 1960s. In addition, within two weeks of the Communist victory in Saigon, the Vietnamese government reopened an old fight with Cambodia by claiming some islands in the Gulf of Thailand. That led to the first clash between the two Communist governments, and although Hanoi recognized Phnom Penh's claim to Poulo Wai, at the May 1976 bilateral meetings the Vietnamese questioned the entire maritime boundary with Cambodia that had supposedly been settled by the Brevie Line in 1939 during the French rule. The incident helped to strengthen Cambodia's apprehensions of Vietnamese expansionist aims. An attempted coup in September 1976, sparked in all likelihood by the government's domestic policy excesses, was alleged to be a Vietnamese plot to overthrow the government through Hanoi Khmer army units. The Pol Pot regime took advantage of the situation to liquidate the remnant of the Hanoi Khmers, which included five members of the twenty-member party Central Committee. The regime's attitude toward Vietnam hardened. The Phnom Penh government refused to hold talks with Vietnam until the latter completely moved out of all territories claimed by Cambodia.

The Khmer–Viet Conflict

Thereafter, Cambodia obviously decided that offense was the best form of defense, an attitude that did not initially receive the full support of its Chinese allies. Beginning in January 1977 and escalating their activities between April and September 1977, Cambodian forces moved into the old Vietnamese sanctuaries where an NEZ was being established. The attack would achieve the multiple purpose of weakening Vietnam's economy, keeping military pressure on it so as to secure the complete evacuation of the sanctuaries, and frustrating Vietnam's alleged plan to integrate Cambodia into a Vietnamese-dominated Indochinese federation.

If the Vietnamese indeed had any such plans, they were not in a hurry to implement them because of their preoccupation with economic problems and domestic dissidence. Their policy of conciliation with Thailand since 1977 and their apparent readiness to endorse the ASEAN concept of a neutral zone in Southeast Asia free of any big-power influence were indicative of their desire to demonstrate even to their non-Communist neighbors that Vietnam sought peace and had no plans of military intervention in other states, at least for several years.

If Vietnam wanted to live within its self-imposed constraints, China and Cambodia seemed determined not to allow it that kind of luxury. Since the conclusion of the Vietnam war, China had emphasized in its relations with Southeast Asian nations that the Soviet Union represented the "present strategic danger to Southeast Asia,"[4] and cautioned them to beware of "the tiger at the back door while repelling the wolf through the front door."[5] From mid–1977, therefore, by holding back further economic aid and building up Cambodia's military strength, China began to exert pressure on Vietnam to condemn Soviet hegemony. Thus between 1975 and 1978, China supplied Cambodia with 130-mm mortars, 107-mm bazookas, automatic rifles, transport vehicles, gasoline, and various small weapons, enough to equip thirty to forty regiments totaling about 200,000 troops. There is no way of knowing how much economic assistance China provided beyond its initial gift of $1 billion, made at the time of Sihanouk's return to Phnom Penh in 1975. An estimated 10,000 Chinese military and technical personnel were sent to Cambodia to improve its military preparedness. In the political circumstances of the time, such tactics could only have been directed against Vietnam, as China had bent over backward in the postwar period to become friendly with Thailand, the only other neighboring country that could be a threat to Cambodian security. Critical of these Sino-Cambodian measures, Vietnam alleged that they were designed to destroy the Vietnamese economy and encircle the country militarily.

At that point, Vietnam had several additional reasons to avoid spoiling for an all-out war with Cambodia. Apart from the diplomatic damage it would cause by destroying the image of sweet reasonableness Vietnam was attempting to create among its Southeast Asian neighbors, a belligerent act of those dimensions would certainly frustrate efforts to secure economic aid from other countries. Second, in the absence of a militarily strong anti–Pol Pot movement, sizable Vietnamese forces would be locked in direct combat with the Cambodian army, supported by China. The Vietnamese leadership therefore attempted to negotiate with the Khmers, but to no avail. They then resorted to large-scale fighting for three months beginning in October 1977, with the limited purpose of securing a Khmer-Vietnamese border treaty. In January 1978, Vietnam proposed that both sides withdraw their troops to five miles from the existing border and submit themselves to an internationally supervised truce commission. In May 1978, Cambodia agreed to peace talks that would begin in 1979, after Vietnam had demonstrated its genuine desire not to integrate Cambodia into an Indochinese federation under Vietnamese control. Vietnam doubted the authenticity of the Cambodian offer, particularly because of the internationalization of the conflict, brought about by Beijing's overt and firm commitment to Phnom Penh and the general deterioration in Sino-Vietnamese relations.

By mid–1978, Sino-Vietnamese relations had sunk to a precipitously low level. China's actions since the turn of the year had shown that it had decided to take sides in the growing Vietnam–Cambodia dispute not because it was convinced either party was right but because of the impact of the confrontation on the relative influence of the Soviet Union or China in the region. In January 1978, Beijing dispatched Teng Ying Chao, a Central Committee member and widow of former Premier Zhou Enlai, to Phnom Penh to show solidarity with the Pol Pot regime. Soon after, China made large-scale arms shipments to Cambodia, including long-range 130-mm and 150-mm artillery, even though the former NLF forces had completely pulled out of Cambodia. Hanoi's intelligence sources indicated a Chinese resolve to support Cambodia in what Beijing expected and perhaps hoped would be a protracted war.

At this point in mid–1978, Vietnam openly abandoned its old policy of friendship with both Communist giants. Hanoi contemplated a quick military action to liquidate the Pol Pot regime before it solidified itself further with Chinese military assistance. In order to bolster its own security in the event of a Chinese attack across the Sino-Vietnamese border to coincide with Vietnamese action in Cambodia, Hanoi decided to move closer to Moscow. On June 29, 1978, it joined the Moscow-dominated COMECON and on November 3 signed with Moscow a full-fledged, twenty-five-year treaty of friendship and mutual cooperation. A partial price of Soviet assistance was Vietnam's consent to Soviet use and development of Da Nang and Cam Ranh Bay as missile bases.

Vietnam's March into Cambodia

Armed with its treaty with the Soviet Union, Vietnam was ready for a brisk war aimed at toppling the Pol Pot regime and installing one favorable to itself. First, it brought the Pol Pot regime's genocidal excesses to international attention through a publicity blitz. Second, in order to make its march into Cambodia politically palatable to the world, Vietnam facilitated the creation of a fourteen-member committee called the Kampuchean United Front for National Salvation, under the leadership of dissident pro-Hanoi Communists such as Heng Samrin and Chea Sim as well as some exiled Cambodian intellectuals and monks. An important element of the new front would be the support of Khmer Krom, the Cambodian minority of more than half a million residents in Cochin China. (It is worth noting that if that minority moved out of Vietnam, it would partly alleviate the food shortages in the country.) Officially, the Vietnamese role would be to help the KUFNS in overthrowing the Pol Pot regime for humanitarian reasons.

Unlike the NLF, the KUFNS did not inspire popular support among Cambodians because its patrons were Vietnamese. The organization was clearly a Vietnamese smoke screen created on the eve of Vietnam's invasion of Cambodia to legitimize its action in the eyes of the world. The success of the seventeen-day Vietnamese blitzkrieg in Cambodia beginning December 25, 1978, owed little to KUFNS or its few supporters inside that country. If the KUFNS and Vietnamese forces did not encounter much opposition, it was because of the public relief over the extinction of the oppressive Pol Pot regime, with its legacy of regimented life, communal kitchens, broken families, and hard, unending labor. Under the leadership of Heng Samrin, the new Cambodian government was successful in controlling most of Cambodia (except the western region) in part owing to the presence of an estimated 160,000 Vietnamese occupation troops, who would not brook any measures to crush serious public opposition.

Pol Pot and his cohorts fled to western Cambodia. For a while, China was able to continue supplying military and economic aid to the anti–Heng Samrin guerrillas thanks to the airstrip at Siem Reap, passages through Laos and Thailand, and the porous 450-mile Cambodian coastline. The Laotian corridor was soon plugged by the pro-Vietnam government, which also expelled Chinese technical and military personnel from Cambodia. The Pol Pot group had no choice but to league with other foes of the Heng Samrin regime, including Sihanouk moderates and even a right-wing organization called the Khmer Serei, led by the former premier Son Sann. (In 1975, the Pol Pot regime had forced the Khmer Serei across the Thai border and into the Cardamom Mountains.) The Khmer Serei's hatred of the military occupation of their homeland by the ancient enemy, Vietnam, far surpassed their antipathy toward the Khmer Rouge. Doubts about the ability of the tripartite coalition resistance forces to overthrow the Vietnam-backed Heng Samrin government may have been responsible for the precipitate Chinese invasion of Vietnam in February 1979. China expected Vietnam to withdraw substantial numbers of its troops from Cambodia to move them to the Sino-Vietnamese frontier, thereby relieving pressure on Pol Pot and his allies in western Cambodia.

Vietnam's Occupation of Cambodia: Goals and Impact

As Hanoi would reveal in September 1989, the eleven-year occupation and war in Cambodia had left 23,000 Vietnamese dead and 55,000 wounded. The impact of the war on the Vietnamese economy, despite all the Soviet economic and military assistance, had been disastrous. Vietnam expended nearly 50 percent of its military budget in Cambodia. Withdrawal from Cambodia would secure the resumption of trade and investment by West European countries, ASEAN, and Japan, which would greatly improve Vietnam's economy and foreign exchange position. (The United States had, with the help of its allies, successfully blocked loans from the International Monetary Fund to Vietnam.) Above all, Vietnam's withdrawal would pave the way for the normalization of relations with the United States. Moreover, ending the military impasse made strategic sense, as the Vietnamese forces would lose during the wet season whatever advances they made on the ground in the dry season. Thus for domestic as well as diplomatic reasons, it became essential for Vietnam to wind down its political, economic, and military commitments in Cambodia.

Hanoi's invasion and occupation of Cambodia was in all likelihood undertaken to enhance Vietnam's security in a variety of ways. It curbed Khmer Rouge attacks on Vietnam's border provinces and removed an unfriendly regime in Phnom Penh. Further, as William Turley put it, it was strategically important for Vietnam to "deny the use of Cambodia by a country seen as hostile, namely, China. Although China was the immediate threat, Hanoi's transcendent concern, based upon experience in two previous wars, was the threat posed by the susceptibility of regimes on Vietnam's Western flank to non-Vietnamese influence."[6]

Vietnam's security concerns were, however, compounded when China and ASEAN enabled the Khmer Rouge to forge an alliance with two non-Communist Cambodian groups—the Khmer People's National Liberation Front (KPNLF), led by Son Sann, and the Armée Nationale Sihanoukiste (National Sihanoukist Army), led by Prince Norodom Sihanouk—to form the Coalition Government of Democratic Kampuchea (CGDK). A new military power equation emerged in the region, with China, the United States, and ASEAN (particularly Thailand) helping the CGDK (which was thus able to secure Cambodia's seat in the UN General Assembly) and the Soviet Union supporting Vietnam and the People's Republic of Kampuchea (PRK).

From the time of its occupation of Cambodia, Vietnam had stressed "security interdependence of the three states of former French Indochina," repeatedly talking of a "special relationship" with Cambodia along the same lines as it had with Laos. With such objectives, Vietnam established trilateral commissions to plan and implement several schemes of economic cooperation that would bring about economic integration among the three states. Vietnam, however, had no intention of becoming bogged down in Cambodia in the manner that the United States had become mired in Vietnam in the 1960s. Hanoi perceived the wisdom of a policy of reducing, if not eliminating, a permanent presence of its troops and political advisers in Cambodia as soon as practicable and instead promoting political, economic, and military self-reliance on the part of the governments in Cambodia and Laos. Even as the CGDK was formed and Western and ASEAN aid offered to it, Vietnam announced in February 1982 its plans gradually to withdraw its troops from Cambodia. The withdrawal did not begin, however, until 1985, due to mounting CGDK resistance in western Cambodia. In that year, Vietnam declared that it would pull all its troops out by 1990, a date that would eventually be advanced to September 1989.

Multipronged Efforts Toward Peace in Cambodia

Major changes that helped the peace process in Cambodia, however, came in 1989. These were preceded by deliberate conciliatory moves on the part of Vietnam on the MIA question and an improvement in relations with China. The first official Sino-Vietnamese meeting in more than a decade took place in January 1989. In the following month, a joint meeting of foreign ministers of Vietnam, Laos, and Cambodia announced that Vietnam would withdraw all its remaining troops from Cambodia before the end of September 1989 "within a framework of a political solution." In May, the PRK amended its constitution to change the country's name to the State of Cambodia (SOC), recognize Buddhism as the state religion, and permit private landownership. Such changes were made as a prelude to more serious talks with the two non-Communist elements of the CGDK and to separate them from the murderous Khmer Rouge. On July 20 the PRK, now the SOC, announced a position of "permanent neutrality" in international affairs, thereby virtually ending the Cambodia–Vietnam alliance treaty. Although the Vietnamese withdrawal of troops was not supervised by any international agency, most of the international community, including the United States, ASEAN, and the Western powers, accepted that but for the presence of a few hundred military and political "advisers," Vietnam's occupation of Cambodia ended in late 1989.

Vietnam's perception that the Khmer government was functioning more effectively also influenced Vietnam's decision to pull out of Cambodia. Moreover, the withdrawal of troops did not mean that Vietnam would abandon its desire to influence the Cambodian government. Thus, in May 1989, the Vietnamese government opened a center in Hanoi to pursue cooperative projects between Vietnam and Cambodia in the fields of economy, science and technology, culture, sports, and tourism. The accomplishments of the Phnom Penh government, particularly since 1986, had encouraged Hanoi to think that it would be able to withstand the political and military opposition of the CGDK, whose solidarity was gravely threatened in 1989 by the possibility that its non-Communist components might break away from it. In case of setbacks, Hanoi would be prepared to rush military and other assistance to Phnom Penh to enable the PRK to defend its position against a major Khmer Rouge offensive in western Cambodia.

By the late 1980s, all the parties directly or indirectly involved in the Cambodian conflict realized that the military stalemate did not give anyone any special advantage. The ASEAN states, notably Thailand, saw no advantage in continuing to be forever a conduit for Chinese arms to the CGDK. On behalf of the ASEAN states, however, Indonesia took the lead in breaking the political and military impasse by bringing all the Cambodian parties together for informal talks at Jakarta. The first two Jakarta Informal Meetings (JIM–1 in July 1988 and JIM–2 in February 1989) linked the withdrawal of Vietnamese troops to the stoppage of all external aid to the CGDK. The second JIM underlined the need for power sharing in Phnom Penh as a postwar solution.

A UN major initiative expressed the all-around desire to find a solution that would mean an "honorable" exclusion of the Khmer Rouge from any future government in Cambodia. On November 3, 1988, with US and Chinese support, the UN General Assembly passed a significant resolution that Cambodia must not return to "the universally condemned policies and practices of a recent past." The vote was 122 for and 19 against. Apparently, both the United States and China seemed satisfied with the progress in Vietnamese plans for withdrawal from Cambodia. Their support—military, economic, and diplomatic—of the Khmer Rouge markedly dropped thereafter.

Just as no solution was found at the first two informal meetings at Jakarta, none came out of the nineteen-nation international conference at Paris, which opened in July 1989. At that venue, the SOC and Vietnam, backed by the Soviet Union, argued in favor of an international agreement preceding an internal settlement on the sharing of power, whereas the CGDK, China, and ASEAN insisted on a comprehensive settlement that would include both internal and international aspects of the problem. On the one hand, the CGDK's demand for a quadripartite division of power in the country was not acceptable to the SOC because it would be left with only one-quarter of the authority, which, it argued, was far removed from the "battlefield realities." Moreover, the SOC was totally opposed to any power sharing that would reward the genocidal Khmer Rouge. On the other hand, the SOC's proposal for a bilateral sharing of power was not acceptable to the CGDK, which claimed total legitimacy of power and sovereignty, in large part based on its holding a seat in the United Nations. One of the few areas of agreement among most of the parties involved was a larger and crucial role for the United Nations not only in the supervision of a cease-fire and disarming of troops but also in the internal administration of the country, on the model of Namibia, pending supervised elections and formation of a coalition government.

The military impasse between the CGDK and the SOC on the battlefields of western Cambodia was now matched by a deadlock at the international negotiations table. Two major international initiatives on the part of the United States and China—the latter's action perhaps as a reaction to the new US stance—significantly helped the peace process. In a dramatic turnaround, Secretary of State James Baker announced on July 18, 1990, at the end of a meeting with the Soviet foreign minister, that after eleven years of backing the Khmer Rouge, the United States would no longer support the seating of the CGDK in the UN General Assembly. Further, the United States declared its readiness to hold direct talks with Vietnam in New York over the Cambodian conflict. Accordingly, on September 29, Foreign Minister Nguyen Co Thach, visiting the UN, met with Baker in New York.

As for China, Gorbachev's initiatives in Afghanistan, Vietnam, and indirectly in Cambodia had contributed in the late 1980s to the decline, if not dissipation, of fears of China's "encirclement" by the Soviet Union and its ally, Vietnam. In January 1990, the Soviet Union declared that it would no longer use the Cam Ranh Bay base. By April, there were reports of the repatriation of about 200,000 Vietnamese workers from the Soviet Union and Eastern Europe, an indication of reduced aid from that quarter to Vietnam. So far, Hanoi had viewed its alliance with the Soviet Union as providing a deterrent to China's use of force against Vietnam. Gorbachev's attempts at forging a Sino-Soviet détente clearly reduced the possibility of the Soviet Union's stepping in if Vietnam and China clashed again. Already, Moscow had manifested a kind of neutrality between Hanoi and Beijing when their rival forces clashed on the offshore Spratly Islands in March 1988.

The visible cracks in the Soviet–Eastern European solidarity and their greatly reduced military and economic support to Vietnam eased China's fears. At the same time, it contributed to Vietnam's desire to improve relations with China itself. In May 1990, China and Vietnam arrived at a "basic agreement" to end the Cambodia conflict through international negotiations. Simultaneously, Moscow announced a normalization of relations with Beijing, implying thereby China's satisfaction that its precondition regarding Vietnam's withdrawal from Cambodia had been met. Reportedly, the two Communist neighbors had agreed to disagree on a number of "minor" points. The much-improved Sino-Soviet relationship prompted Vietnam to open a dialogue with China. Secret talks between the two countries at the highest level, the first since 1976, took place in early September 1990. The Vietnamese delegation, headed by party secretary-general Nguyen Van Linh, included Prime Minister Du Muoi and former prime minister, Pham Van Dong; its Chinese counterpart was led by party chief Jiang Zemin and Premier Li Peng.

With the change in attitude of the two major supporters of the Khmer Rouge—namely, the United States and China—the international climate became conducive as never before to a settlement of the Cambodian problem. The impasse over the twin questions of power sharing and the SOC's apprehension of an enhanced UN role in the transitional period was overcome by an Australian proposal presented to a meeting of the five permanent members of the UN interim administration of Cambodia pending general elections. The proposal suggested that the CGDK be asked to vacate its seat in the UN General Assembly. Although the five permanent members of the Security Council approved the Australian plan in principle, only three of the four Cambodian factions endorsed it, the most vociferous dissenter being the Khmer Rouge. The differences between the Khmer Rouge and its CGDK partners became even sharper at JIM–3 in February 1990. Earlier the same month, Sihanouk announced the renaming of the Coalition Government of Democratic Kampuchea as the National Government of Cambodia, thus distancing the two Communist components of the former CGDK from the Khmer Rouge, whose disreputable government from 1975 to 1978 was known as Democratic Kampuchea.

In spring 1990, there was no appreciable progress toward adoption of the UN plan, despite intense diplomatic pressure on the different Cambodian factions by their former external supporters. Finally, on August 28, 1990, a collective initiative on the part of the nineteen-nation Paris Conference on Cambodia (PCC), cochaired by Indonesia and France and including the five permanent members of the Security Council, resulted in a unanimous agreement on a framework for settlement of the Cambodian conflict. All four Cambodian factions endorsed the framework document. Thereafter, the negotiations progressed faster, eventually culminating in a final settlement in October 1991 at three interdependent levels: the Cambodian factions meeting in Jakarta, Indonesia, and Pattaya, Thailand; the PCC meetings; and the PCC cochairs working jointly with the five permanent members of the UN Security Council and the UN secretary-general's representative, Rafeeuddin Ahmed. Underlying these developments, however, were cataclysmic changes on the global level that created a climate conducive to the international settlement of the Cambodian conflict: the collapse of the Soviet Union and Eastern European states, the manifestation of the sole superpower role by the United States in the Gulf War, and the readiness of China and Vietnam in the altered international context to mend their relationship.

Progress followed more quickly in the aftermath of the Seventh Congress of the VCP in June 1991. At the Pattaya meeting in the same month, Sihanouk, with Hun Sen of the Cambodian People's Party (CPP), announced that he would return to Phnom Penh as head of a Supreme National Council (SNC), a body of representatives from each of the four Cambodian factions (including the Khmer Rouge) that would govern the country under UN supervision. In the last week of August, at the second meeting at Pattaya, which Sihanouk chaired and representatives of the PCC countries attended, the SNC announced unanimous agreement on all major points: cease-fire and cessation of foreign military assistance; demobilization of the military forces of the four factions; the establishment of a United Nations Transitional Authority in Cambodia (UNTAC); Cambodia's future political framework; human rights and principles of a new constitution for Cambodia; and international rehabilitation and reconstruction aid.

Paris Agreements and the UNTAC's Mission

The Pattaya consensus became the basis of the PCC's agreements on a comprehensive settlement of the Cambodian conflict on October 23, 1991. The settlement represented the most ambitious and elaborate peacekeeping effort ever attempted by the United Nations. Principally brokered by external powers, it was accepted by all Cambodian parties, though as subsequent events showed, with great reluctance and perhaps under duress by the Khmer Rouge (KR). The settlement created the UNTAC to wield substantial power over the government of Cambodia for a period of eighteen months to two years. The UNTAC would deal with the SNC, which would exercise Cambodian sovereignty in the UN and deal with foreign nations and international financial agencies.

The SNC would consist of twelve members—six from the existing government of Cambodia, referred to as the State of Cambodia and identified with the ruling party; the CPP; and two each from the three rebel factions: FUNCINPEC (the French acronym for National United Front for an Independent, Neutral, Peaceful, and Cooperative Cambodia), Prince Norodom Sihanouk's party, headed by his son Ranaridh; the KPNLF under former Cambodian prime minister Son Sann; and the KR. Norodom Sihanouk would be chairman of the SNC. He, along with UNTAC chief Yasushi Akashi, a former Japanese diplomat with considerable experience in UN peacekeeping operations, would have final decision-making powers. The UNTAC would, through its own senior officials, directly oversee the work of the Ministries of Foreign Affairs, Defense, Finance, Public Security, and Information. It would protect the civil rights of all Cambodians, including the estimated 350,000 refugees in Thailand, who would be returned and resettled in Cambodia through the assistance of the United Nations High Commissioner for Refugees (UNHCR). During the first phase, the UNTAC would separate, canton, and disarm the forces of the various factions and demobilize 70 percent of each of them; the remaining 30 percent would be allowed to stay in cantonments with weapons under UNTAC control. By the middle of 1992, the UNTAC had deployed nearly 16,000 troops, 3,500 civilian police, and 3,000 civilian officials, including those in charge of organizing the elections. The entire operation was estimated to cost $1.9 billion in addition to $600 million for the repatriation and rehabilitation of refugees by the UNCHR.

On the political plane, the UNTAC was entrusted with the task of holding national elections to a constituent assembly in mid– or late 1993. All Cambodians above the age of eighteen, including the returning refugees, would be eligible to vote. After the elections were certified by the UN as fair and free, the constituent assembly would draft a constitution within three months on the lines of democratic liberalism, pluralism, universal franchise, and human rights. Thereafter, the constituent assembly would be transformed into a legislative assembly with a new government responsible to it.

A major flaw in the agreements was that the SOC and the resistance factions were allowed to continue to administer the areas and populations under their respective control. Although the FUNCINPEC and KPNLF cooperated, the KR refused the UNTAC teams access to the territories it controlled and would not commit its troops to the cantonments or facilitate their disarmament. KR forces frequently opened fire on UNTAC helicopters and mined roads leading to KR bases. In mid–1992, the KR accused the UNTAC of failing to create the neutral political environment envisaged in the Paris agreements. It alleged that the SOC was exercising a degree of control over Cambodian life that made fair political competition for other parties impossible, that there were hundreds of thousands of Vietnamese soldiers in the guise of settlers who could not be distinguished from genuine settlers, and that therefore all Vietnamese must be expelled from Cambodia in order to make the elections fair. The KR made compliance with its demands a precondition for cooperation with the UNTAC. In fact, it launched a campaign to eliminate the *youn*, the pejorative Khmer term for the Vietnamese. The campaign assumed alarming proportions by late 1992; it proved to be popular with the Cambodian masses, the KR exploiting their historical hatred of the Vietnamese. Not surprisingly, no individual leader or political party, with the sole exception of Norodom Sihanouk, condemned the atrocities against unarmed Vietnamese civilians. A factor contributing to Khmer intransigence was its financial independence, thanks to its lucrative timber and gem trades with Thai businesspeople and military leaders across the border.

Despite the lack of cooperation from the KR, the UNTAC went ahead with the implementation of the Paris agreements. A crucial boost to its activities was provided by the Security Council's unanimous resolution of October 13,

1992, that elections would be held in Cambodia in May 1993 with or without the participation of the KR. The resolution also authorized the PCC cochairs, Indonesia and France, to intercede with the KR to allow the UNTAC access to KR territories and help in the process of disarming and demobilizing KR troops. The UN Security Council resolution proposed economic sanctions, including cutting off gasoline supplies to the KR, and requested the "neighboring states," meaning Thailand, to respect the moratorium on the export of logs, gems, and minerals from Cambodia. Neither the UN resolution nor a subsequent ten-nation conference in Beijing in November 1992 produced any positive reaction from the KR.

Despite Khmer threats, 90 percent of the eligible voters exercised their right to vote in the UNTAC-organized general elections of May 23–28, 1993. A UN force of 700 volunteers drawn from more than thirty countries helped with the election process. The KR boycotted the elections because it expected a rigged victory for the incumbent CPP. Instead, FUNCINPEC won with 45.5 percent of the vote and fifty-eight seats in the National Assembly; the ruling CPP received 38.2 percent of the vote and fifty-one seats; the Buddhist Liberal Democratic Party (BLDP) won ten seats; and Moulinaka (an offshoot of FUNCINPEC) one seat. No one had an absolute majority, let alone the two-thirds majority required for passing constitutional proposals.

The transition of authority was not completely peaceful. The ruling CPP challenged the election results in four provinces. The SOC threatened to use the forces under its control—100,000 soldiers and 45,000 police—to retain the status quo and deny the electoral results. The leadership of both CPP and FUNCINPEC were divided with regard to the question and modalities of sharing power. A deputy prime minister in the SOC, Prince Chakrapong (a son of Norodom Sihanouk, who had differences with his father), led a dissident coup and fled the country but was allowed to return without punishment. The national mood was of reconciliation, a feeling that if Cambodia missed the opportunity presented by a peaceful, internationally supervised election, democracy in the country would be doomed. The only person in the fragmented political spectrum who seemed to command the general respect and confidence of the people was Norodom Sihanouk, who had on so many occasions in the past played a central role in the nation's politics. His efforts finally put together a national government of "peace and reconciliation."

During the transition, Sihanouk emerged as a focal point of national unity and reconciliation: First, on June 3, 1993, he declared that he was officially assuming the functions of head of state, premier, and commander of the armed forces in his capacity as "father of the nation, father of national unity, father of reconciliation." On June 14, the newly elected assembly ratified the arrangements and gave Sihanouk whatever powers he deemed necessary to "save the Cambodian nation." Sihanouk reconciled the differences between the CPP and FUNCINPEC by creating two coequal deputy premiers, his own son Ranaridh and Hun Sen. The governing coalition, which also included the BLDP and Moulinaka, would be in power until the newly elected assembly drafted a constitution and formed a regular government.

The new constitution promulgated on September 24, 1993, restored the monarchy of Cambodia, with Norodom Sihanouk as king. It also revived the flag and the national anthem of the Sihanouk era. As noted in chapter 6, in 1955 Sihanouk had abdicated his throne in favor of his own father, Suramarit. After the death of King Suramarit in 1960, the parliament elected Sihanouk as head of state and abolished the monarchy. Twenty-four clauses in the new constitution defined and limited the authority of the king, who would be advised by a seven-member throne council. The new constitution provided for a pluralist liberal democracy, a state-guided market economy, and a social system guaranteeing economic, social, cultural, and educational rights to all citizens.

Unstable Government and Khmer Rouge Intransigence

The government of Cambodia under the new constitution was a coalition of FUNCINPEC, CPP, and BLDP, with Norodom Ranaridh of FUNCINPEC the first prime minister and Hun Sen of the CPP the second prime minister. Despite frequent disagreements over some issues, the coalition worked until June 1997. At least three factors helped to hold the coalition together. First was the royal influence of the ailing but alert Norodom Sihanouk, who threatened to quit his office every time the coalition was beset by internal dissension. Second was the widespread corruption bolstered by plentiful funds from international agencies, including the International Committee on Reconstruction of Cambodia (ICRC) that met every year and pledged loans and grants for debt relief, economic adjustment, and reform programs. In early 1994, the thirty-two countries of the ICRC approved $700 million for Cambodia in addition to the US grant of $15 million for clearing land mines; in May, the IMF approved a three-year "enhanced structural adjustment facility" of $120 million. In March 1995, the ICRC approved a $1.3 billion package for 1995–1996, $430 million for fiscal 1997, and $870 million for 1998. Additionally, the Forum for Comprehensive Development of Cambodia and Vietnam meeting in Tokyo in the same month approved an additional 2.6 billion yen. Considerable amounts of those funds remained unused because of Cambodia's inadequate absorption capabilities, but they allowed bureaucrats and politicians to line their pockets. Third, the KR provided a common focal point of hostility for the governmental coalition partners.

The continued intransigence of the KR led to orders to close the KR offices in Phnom Penh on June 17, 1993; three weeks later the National Assembly declared it an outlaw organization. The government offered six-month amnesty for Khmer forces to surrender, after which they would be subject to thirty-year prison terms. In response, the KR announced the formation of the Provisional Government of National Union and National Salvation, with headquarters in the northwestern province of Prey Vihear. More than 2,000 KR soldiers took advantage of the amnesty, but an estimated 5,000 to 10,000 remained at bay, fighting the government forces in western Cambodia.

Khmer Rouge and Pol Pot

The KR's forces were decimated by large-scale defections and the government's success between 1993 and 1998 in destroying their strongholds in western Cambodia. Remnants of the KR were badly divided; a fairly strong faction under the much-feared KR chief of staff, Ta Mok, headed the KR "government" in the heavily mined Anlong Veng. In July 1997, Ta Mok brought Pol Pot to "trial" by a "people's tribunal" that sentenced him to life imprisonment. At the so-called trial, Pol Pot refused to accept responsibility for the mass murders and insisted that evidence such as that found at Tuol Sieng prison in Phnom Penh was fabricated by the Vietnamese. A few months later, in March 1998, it was Ta Mok's turn to face a mutiny when an estimated 1,000 KR guerrillas rebelled against him. Government troops pushed forward to rendezvous with guerrilla renegades as they pursued Ta Mok and his "prisoner"—Pol Pot—east toward Preah Vihear. By the end of the year, virtually all of the KR leadership—including its political chief, Khieu Samphan, and its chief ideologue, Nuon Chea—surrendered to government forces. Ta Mok was captured on March 6, 1999, on the Thai border, thereby marking the end of the twenty-five-year long KR insurgency.

At some point during the government's drive against Ta Mok, the latter was reported to be considering handing Pol Pot over to the government to stand trial. Such reports may have prompted Pol Pot to commit suicide on April 15, 1998, although there were rumors that he may have been poisoned by Ta Mok or his men.

Hun Sen Takes Power

In July 1997, the same month as Pol Pot was brought to trial, the coalition government fell apart when the second prime minister Hun Sen ousted the first prime minister Prince Ranaridh. The CPP's superior forces overpowered those loyal to the royalist faction, imprisoning and executing forty-three of Ranaridh's supporters. Hun Sen declared that the FUNCINPEC foreign minister Ung Huoi had replaced Ranaridh as the second prime minister. The "revolution" threatened to wreck the underlying spirit of the coalition government so painstakingly put together by the UNTAC and the international donors, notably Japan. They pressed and prevailed upon Hun Sen to hold a "show trial" of Prince Ranaridh, who had been accused of consorting with the Khmer Rouge and smuggling weapons, and then acquit him through the king's power to pardon.

Since the "coup" of July 1997, Cambodia virtually has been ruled by Hun Sen, whose CPP scored decisive electoral victories in the national elections held in July 1998 and July 2003. Although his party won seventy-three seats— the highest of all parties—it did not meet the constitutional requirement of two-thirds majority to form a government and was compelled to form a coalition government on both occasions.

The FUNCINPEC has progressively lost from its majority of fifty-eight seats in 1993 to forty-three in 1998, and only twenty-six in 2003 out of a total of 123 seats in the National Assembly. The opposition Sam Rangsi Party (SRP) moved from fifteen in 1998 to twenty-four in 2003, scoring 22 percent of the popular vote as against FUNCINPEC's 21 percent and CPP's 47 percent. The 2003 election was preceded by a number of political murders of medium-level opposition politicians and their supporters in the media and entertainment worlds.

Both FUNCINPEC and SRP alleged election-rigging by Hun Sen–led government on a large scale. Their challenges before the election tribunal delayed the formation of the coalition government until November 2003. the CPP and FUNCINPEC formed the government with the SRP serving as the official opposition.

The Khmer Rouge Trial

With the defeat and capture of the Khmer Rouge leadership in early 1999, both domestic and international organizations clamored for legal proceedings against those who had perpetrated torture and mass killings in the country for a quarter century. Prime Minister Hun Sen himself had an unsettling relationship with senior members of the Khmer Rouge, having been a KR member from 1970 to 1978, when he fled to Vietnam. Hun Sen accompanied the Vietnamese invaders to Cambodia and joined the anti-KR Vietnam-backed Heng Samrin government as its foreign minister and became prime minister in 1985 at the early age of thirty-three. In December 1998, when major leaders of the Khmer Rouge—Khieu Samphan and Nuon Chea—surrendered, Hun Sen at first offered an amnesty. His reluctance to punish the KR may be selective, but in general the successive governments he has headed have been less than enthusiastic about bringing the Khmer Rouge leaders to trial.

A reluctant Hun Sen, perhaps under acute international pressure, joined his co-prime minister Ranaridh in June 1997 to approach the UN for assistance in organizing the process for KR trial. Following a UN resolution of December 1997, Secretary-General Kofi Annan sent, in the following August, a group of experts to Cambodia to devise measures for the trials "as a means of bringing about national reconciliation, strengthening democracy and addressing the issue of individual accountability." Although the Hun Sen government appointed a task force for cooperation with international legal experts and prepared for the trials, negotiations among Cambodian, UN, and third-party intermediaries dragged on through the next five years. Prime Minister Hun Sen supported a trial of former KR leaders for crimes against humanity, but with the qualification that those who supported them should also be brought to justice in accordance with the Cambodian judicial system, with international legal assistance, including foreign judges and prosecutors. As against the demand of Western countries and the United States that the trial's focus should be on the period of the Khmer Rouge (1975–1979), Hun Sen demanded that the period be extended from 1970 to 1998 so as to include US bombing of Cambodia in the early 1970s and the years of support by China, Thailand, and the United States to the Khmer Rouge after 1979. A draft agreement of 1999 was thrown out—even after it met the approval of the Cambodian National Assembly in August 2001 on grounds that it violated the Cambodian constitution on certain points such as the death penalty.

In disgust, UN negotiators withdrew from Cambodia in February 2002. The issue, however, did not disappear from the UN radar. On November 20, 2002, The UN General Assembly's Social, Humanitarian, and Cultural Committee voted 123–0, with thirty-seven abstentions, to approve a resolution sponsored by France and Japan urging UN Secretary-General Kofi Annan to resume negotiations. On March 17, the UN's chief negotiator, Hans Corell, announced a draft agreement that would provide for a bicameral (in place of the previously proposed tricameral) judicial structure consisting of a Trial Chamber and a Supreme Court Chamber.

The scope of the trial would be limited to crimes committed by senior leaders of the Khmer Rouge between April 17, 1975—the day the KR government under Pol Pot took over—to January 6, 1979, when the Vietnamese invasion overthrew it. On October 1, Karsten Herrel was appointed coordinator for UN Assistance to Khmer Rouge Trials (UNAKRT) while several countries, including Sweden, Great Britain, and Australia, undertook to meet the expenses of the task force and the trials. As of mid–2004, the trials had not commenced.

Cambodia's Economic Reconstruction

The Pol Pot's regime's excesses completely destroyed the economic infrastructure of the country that in the first place was hardly developed under French colonial rule. During the Pol Pot period, an entire generation of professionals—teachers, university academics, bureaucrats, small businessmen—had been wiped out, leaving an enormous, young population with little opportunity for guidance from elders and little respect for the country's culture or heritage. The decade of Vietnamese occupation of Cambodia—1979 to 1989—did little to revitalize the Cambodian economy; in fact, years of sporadic warfare with the Khmer Rouge forces did not help the building of a viable national economy.

The Khmer Rouge remnants fighting government forces in the western parts of the country had no respect for heritage, and they engaged in smuggling carvings from Angkor Wat and Angkor Thom across Thailand to sell to antiquities dealers in the West. In the 1990s, with UNESCO's support, the Cambodian government was able to seek the cooperation of enforcement agencies of Western nations and Interpol to arrest the loot of national treasures; in November 1999, Thailand, a fellow-member of the ASEAN, handed over to the visiting Cambodian foreign minister more than 100 illegally traded antiquities apprehended by the Bangkok authorities from local markets.

The Cambodian economy began to pick up only after the Paris accords and the pumping of large funds donated by several Western countries and Japan. In the late 1990s, with relative peace prevailing in the country, the normal economy based on rice and fish revived and brought back the traditional contentment to the peasantry. The infusion of foreign aid and capital helped the growth of the textiles and garments manufacturing sector, with popular Western brand names exploiting Cambodia's low-wage structure. More than 100 new factories sprang up to take advantage of the US market. The imposition of quotas by the United States, however, toward the end of the 1990s and the signing of the bilateral trade agreement (BTA) between the United States and Vietnam in July 2000 began to affect the industry in Cambodia.

Poor economies often impel the depredation of natural wealth. In 2000, an Asian Development Bank study characterized Cambodia's forest management program "a total system failure." In January of the same year, the government claimed to take stringent measures against illegal logging, while the opposition parties appealed to foreign aid donors to make their assistance to government conditional on adoption of genuine measures against illegal logging operations in western Cambodia. A major problem in the drive against illegal loggers has been their collusion with army commanders, who have been virtual rulers of some districts, making law enforcement ineffective in those areas. With the progressive demobilization of military forces, the problem may get even worse unless the government assists the enforcement tasks with gun-mounted helicopters to survey the affected regions.

CHAPTER 9

Vietnam's Relations with China, the Soviet Union, and ASEAN

Contrary to the DRV's pre–1975 professed stance of spearheading communist revolution in Southeast Asia, by the end of the 1980s the Communist government of unified Vietnam moved to become a responsible member of the international community. It desired not only peace and good relations with its neighbors but even membership in the largely pro-Western ASEAN, with which it had had a mutually adversarial relationship since ASEAN's birth in 1967. By 1989, it had pulled out its troops and ended its occupation of Cambodia, and in October 1991, together with eighteen other countries, it signed the Paris peace accords on Cambodia. At that point Vietnam raised the hopes of the international community that it, along with Laos and Cambodia, would "be formally integrated into the rest of Southeast Asia, thereby erasing an ideological divide—a legacy of the Cold War—in which the region was polarized into two opposing ideological blocs, namely, a Communist Indochina and a non-Communist Southeast Asia."[1]

By the mid–1990s, Vietnam had succeeded in normalizing its relations with its former enemy number one, the United States. It had also succeeded in joining ASEAN as a full member. Above all, it had liberalized its economic policies to transform its economy along capitalist lines, promoting close economic ties with the United States, Western Europe, Japan, and pro-West world agencies such as the World Bank and the IMF. In this, Vietnam had followed the Chinese example of adopting economic liberalization and globalization without allowing substantially greater political openness or modifying the political process that gave a monopoly of power to the Communist Party.

Vietnam and China

Vietnam–China relations are best understood in terms of the nations' rival long-term ambitions in Southeast Asia. Communist China through the past five decades has periodically published maps showing most of Southeast Asia as lying within China's sphere of influence. For its part, the Vietnamese Communists had, since the establishment of the Indochina Communist Party in 1930, indicated their plans to dominate the territories formerly under French rule.

Vietnam's ambition for a regional leadership through assistance to Communist movements and domination of governments could be attributed to other than purely ideological reasons. Its desire to create a strong independent center of power is partly a quest for enhanced security born of a traditional fear of Chinese domination of Vietnam. Historically, Vietnam has been a fiercely freedom-loving country apprehensive of its northern neighbor's expansionism. The several revolts during the thousand-odd years of Chinese rule extending over the first millennium (111 BC–AD 939), the successful overthrow of the Chinese rule again in the fifteenth century (1407–1428), the readiness to sign an agreement to allow the return of the French—only to get the Chinese occupation troops out in 1946, and the reluctant acceptance of the cease-fire along the 17th parallel in 1954 at Geneva—all demonstrate Vietnam's intense distrust and suspicion of China under whatever government, imperial, nationalist, or Communist.

During the greater part of the thirty-year struggle that ended in 1975, the Viet Minh and later the DRV and the NLF had to maintain cordial relations with China in order to continue to receive much-needed military assistance. Although no reliable figures on Chinese aid to North Vietnam exist—even official Chinese estimates vary from $14 billion to $21 billion—there is no doubt that Chinese economic and military assistance was crucial for the Communist success in South Vietnam. Despite such dependence, Hanoi retained its political autonomy; it refused, for instance, to enter into a formal military alliance with China and politely declined to "invite" Chinese volunteer forces to aid the Vietnamese liberation movement. Until 1965, there was greater consensus between Chinese and Vietnamese strategy and tactics, the Vietnamese being more appreciative of the Chinese than of the Soviets owing to the former's support to wars of national liberation. Also, until that point Chinese aid to

Vietnam was far more, almost double the amount proffered by the Soviet Union. The situation changed in early 1965 with the beginning of US strategic bombing of North Vietnam, whose need for sophisticated defense equipment, including surface-to-air missiles, could be met by the Soviet Union rather than China. Thus far, the North Vietnamese had relied more on guerrilla warfare and much less on mobile warfare to carry on the struggle in the south. In mid–1965, the North Vietnamese strategists judged the time had come to switch to mobile warfare and, in some instances, even to positional warfare. Such an advanced war strategy was not condoned by the Chinese, who preferred a protracted war in which the Vietnamese would depend for indefinite periods on China's assistance in the form of small weapons. Chinese defense minister Lin Biao's celebrated doctrine of the "wars of national liberation" launched on September 3, 1965, emphasized a policy of self-reliance, an indirect exhortation to Vietnam to reduce its dependence on the Soviet Union.

During the Cultural Revolution in the late 1960s, the Chinese authorities acted deliberately to impede the flow of Soviet military aid to North Vietnam. For example, China asked the Soviet Union to pay in US dollars the freight for transporting armaments by Chinese rail, then made sure that railroad wagons were rarely available to the Soviets. From 1967 until the end of the war, the Soviet Union consequently had to supply by sea both large and small weaponry, which included surface-to-air missiles (SAMs), MiG aircraft, bombers, helicopters, antiaircraft batteries, a radar defense system, and all kinds of transport vehicles. Annual Soviet military aid to North Vietnam soon surpassed that of the Chinese.

Vietnam and the Sino-Soviet Rivalry

The more recent phase of Sino-Vietnamese differences began in 1971 with the Chinese and US moves toward rapprochement. Hanoi regarded US efforts to end the Vietnam conflict by asking China to stop its military aid to Vietnamese Communists and China's subsequent emphasis on a struggle against revisionism rather than Western imperialism as Beijing's move to subordinate Vietnamese interests to those of China. At the Geneva conference in 1954, at China's insistence, the North Vietnamese had reluctantly agreed to the partition of their country in the interests of the global communist policy of peaceful coexistence. By the early 1970s, the Vietnamese suspected that China did not want to see a strong, reunified Vietnam emerge as a potential competitor for influence in Southeast Asia. Additionally, they found themselves on the opposite side of the Chinese in regard to the US presence in Asia, which China regarded as a desirable counterbalance to Soviet ambitions in the area.

With the end of the war in South Vietnam, it was only a matter of time before the two halves of the country would unite to create a single state. China was certainly not happy at the prospect of the emergence of a strong state on its southern borders. It would not be a spectator to Hanoi's suspected ambitions to dominate Laos and Cambodia and lend assistance to fraternal Communist parties in Southeast Asia, traditionally an area of China's political influence. In order to force Vietnam to reassume its historical role as China's vassal state, China threatened to stop its loans and grants to Vietnam if it did not join China in condemning Soviet hegemony. When the Vietnamese gently pointed out that the late premier Zhou Enlai had made a commitment in June 1973 to continue economic and military aid at the then existing level for five years, the Chinese "explained" that a prior agreement between Zhou Enlai and Ho Chi Minh called for termination of aid after the Vietnam war ended. China did not make an exception even on humanitarian grounds. Thus, when Vietnam was hit by severe food shortages during 1976–1977 because of adverse weather conditions, China did not send any food grains across its southern borders. In contrast, the Soviet Union supplied 450,000 of the 1.6 million tons of food rushed to Vietnam by external agencies.

Vietnam alleged that China thereafter attempted to "contain" it by organizing a coalition with the United States, Thailand, and Cambodia as a counterweight to Vietnamese influence on mainland Southeast Asia. The steady deterioration of Sino-Vietnamese relations was aggravated by two specific issues: the offshore islands and Vietnamese of Chinese ethnic origin. The real issues were political, centering on the question of political hegemony, in the short run over Indochina and eventually over all of Southeast Asia.

The Islands Issue

The question of sovereignty over two groups of islands in the South China Sea—the Spratlys and the Paracels—has been a bone of contention between China and Vietnam for more than a century and a half. Vietnam asserts that the Paracels and the Spratlys were included in the territories under the control of emperors Gia Long and Minh Mang. China counters such historical claims by pointing out that until 1885, Vietnam itself was a protectorate of China and therefore the islands, too, were legally under Chinese sovereignty. China points out that the Sino-French convention of 1887 stipulated that the islands lying east of a delimiting line (both island groups are east of that line) belong to China.

Between 1930 and 1933, France sent its gunboats to eight Spratly Islands, occupied them, and made them a part of the Baria Province. In the latter year, France raised through diplomatic channels the question of sovereignty over the Paracels, and in 1938, following Japan's attacks against China, it occupied the Paracels.

During World War II, Japan occupied both island groups, incorporating them into Taiwan (then under Japan's control) under the name of Shinna Gunto. Subsequently, Japan used one of the Spratly Islands, Itu Aba, as a submarine base for its attacks on the Philippines. After the war, Japan turned over the islands to China. France protested the action and between October 1946 and January 1947 sent ships to occupy the principal islands of both groups. In August 1951, the People's Republic of China asserted its claims to the Spratlys as well as the Paracels.

In the mid–1950s, when geologists indicated that there were large reserves of oil and gas in the seabed of the Spratlys, not only China and France but also Taiwan, the Philippines, Malaysia, and South Vietnam claimed the territory. In 1956, the Philippines announced its sovereignty over the Spratly group based on the discovery and occupation of thirty-three islands and reefs of the Spratlys by a Filipino, Tomas Cloma. It pointed out that the French had never "officially transferred" the islands to either government in Vietnam. The government of South Vietnam promptly reacted by sending troops to some of the Spratly Islands, declaring that all Spratlys would thereafter be assigned to Phuc Tuy Province. In the following year, Saigon occupied Robert Island, Pattle Island, and Money Island of the Paracels. It sent its gunboats in February 1959 to Duncan Island in the same group, took numerous Chinese fishermen as prisoners, and over Beijing's protests announced the incorporation of the Paracels as part of Quang Nam Province. In the aftermath of the Paris agreements and in the face of the global oil crisis, the South Vietnamese government officially incorporated eleven oil-rich main islands of the Spratly group into Phuc Tuy Province in September 1973. Two months earlier, Saigon had begun to issue oil exploration permits in the Spratlys to Western companies. By the end of the year, Saigon sent gunboats and troops to several islands at the urging of its National Petroleum Board, which hoped to preempt the continental shelf between the Spratlys and the Vietnamese mainland.

Perhaps because the Spratlys were 550 miles farther south and beyond the range of Chinese air support, China took no action to prevent South Vietnam from occupying them. But Beijing did take strong naval and air action in January 1974 against South Vietnam's movements on the Paracels. It conducted air raids against Robert, Pattle, and Money Islands and landed troops on Robert and Drummond Islands. Chinese boats equipped for firing short-range missiles, located on the naval base of Yulin on the Hainan Islands, showed their clear superiority over South Vietnam's coast guard cutters, destroyer escorts, and patrol boats in the engagements of January 19–20, 1974. The Paracel group was important to Beijing because of the presence of a

Chinese naval complex and sophisticated radar facilities on one of the islands since 1971.

Until 1974, North Vietnam officially recognized both island groups as Chinese territory not because it believed China's claims but, as it explained later, because of the need to solicit China's support against the United States during the Vietnam war. In fact, even before the end of that war and just before the takeover of Saigon, in April 1975, Hanoi sent its troops to occupy the six islands in the Spratly group that had been occupied by the South Vietnamese government in 1973. In late 1975, Hanoi issued a new map showing the reunited Vietnam that included the Paracels and the Spratlys. According to Chang Pao-min, this was part of Hanoi's strategy to present China with a fait accompli.[2]

The claims of numerous states to the two island groups were recast in light of the 1982 convention on the Law of the Sea. The convention extended territorial sea limits from three to twelve nautical miles, recognized a state's "contiguous zone" by another twelve nautical miles, and acknowledged the state's exclusive right to exploit the natural resources on and below the continental shelf as well as an exclusive economic zone (EEZ) extending up to 200 nautical miles. Predating the convention, Vietnam proclaimed in May 1977 its twelve-nautical-mile territorial sea, an adjacent twelve-nautical-mile contiguous zone, and an EEZ stretching from the baselines to the 200-nautical-mile mark, and its claim to the natural resources of its continental shelf. In 1978, the Philippines, in 1980, Indonesia and Malaysia, and in 1982, Brunei, all declared their 200-nautical-mile EEZs in the South China Sea based on their baselines. Malaysia and the Philippines allegedly built fortifications on the islands under their control, equipping them with heavy coastal artillery and antiaircraft guns. China maintained that it, too, had a right to an EEZ but would not declare it to avoid repercussions from other coastal states. China also argued that the demarcation of continental shelves and EEZs by rival states would create overlapping regions of jurisdiction in the South China Sea, without leaving any areas as high seas. Meanwhile, Hanoi began issuing permits to several European and Japanese companies to engage in the exploration and exploitation of the Spratlys' seabed.

Following the 1982 international convention, Hanoi officially declared on November 25, 1982, that its territorial waters included the Spratlys and the Paracels. In the following year, it occupied six more islands in the Spratly group and stationed about 350 troops there. In the late 1970s, it had built an airstrip on the main island of the Spratly group that could handle small aircraft such as the Soviet-made CN–212 light transport planes. In 1987–1988, China accused Vietnam of occupying several more islands and reefs in the

Spratly group—the most important of them the island of Bai Jiao—from which China hoped to exploit the oil lying beneath the continental shelf.

Although there seemed to be a tacit understanding among the Southeast Asian countries not to engage in armed conflict over rival claims to the Spratly Islands, a skirmish broke out between China and Vietnam in 1988. In the previous year, China had completed a maritime survey and decided that Fiery Cross Reef (Yongshu Jiao) was suitable for setting up marine observation posts of the kind specified by the United Nations Educational, Scientific, and Cultural Organization (UNESCO). In a bid to have a permanent military presence as well as marine observation stations in the Spratlys, China sent several crane ships, dredgers, bulldozers, and transport and naval patrol vessels to Fiery Cross Reef in February 1988. Thereafter, the Chinese navy dispatched several missile destroyers and other vessels on a patrol and escort mission in the Spratlys.

Serious clashes between Chinese and Vietnamese armed forces took place in March and April 1988 when the Vietnamese attempted to prevent the Chinese from building an observation post on a reef called Chigua Jiao in the Spratlys. Although Beijing reported no losses, Hanoi acknowledged that three Vietnamese sailors had been killed and seventy-four were missing in action.

In the decade since those clashes, both China and Vietnam have favored negotiations for settlement of the dispute. Despite overall and substantial improvement in Sino-Vietnamese relations, however, no formal talks on the islands question have taken place, leaving the issue as a potential powder keg between the two Communist neighbors.

The Ethnic Chinese Issue

The "overseas Chinese" in Vietnam were as much hated by the local people as they were elsewhere in Southeast Asia owing to their superior economic standing. Their loyalty to Vietnam was always suspect. Their unruly and disruptive behavior during the years of the Cultural Revolution was least appreciated in Vietnam. After the Communist victory in Saigon, the large Chinese population, noted for its industry and wealth, received special attention from the new government. The community's cooperation was vital for keeping the economy going until the government gradually moved to eliminate the private sector. By 1977, such cooperation was not as badly needed. The Vietnamese Chinese were then grouped along with intellectuals, devout Buddhists, and Catholics as potential opposition to the spread of socialism. Although the Vietnamese Chinese were not specifically named as "capitalist" opponents of the new government, the frequent mention of the areas in which the Chinese predominantly lived as being the cesspools of black marketing and corruption was an indirect condemnation of the community. In the campaign for "ideological certification" of the "misfits," the Chinese were progressively moved to the NEZs in the countryside, which included the border province of Tay Ninh. There the Chinese would also serve as a buffer between the Vietnamese and Cambodia.

The Vietnamese government came down most openly against the Chinese community in March 1978, not long after China began an initiative to win the loyalty and support of the overseas Chinese. Beijing's campaign was perhaps launched with the twin objectives of drumming up support for itself vis-à-vis Taipei and for securing technical and financial assistance from the overseas Chinese in Southeast Asia and the United States to help China's program to modernize its economy. The vigor of the campaign unnerved many Southeast Asian states with large Chinese minorities because of its political implications. Was the Vietnamese government's action against the ethnic Chinese a reaction to China's new policy toward the overseas Chinese, or was it—as seems more likely—a response to China's decision to help Vietnam's enemy, the Pol Pot regime, in Cambodia? In any case, the Vietnamese government's policy toward the ethnic Chinese went far beyond mere verbal attacks. It resulted in the migration of a large number of them, providing the most visible and dramatic evidence of the growing gulf between Beijing and Hanoi.

In the name of carrying out the rapid socialization of the economy, the Vietnamese government raided the Cholon area of Saigon where the Chinese lived and ordered their assets frozen. Of note was the official reclassification of the Vietnamese Chinese in May 1978 as an ethnic minority, abolishing the special-category status the Chinese had enjoyed thus far. The change indicated the government's firm resolve to integrate the Chinese, along with other ethnic minorities, into the national community. The Chinese community thus was faced with choosing one of two alternatives: the obligations to the state that were implied in the acceptance of Vietnamese citizenship or the handicaps of alien status.

The government saw in the mainly urban Chinese community a partial but multifaceted solution to a complex, depressing economic malaise: It could lay its hands on the commercial establishments of the Chinese community by forcibly moving large numbers of ethnic Chinese to the countryside. The government also decided to relocate many urban Chinese to the NEZs close to the Cambodian border, where their numbers dwindled in the cross fire of binational conflict. The Vietnamese shed few tears over these human losses because of their traditional prejudice against the Chinese. Moving the ethnic Chinese out of Ho Chi Minh City and Cholon opened up commercial as well as general job opportunities to Vietnamese unemployed youth in urban centers, notably in Ho Chi Minh City. The large-scale hardship and discontent caused by the new policy forced many Chinese to flee the country. A puzzling point of this exodus was that a substantial number of Chinese from North Vietnam also crossed the border into China, indicating that the feeling of insecurity had political roots and had permeated the Chinese community throughout Vietnam, not just in the south.

It is doubtful the Chinese government was genuinely concerned about the plight of the overseas Chinese in Vietnam.[3] To be sure, China had all along maintained its interest in the overseas Chinese, but never enough to go to war with any country in Southeast Asia. As for South Vietnam, China had specifically protested against the South Vietnamese government's legislation in 1955 compelling the Chinese community to accept Vietnamese citizenship. In 1965, North Vietnam agreed to settle the question in consultation with China after the "liberation" of South Vietnam. In practice, however, the Chinese government had done little to protect the overseas Chinese, whether in Indonesia during the second half of the 1960s or in Cambodia before and after the Communist takeover. Vietnam, therefore, may have assumed that its persecution of its Chinese minority would not provoke Beijing. After all, of the 1.5 million Vietnamese Chinese, 90 percent had lived in the south, amassed fortunes by exploiting the prolonged situation created by the Second Indochina War, and generally supported a capitalist way of life.

The indignation of the Chinese government at the "racial" discrimination of Vietnamese Chinese can be explained only in political terms as an attempt to find an additional excuse to attack Vietnam. This hypothesis is reinforced by the halfhearted manner in which China tried to evacuate the Vietnamese Chinese. In June 1978, China sent two ships, the *Minghua* and the *Changli*, to Saigon and Haiphong to bring back the Chinese. The two ships remained off the coast during the six weeks of fruitless negotiations with Vietnamese officials over an acceptable evacuation procedure. On July 11, China closed its borders to the thousands of Vietnamese Chinese trying to enter China by land. The Chinese authorities would accept only those refugees who could produce exit visas issued by the Vietnamese government, along with repatriation certificates from the Chinese embassy in Hanoi. Insistence on such documentation, particularly repatriation certificates, once again demonstrated that the Chinese government's concern for Vietnamese Chinese was not genuine.

The Sino-Vietnamese Conflict of 1979

As detailed in the previous chapter, the deteriorating relations between Vietnam and Cambodia in 1977–1978 culminated in Vietnam's decision in late 1978 to invade Cambodia. By that time, China had already resolved to support the Khmer Rouge regime both diplomatically and militarily. Fearing a Chinese attack across its southern border in response to its march into Cambodia, the Hanoi government decided to step up its economic and military dependence on the Soviet Union. On June 29, 1978, it joined the Soviet-dominated COMECON and on November 3, 1978, signed with the Soviet Union a formal twenty-five-year treaty of friendship and mutual cooperation, which was clearly an anti-China pact.

China retaliated against the first of these actions on July 3, 1978, by formally terminating all its economic, military, and technical assistance to Vietnam and ordering the Chinese personnel there to head home. In the previous month, Vietnam had rejected Chinese requests to open consular offices in Saigon, Da Nang, and Haiphong; in a reciprocal action the Chinese government asked Vietnam to close its consular establishments in Canton, Nanning, and Kunming. Beijing alleged that the USSR and Vietnam had a three-part plan to "encircle" China: first, by removing the Vietnamese Chinese from positions of authority; second, by compelling Laos and Cambodia through military threats to join an Indochinese federation nominally under Vietnamese control but in fact under Soviet domination; and last, by implementing Leonid Brezhnev's plan for Asian security, thereby bringing all of Southeast Asia into the Soviet sphere of influence. China accused Vietnam of being the "Cuba of Asia," a satellite of the Soviet Union that was assisting the latter in its strategic aims in Asia.

The two wars—one at the turn of 1978, the other in early 1979 in Indochina, and both involving Vietnam—made that portion of Asia once more an area of instability and insecurity. For the next decade, China and Vietnam had to keep their forces deployed on two fronts: China on its borders with the Soviet Union and Vietnam, Vietnam on its Chinese borders and against the Chinese-backed forces of Pol Pot in Cambodia. All the regional states involved in those conflicts came out losers; only the Soviet Union succeeded in augmenting its influence in the region. Cambodia was the greatest loser of all, its independence and integrity badly compromised, its domestic disorder worsened by a new civil war in which the two sides were supported by China and Vietnam. Vietnam lost on several grounds. Vietnam's military and political domination of Cambodia was achieved at tremendous costs to its own security, stability, economy, and international image. Its Second Five-Year Plan (1976–1980) was practically scrapped as the government had to set new priorities in defense outlay and was forced to postpone several reconstruction projects. The country's military and diplomatic dependence on the Soviet Union and Eastern European countries became as complete as its isolation from most of the third world. Moreover, its chances of getting developmental assistance from the United States, Western Europe, and Japan disappeared. Additionally, Hanoi's new stance drastically diminished its credibility among ASEAN states as a nation committed to carving a zone of peace in Southeast Asia. Finally, Vietnam's continued control and domination over Laos and Cambodia became contingent on its dependence on Soviet economic and military assistance, thus diluting its own hard-earned independence and making it vulnerable to the charge of being Moscow's agent for acquisition of power and influence in Southeast Asia and for the containment of China.

Vietnam's successful overthrow of the Beijing-backed Pol Pot regime was a serious blow to China. In February 1979, when Chinese forces marched across the border into Vietnam, Beijing's public posture was that it wanted to teach Vietnam a lesson for its behavior toward Cambodia and the ethnic Chinese. On neither count did Hanoi learn any lesson. Vietnam did not withdraw its forces from Cambodia. Additionally, it made Laos end China's enormous influence there by asking all Chinese technical personnel to leave the country. Further, Vietnam stepped up its persecution of the ethnic Chinese, causing a mass exodus in the first half of 1979.

The monthlong border hostilities did not by any measure establish China's military superiority over its much smaller southern neighbor. Hanoi did not even commit its crack regiments to the border war—most of the fighting being carried out by its militia forces. If anything, the conflict laid bare severe weaknesses in the Chinese military machine, which had not seen action since the border war with India in 1962, had not fully recovered from the severe discipline problems it had experienced during the Cultural Revolution, and perhaps lacked certain categories of equipment previously supplied by the Soviet Union during the days of Sino-Soviet amity and alliance. The Chinese casualties were estimated at 20,000. The little war convinced the Chinese leaders that their defense outlay had to be enhanced even at the expense of their plans to modernize their economy. An additional strain on the economy arising from the conflict with Vietnam was the substantial expenditure on an estimated quarter of a million Chinese refugees from Vietnam.

Vietnam and the Soviet Union

Toward the end of 1978, the only party that stood to gain from major conflicts in Indochina was the Soviet Union. Moscow's actions to draw Vietnam closer to the Soviet Union politically, economically, and militarily should be seen in the context of its dual policy to weaken the new Sino-US rapprochement and to frustrate the Chinese attempt to enhance its influence in Southeast Asia. The Soviet policy was, in fact, a continuation of its decade-long diplomatic offensive to win all the countries of South and Southeast Asia to its side—or at least wean them away from Beijing. Such efforts were supplemented by military (though decidedly low-key) activity, particularly in the Indian Ocean.

The steadily increasing diplomatic and naval activity of the Soviet Union in South and Southeast Asia since 1968 must certainly be seen in the context of the US withdrawal from the region and the growing US–Chinese friendship. Traditionally, Southeast Asia has never figured importantly in Soviet ambitions. Since it is partly an Asian country, however, the Soviet Union cannot countenance with equanimity the exclusive domination by any other major power, particularly China, over large parts of Asia. Moscow did not want to allow its ideological rival, Beijing, the prestige of becoming the standard-bearer of a Communist revolution not only in Southeast Asia but throughout the world.

Yet the Soviet Union was far from eager to become the police force of Asia—an ambition any power geographically distant from the region should be able to resist after the glaring failure of the United States. Even during the Vietnam conflict, the Soviet Union begrudged the heavy costs of assisting North Vietnam and the NLF in the form of war materiel and sophisticated equipment. The Soviets were also unhappy at the Vietnamese situation in the late 1960s, which impinged upon the progress of Soviet talks with the United States on a wide range of topics aimed at détente. In 1968, a month before the initiation of the Nixon Doctrine, Soviet leader Brezhnev proposed a system of collective security for Asia wherein the local military and economic resources would be supplemented by the Soviet Union. No Southeast Asian nation, including North Vietnam, joined the proposed system because none wanted to give the impression of ganging up against China, although Moscow denied that the Brezhnev plan sought to contain China.

Rationally speaking, the long-term interests of the superpowers—both of them geographically distant from Southeast Asia—lay in denying any power an opportunity to dominate the area and to achieve such a goal through promotion of a regional balance of power. In the short run, however, the Sino-US rapprochement, the almost complete withdrawal of US forces from Southeast Asia, and the Sino-Soviet race to win the allegiance of the new Communist regimes in Indochina accelerated immediate Soviet involvement in the region. The Soviet Union had no leverage with the Pol Pot regime, which decried the former's recognition of the Lon Nol government right up to its downfall in March 1975. China compelled Vietnam to choose between Moscow and Beijing in October 1975, when the secretary-general of the Vietnamese Communist Party, Le Duan, visited China. Le Duan refused to comply with his host's wishes to condemn Soviet "hegemonism." Thereafter, China stopped any further aid to Vietnam, whereas the Soviet Union came forward to support Vietnam generously, intensifying Vietnamese dependence on the Soviet Union.

During 1978, Moscow apparently persuaded the Hanoi leadership to think that a continuing state of tension between a Chinese-backed Cambodia and

Vietnam would constitute a festering economic sore for Vietnam. Moscow urged that the question be resolved expeditiously at least in the interests of economy. In 1978–1979, Vietnam was in dire need of food assistance amounting to 4.3 million tons due to successive crop failures. It was this desperate economic situation that made Vietnam finally succumb to Soviet pressures to join COMECON. Also, because the United States normalized its relations with China, the Soviet Union stepped up its pressure on Vietnam for a formal anti-China military alliance. There is reason to believe that an overt anti-Chinese alliance was the price Moscow extracted for bailing Vietnam out of its economic crisis. The Soviet-Vietnamese treaty of friendship, signed barely six weeks before the Vietnamese march into Cambodia, provided Vietnam a Soviet shield of protection from a Chinese attack. Article 6 of the treaty clearly stated that in the event of an attack or a threat of attack, Vietnam and the Soviet Union would consult with each other and take "appropriate and effective measures" to "eliminate" that threat. The treaty indeed marked a high point of Moscow's diplomatic success in Indochina.

Through the next decade, Vietnam had to pay a heavy price for the Soviet assistance, military and economic. It had to grant the Soviet Union port facilities at Cam Ranh Bay, which remained thereafter until the collapse of the Soviet Union's most important strategic base, the only one between Vladivostok and East Africa. Its value to the Soviet Union was inestimable, particularly because of its proximity to the largest overseas US naval base at that time, in the neighboring Philippines.

The Soviet Union's economic assistance was crucial to the success of Vietnam's five-year plans. The Soviet Union's military assistance enabled Vietnam to augment its military forces from 600,000 in 1975 to 1.1 million in 1978–1979 and to keep up military presence of about 160,000 troops in Cambodia and 40,000 to 50,000 in Laos. The costs of maintaining the fourth largest army in the world would have been impossible for Vietnam but for Soviet assistance, which was estimated at between $1 billion and $1.5 billion annually from 1979 to 1983. Thereafter, until 1987, the military component of assistance was reduced in favor of the economic. At the same time, agreements for Vietnamese repayments included not only raw materials but also Vietnamese "guest workers" in the Soviet Union, perhaps as many as 50,000 persons, part of whose wages were used to offset the Vietnamese debt burden to the Soviet Union.

Such major concessions were galling to the self-esteem of Vietnam, which prided itself on the sacrifices involved in the long struggle of liberation against another superpower. By the mid–1980s, readjustment of relations with major powers as well as neighbors was deemed prudent and vital. The Sixth Party Congress in December 1986 therefore voted in favor of restoration of good relations with China, improvement of economic ties with the West, Japan, and

ASEAN, and above all, a negotiated political settlement of the Cambodian problem.

The political and economic collapse of the socialist systems in Eastern Europe and the Soviet Union in the late 1980s further underlined the need for completely redirecting Vietnam's international relations. Even before its collapse, the Soviet Union had manifested its inability to continue funding the Vietnamese occupation of Cambodia. With the end of Soviet aid and because both China and the United States stipulated withdrawal of Vietnamese troops from Cambodia as a precondition for the normalization of their relations with Vietnam, Vietnam found it necessary to end its misadventure in Cambodia.

Sino-Vietnamese Relations After Withdrawal from Cambodia

Along with normalizing relations with the United States, Vietnam focused on improving its relations with China in the 1990s. To facilitate the process, it removed its anti-China foreign minister, Nguyen Co Thach, and appointed Nguyen Manh Cam in his place in June 1991. The following month, Le Duc Anh, the second-ranking Politburo member, visited Beijing to end the decade of "abnormal relations" between the countries. In November, the two governments announced the normalization of relations with the visit to Beijing of the VCP's new secretary-general, Do Muoi, and the new prime minister, Vo Van Kiet. Vietnam and China signed numerous agreements for opening border trading points and restoring air, sea, and telecommunications links. Yet it took an additional four years before the two countries signed a formal agreement in December 1995 to reopen rail links that had been severed following the border war in 1979.

After nearly a decade, China showed renewed interest in the Spratly Islands by seizing a few atolls in that group in 1988. In January 1992, China's National Assembly passed a law on the country's territorial waters, claiming numerous islands in the South China Sea, among them the Spratlys. New Chinese maps indicated China's sovereignty over most of the China Sea, along with all its seabed oil and gas reserves. In the following month, however, China appeared conciliatory during the visit to Vietnam of its foreign minister, Qian Qichen; it agreed to hold a meeting of experts from both sides to discuss all territorial disputes, including the offshore islands. In May 1992, however, China unilaterally granted the Colorado-based Crestone Energy Corporation the right to explore for oil within what Vietnam claimed was a part of its continental shelf. Hanoi protested the action, complaining as well about China's continued occupation of thirty-six small areas along the common land border.

Despite their stakes in improving relations, there was fresh tension between the two Communist neighbors in October 1994 as China expressed serious concern over Vietnam's oil-prospecting activities, and Vietnam accused China of systematic territorial violations. China allegedly sent warships to blockade a Vietnamese oil-drilling rig operating in the disputed area. In the decade of the 1990s, China quietly extended its naval hold by stationing permanent garrisons over some nine atolls, including Fiery Cross, Johnson South Reef, Gaven Reef, and Mischief Reef. The Chinese forces, estimated at 2,000, have the benefit of helipads, air-raid shelters, antiaircraft guns and capability for augmenting their supplies through ships capable of docking. China has, in fact, insisted on its claim over the entire South China Sea, a vital artery for the strategic defense and commercial traffic between East Asia and Southeast Asia. Pertinent in this regard is the 1982 United Nations Convention on the Law of the Sea, ratified by China, which acknowledges a country's right to an exclusive economic zone of up to 200 nautical miles. This would cover part of China's claims in the South China Sea but would exclude many of the Spratly and Paracel Islands.

China's new posture in the South China Sea has worried Vietnam, which would like to avoid a military confrontation. Yet since the late 1970s, Vietnam had used China's aggressiveness to mend its relations with the United States and ASEAN by offering to act as a counterweight to China's growing military and economic strength. After Vietnam acquired the status of an observer state in ASEAN in July 1992, it took up the question of the Spratly Islands with other members. President Fidel Ramos of the Philippines, who shared Vietnam's concern over China's seizure of atolls in the Spratly Islands and its claims to the entire South China Sea area, called for the six countries with claims in the disputed Spratly group—Brunei, China, Malaysia, Philippines, Taiwan, and Vietnam—to demilitarize the area.

The Sino-Vietnamese dispute over the islands has defied solution. There were serious tensions between the two neighbors in 1994, 1996, and 1997 because of substantial recoverable gas and oil deposits. Diplomacy and negotiations, however, have inhibited the use of force. In 1996, Vietnam offered to a rival company, Conoco, two exploration blocs adjacent to the areas given to Crestone by China.

Curiously, in June 2003, China ratified ASEAN's 1976 Treaty of Amity, a procedure to settle interstate disputes that was extended by the 1992 Declaration on the South China Sea to include the disputed islands. The declaration laid down a "code of conduct" for settling disputes. China's ratification commits it not to "participate in any activity which shall constitute a threat to the political and economic stability, sovereignty, or territorial integrity" of ASEAN member states, including Vietnam. At the Sixteenth Chinese Communist Party Congress and generally since 1996, Chinese leaders concerned with the United States's growing influence in Southeast Asia have underlined China's policy of strengthening ties with its neighbors by settling territorial, border, and fishing disputes. In November 2002, China signed at the Eighth ASEAN Summit in Phnom Penh several agreements, including the Declaration on Conduct of Parties in the South China Sea, by which it agreed to exercise restraint and give advance notice even for military exercises in the South China Sea. While China's action brought considerable relief to Southeast Asian states wary of its rising economic and military strength, the 1976 treaty ratification in 2003 may have, in reality, given China's maritime claims an indirect recognition and a "place at the table" with several ASEAN states asserting overlapping claims to several islands in the region.

Vietnam and ASEAN

The pro-Western states of Southeast Asia formed the Association of Southeast Asian Nations in August 1967 in part because they feared that a Communist victory in Vietnam could encourage Hanoi's ambitions to spread the revolution to neighboring countries. Most members of the new organization also wanted to improve relations with China in case the United States suffered a military defeat in Vietnam and generally withdrew from the region. Its constitution left membership open to all states of the region that subscribed to the association's "aims, principles and purposes." In time, ASEAN succeeded in building regionalism with relevance in many domains—economic, social, cultural, technical, and political.

In the wake of the Paris Accords on Vietnam in January 1973, the foreign ministers of the ASEAN states proposed that the association be expanded to include all countries of Southeast Asia and that it participate in the rehabilitation of Vietnam. The DRV, however, rejected the proposal, condemning ASEAN as a new version of SEATO and a puppet of US imperialism. It pointed out that troops of two ASEAN members—Thailand and the Philippines—had served on the US side in the Vietnam war. By 1976, all Southeast Asian members established diplomatic ties with Vietnam, and although Vietnam rejected the offer, ASEAN continued to try to persuade Vietnam to accept the ASEAN resolution to create a zone of peace, freedom, and neutrality (ZOPFAN) covering all of Southeast Asia.

By late 1978, with its impending plans to invade Cambodia and topple the Khmer Rouge regime there, Vietnam needed better relations with its other neighbors, notably ASEAN. In September 1978, Vietnamese premier Pham Van

Dong offered his country's accession to the treaty of amity and cooperation (the so-called Bali treaty signed by ASEAN members in 1976). It was now ASEAN's turn to question Vietnam's bona fides, particularly because Vietnam had by that time joined the Soviet-dominated COMECON and signed a mutual assistance treaty with the Soviet Union. The Vietnamese invasion of Cambodia in December 1978 reinforced ASEAN's apprehensions of Vietnam's expansionist ambitions and drastically diminished Hanoi's credibility among ASEAN states as a nation committed to carving out a zone of peace in Southeast Asia. The invasion marked a gross violation of ASEAN's nonaggression principles as enshrined in the Bali treaty. ASEAN favored a political status quo in Southeast Asia and, therefore, continued to recognize the Democratic Republic of Cambodia and support the place of the Khmer Rouge in the United Nations. For the next ten years, the Cambodian issue dictated and aggravated ASEAN-Vietnam relations; it also held together two divergent groups within ASEAN.

Among ASEAN members, Indonesia and Malaysia had long believed that it was not Vietnam but China that held the key to the political future and posed a potential threat to the security of Southeast Asia. In 1980, Indonesia sought to recognize Vietnam's dominant role in the other countries of Indochina. As for Malaysia, by the early 1980s, its fears—that the Vietnamese of Chinese origin who arrived on its shores as boat people would upset the country's delicate racial balance—had dissipated. In contrast, Thailand, with its common land and sea borders with Cambodia, feared the Vietnamese occupation as an immediate threat to Thailand's security. Singapore, too, opposed the occupation because it feared that it might set a precedent for similar action on the part of its neighbors, Indonesia and Malaysia, directed against Singapore.

The ASEAN states viewed Vietnam's withdrawal from Cambodia in 1989 as a recognition of ASEAN's policy of maintaining the regional status quo and an indication of Vietnam's desire to contribute positively to the region's security. There was a spate of visits by heads of governments of the ASEAN states to Vietnam and reciprocal visits by Vietnamese premier Vo Van Kiet, all of which highlighted the new phase of bonhomie and economic cooperation between Vietnam and the ASEAN members. Thus in 1990, President Suharto of Indonesia visited Vietnam. In the following year, Malaysia removed restrictions on business travel to Vietnam, and in April 1992, Malaysian prime minister Mahathir, accompanied by about 100 businessmen, paid an official six-day visit to Vietnam, during which he inaugurated a joint-venture branch of a Malaysian bank and offered assistance in rubber technology and in joint oil exploration. His general theme was to emphasize ASEAN's belief that economically stable and prosperous neighbors would contribute positively to the peace and security of the whole region.

In January 1992, Prime Minister Anand Panyarachun of Thailand visited Vietnam. Thailand was happy to note that Vietnam's withdrawal from Cambodia "restored a buffer zone" and made mutual trust between Bangkok and Hanoi possible. The appeal by Foreign Minister Prasong Soonsiri to turn "battlefields into a marketplace" signaled the end of a hard line and the opening of an "economic engagement" among Thailand, Vietnam, Cambodia, and Laos.[4] Thailand offered to establish a network of economic cooperation that would give the countries a stake in maintaining peaceful and friendly relations. It signed agreements with Vietnam for joint projects such as a gemstone company and an international banking facility in Bangkok for the reconstruction of Vietnam, Cambodia, and Laos.

Even before its normalization of relations with Vietnam, Singapore had emerged by the mid–1980s as the largest ASEAN trading partner of Vietnam. Following the visit of Vo Van Kiet to Singapore in October 1991 and the reciprocal visit of the father of modern Singapore, Lee Kuan Yew, to Vietnam, the two countries took a number of measures to increase their bilateral trade. In November 1991, Singapore lifted the ban on investment in Vietnam and agreed to help Vietnam develop its ports.

If the ASEAN states were aware that a prosperous Vietnam would lead to a stable and peaceful Vietnam, the latter seemed to think that with the collapse of the Soviet Union and a less than friendly and dependable China, it would best serve Vietnam's security interests to become a member of ASEAN rather than allying itself to an external power. In fact, there was no major power in the Communist world with which to align. Hanoi therefore modified its foreign policy to bring it in line with that of ASEAN, hoping to ride on the group's influence and clout. Hanoi viewed ASEAN as a major player in the international community, notably the United Nations and European Community, which could help it mobilize diplomatic support in the event of a conflict with its powerful northern neighbor. Vietnam also noted that ASEAN itself had dramatically improved its relations with China in the aftermath of the US debacle in Vietnam in the early 1970s. Indonesia re-established diplomatic relations with China in September 1991, followed by Singapore and Brunei. Hanoi was aware, however, that Malaysia and Indonesia continued to regard China as a threat, even though communism itself had lost its appeal to the people of those states. These ASEAN members shared a concern with Vietnam over China's renewed aggressiveness in the South China Sea and reports of China's buying sophisticated armaments from Russia and projecting power far beyond its borders through a rapid-deployment force, air-refueling equipment for its new SU–27 fighters, a blue-water naval system, surface-to-surface missiles, electronic warfare technology, and missile guidance equipment. Indeed, the international politics of Southeast Asia had completely altered in the decade and a half since Vietnam's reunification. As Mike Yeong observed in 1992, "It is . . . an irony that in the past, some ASEAN members had viewed Vietnam as a bulwark against an aggressive China, and now Hanoi views ASEAN as a potential protector against a China which is intimidating Vietnam at will."[5]

Vietnam was and is attracted to ASEAN for economic reasons as well. In the 1980s, ASEAN attracted world attention due to its spectacular economic growth, averaging 7 percent. Except for the Philippines, all other member states registered impressive development in all areas of economic activity, making the ASEAN region a new center of world economic power. Trade among the six member states constituted 17 percent of their total trade, which was bolstered by a preferential tariff agreement among them. In July 1992, the association resolved to implement the ASEAN Free Trade Agreement (AFTA), under which tariffs on goods with 40 percent or more ASEAN content would fall to 0 percent to 5 percent by 2008. The move was regarded as a first step in the direction of establishing an ASEAN common market to meet the threat of increasing protectionism in Europe and the United States.

Ever since its birth in 1967, ASEAN has evinced a remarkable ability to contain tensions and to try to resolve interstate problems peacefully. Numerous bilateral and multilateral disputes have persisted, but the lines of communication have remained open. Consultation, cooperation, and conciliation have eschewed confrontation and conflict, enhancing the security of the entire region. Moreover, since the 1980s, ASEAN has served as an effective voice for regional issues. The foreign ministers of the ASEAN states have demonstrated impressive skill in ironing out contentious issues in their annual consultative sessions with their counterparts from the European Community, the United States, Australia, New Zealand, and Japan. Due to the member states' common stand on many issues—notably the nagging problem of the 1980s and Cambodia—ASEAN has emerged as an international actor.[6] As aspirants to membership, Vietnam, Laos, Cambodia, and Myanmar must have perceived these achievements and the potential for containing conflicts as some of the greatest advantages of ASEAN participation.

For its part, ASEAN saw the new Vietnam—particularly after its leadership ushered in *doi moi*—as a chastened and pragmatic country, no longer with a will or a program for spreading the Communist revolution. In fact, Vietnam's movement toward globalization of its economy would not only afford an opportunity to the ASEAN member states to trade with and invest in Vietnam, but the liberalization process itself would help the regional political status quo. With the admission of the states of former Indochina and Myanmar to the organization, ASEAN could become a truly regional organization rather than a merely subregional one. Parenthetically, Vietnam, with its geographical proximity to China, might serve as a buffer between China and the ASEAN states, thereby preventing China from attaining its perceived goal of bringing Southeast Asia under its sphere of influence.[7]

Full membership within ASEAN finally materialized for Vietnam on July 28, 1995, as it became the first Communist member of an organization that was founded almost three decades earlier as an avowedly anti-Communist body. Progress toward full membership came in steady but sure steps following Vietnam's withdrawal of its troops from Cambodia in 1989 and the signing of the Paris settlement of the Cambodia question. In anticipation of attending ASEAN's meeting in Manila in July 1992 for the first time as an observer, Premier Vo Van Kiet visited all ASEAN states to assure them of Vietnam's interest in developing cordial relations with all its neighbors and promoting peace in the entire region. At Manila, Vietnam, along with Laos, signed the 1976 Bali treaty underlining respect for independence, territorial integrity, noninterference in domestic affairs, and renunciation of the threat or use of force in international relations. Thereafter, the movement toward full membership was somewhat delayed by Vietnam's ongoing negotiations with the United States; once relations between the two countries were normalized on July 11, 1995, membership in ASEAN quickly followed.

Vietnam's membership opened the doors for Cambodia to be accorded the status of an observer; Laos had been granted a similar status in 1992. All three Communist states of the former French Indochina were also invited to attend the ASEAN regional forum, which meets annually to discuss security and defense affairs in Asia and the Pacific. Although Laos and Myanmar were granted full membership in the organization, Cambodia was declined that status in July 1997 owing to renewed political instability after the ouster of Copremier Prince Ranaridh in the previous month. The hurdle to Cambodia's membership of the ASEAN was removed with the UN action in December 1998 reinstating that country's seat in the UN General Assembly. With the formal admission of Cambodia to the ASEAN on April 29, 1999, that organization became truly the Association of Southeast Asian Nations.

In 1971, the then five-member fledgling ASEAN had resolved to establish a zone of peace, freedom, and neutrality in Southeast Asia; in December 1995, all states of Southeast Asia (including Vietnam) signed, under ASEAN's auspices, a treaty creating a Southeast Asian Nuclear Weapons-Free Zone that prohibits manufacture, possession, or use of nuclear weapons. It covered the land area, territorial waters, the two-hundred-mile exclusive economic zones, and continental shelves of the signatory states. Since none of the Southeast Asian states is a nuclear power, the treaty is symbolic, reflective at best of the desires of a people who have suffered from actual war or from the tensions of a war raging in a neighboring country for decades.

ASEAN and Vietnamese Economy

In the deliberations between ASEAN and Vietnamese officials preceding Vietnam's membership, Vietnam had agreed to take measures to fall in line with trade relationships within ASEAN. One of the first acts for Vietnam after its entry into ASEAN was to attend its Fifth Summit in Bangkok and sign on December 15, 1995, the Common Effective Preferential Tariff scheme (CEPT) for the ASEAN Free Trade Area. Vietnam thereby agreed to extend, on a reciprocal basis, most-favored nation (MFN) and National Treatment to ASEAN member states; provide relevant information on her trade regime as and when requested; prepare a list for tariff reduction and engage in a ten-year tariff reduction program beginning January 1, 1996, and ending at 0.5 percent tariff rate on January 1, 2006. Accordingly, on January 1, 1996, Vietnam published a list of 857 tariff lines in the Inclusion List, representing 39 percent of a total of 2,218 tariff lines. Of these, 1,189, or 54 percent, were placed in a Temporary Exclusion List (TEL). Of the 857 lines in the Inclusion List, 548 had zero tariff, while the remaining 309 were in the 1 percent to 5 percent tariff range. Beginning January 1, 1999, the TEL products would be phased into the CEPT Scheme in five annual installments, ending January 2003, bringing in a total of 2,046, or 92 percent, of all tariff lines in the CEPT. Included in the remaining 172 lines were 26 in the "Sensitive List," representing unprocessed agricultural products that would be phased into the CEPT for ten years beginning January 1, 2001.

The impact of this agreement has been far-reaching on Vietnam's international trade and international relations. It has helped Vietnam's effective participation in regional affairs and in the globalization of Vietnam's economy. The growing economic competition with the ASEAN states has required greater efficiency in the allocation of resources in Vietnam. It has generated pressures on the Vietnamese State-Owned Enterprises and to the privatization of unproductive ones among them. The discipline required by the CEPT and AFTA agreements has brought increasing Vietnamese compliance with legislation in other countries on intellectual property, environmental protection, and guarantees on repatriation of FDI funds.

Importantly, Vietnam's newly liberalized regime on trade and investment has helped Hanoi in its plans to join the World Trade Organization (WTO) with support from fellow members in ASEAN and their influence with Western countries, including the United States.

CHAPTER 10

US–Vietnam Relations and Vietnamese Americans

Despite the fall of Saigon in 1975, the official US position favored normalizing relations with Vietnam. As early as November 1975, US Secretary of State Kissinger declared,

> As for our relations with the new government in that region, these will not be determined by the past; we are prepared to look forward to a more hopeful future. The United States will respond to gestures of goodwill. If these governments show understanding of our concerns and those of their neighbors, they will find us ready to reciprocate. This will be especially the case if they deal constructively with the anguish of thousands of Americans who ask only an accounting for their loved ones missing in action and the return of the bodies of Americans who died in Indochina. We have no interest to continue the Indochina war on the diplomatic front; we envisage the eventual normalization of relations.[1]

Although Kissinger referred to the states of Indochina, his statement was directed mainly to Vietnam. The United States stipulated three conditions for the new Vietnam to meet before the process of normalizing relations could begin: peaceful relations with the ASEAN countries, an accounting of Americans missing in action, and the return of bodies of US troops who had died in Vietnam.

Preconditions to Normalization of US–Vietnam Relations

To these conditions, in the early years of their victory, the Vietnamese added a fourth condition—namely, reconstruction aid promised by the United States to Vietnam under article 21 of the Paris Accords of January 1973. In support of its claim, Vietnam publicized a letter of February 1, 1973, from President Nixon to Prime Minister Pham Van Dong confirming the intent of article 21 and offering reconstruction aid of $3.3 billion for a period of five years.[2]

In mid–1975, within two months of Hanoi's victory in the south, Pham Van Dong called for normalization of relations with the United States and the fulfillment of the pledge to provide aid for reconstruction. The United States rejected the Vietnamese demand for aid by arguing that Hanoi had completely violated the understanding at Paris by invading and taking over South Vietnam in April 1975, thereby forfeiting any claim to US assistance. Badly needing Western assistance for economic development, the Vietnamese government told a visiting US mission under Leonard Woodcock (President Jimmy Carter's special envoy) in March 1977 that it would not insist on aid as a precondition to normalization of ties.[3]

In an atmosphere of bonhomie at a May 1977 US–Vietnam conference of deputy foreign ministers, the United States declared that it would not exercise its veto on the question of admission of Vietnam to the United Nations. Immediately after that conference, however, the US House of Representatives resolved on May 6 to prohibit the State Department from giving any aid to Vietnam. Such an explicit resolution must have angered Vietnam, which thereupon reverted to its previous position of making the normalization of relations contingent upon US payment of reconstruction aid.

Hanoi's need for better relations with the United States changed in the next two years because of Vietnam's hostile relations with China over the question of Vietnamese occupation of Cambodia and the status of ethnic Chinese in Vietnam. In 1978, while negotiating its twenty-year friendship treaty with the Soviet Union, Hanoi hoped to counterbalance the increasing Soviet influence in Vietnam by improving its relations with the United States. In July 1978, Vietnam again declared its readiness to normalize relations with the United States without any preconditions. Although Cyrus Vance and Richard Holbrooke at the Department of State viewed the new diplomatic development favorably, the national security adviser, Zbigniew Brzezinski, opposed any reconciliation with Vietnam; using the same language as had the Chinese, he called Vietnam an "Asian Cuba" that was fighting China and Cambodia as a proxy of the Soviet Union. He argued further that Beijing would view any US understanding with Vietnam as an anti-China move that would help Soviet "hegemonistic" ambitions in Southeast Asia. President Carter opted for Brzezinski's position, thereby reversing, on October 11, 1978, the State Department's verbal agreement of September 29 with Vietnam's vice foreign minister, Nguyen Co Thach, that the US government "in principle" approved normalization of relations with Vietnam from November 1978.[4]

The adoption of a stronger US stand against Vietnam was followed on November 3, 1978, by the signing of the treaty of friendship and cooperation between the Soviet Union and Vietnam. According to Gareth Porter, Vietnam had delayed the conclusion of that treaty because of the prospect of normalized relations with the United States. Hanoi interpreted the US adoption of Brzezinski's argument to mean that Washington had chosen China over Vietnam, thereby augmenting Vietnam's needs for superior weapons systems from the Soviet Union to combat China.[5] Although the US policy cannot be directly faulted for the Vietnamese-Soviet treaty and subsequent Vietnamese invasion of Cambodia, it is clear that it opened the way for closer Vietnamese dependence on the Soviet Union.

The Vietnamese invasion of Cambodia brought the United States vociferously down on the side of the ASEAN countries, which not only condemned Vietnam for its aggression but also launched a diplomatic war to ostracize it from international organizations. There were substantial segments of US public opinion, however, that were horrified at the revelations of the genocidal excesses of the Pol Pot regime and therefore opposed its return to power. The Carter administration, espousing Brzezinski's viewpoint, welcomed the Chinese invasion of Vietnam, as it could force Vietnam's pullout from Cambodia.

With China's failure to teach Vietnam a "lesson," Soviet influence in Vietnam mounted. It soon extended to the use of Cam Ranh Bay as a naval base. The coalition of anti-Vietnamese forces—the United States, Western Europe, Japan, ASEAN, and China—led to increased Vietnamese economic and military dependence on the Soviet Union during the subsequent decade. There was no longer any serious talk of normalization of US relations with Vietnam; indeed, Vietnam's withdrawal from Cambodia became an additional precondition to renewed talks.

The MIA Issue

In the 1980s, Hanoi moved specifically to improve relations with the United States by taking action on the MIA issue. In February 1982, for the first time, Vietnam turned over some MIA remains to a US delegation to Hanoi led by

Deputy Secretary of Defense Richard Armitage. In June 1985, Hanoi informed the United States that it was willing to settle the MIA issue within two years. Two months later it released the remains of twenty-six Americans, the largest single transfer since 1982. In November, it allowed the first US–Vietnam joint excavation of a B-52 crash site in order to uncover MIA remains.

A major breakthrough on the MIA question came after the Sixth Congress of the Vietnamese Communist Party decided, in December 1986, to seek and facilitate a political settlement of the Cambodia problem. In 1987, Vietnam agreed to have the former chairman of the Joint Chiefs of Staff, General John Vessey, visit Hanoi as President Ronald Reagan's special representative and discuss the problem of searching for MIAs.

The first Vessey mission, which included several officials and nonofficials—notably, representatives of the National League of POW–MIA Families—emphasized the humanitarian issues of mutual interest and resulted in a joint communiqué on August 3, 1987, whereby Vietnam delinked the MIA issue from the question of normalization of relations. Later in the same month, two conferences were held simultaneously in Washington and Hanoi to discuss the MIA question and that of urgent humanitarian assistance for Vietnam.[6] The Reagan administration officially agreed to encourage charitable assistance from the United States to Vietnam, including the establishment of a private foundation to reinforce such activities. These would include an immediate supply of artificial limbs for about 60,000 Vietnamese disabled veterans. It was the first time since 1975 that the United States had offered financial aid of any kind in return for Vietnamese assistance in accounting for MIAs or returning MIA remains. Hanoi also agreed to allow joint US–Vietnam technical teams to work together to find the remains of missing service people. By September 1990, the United States had received the remains of only 100 MIAs from the Vietnamese government. The United States listed 1,750 Americans as missing in Vietnam; the total figure in all of Indochina was 2,387.

In July 1990, the United States announced the first major shift in relations with Vietnam, as a consequence of which Vietnam's foreign minister, Nguyen Co Thach, then visiting the United Nations, and US Secretary of State James Baker met in New York on September 29, 1990. This was the first such high-level meeting between the two countries in seventeen years. Following the meeting, the United States granted a onetime waiver of the restriction prohibiting Vietnamese officials from traveling beyond a twenty-five-mile radius of the United Nations. Thach thus was able to proceed to Washington, DC, to discuss the MIA question with General Vessey and to meet with the Senate Foreign Relations Committee for an informal closed-door session.

During the New York meeting, Vietnam agreed to allow the United States to establish an office in Hanoi to gather information about MIAs. The visiting

foreign minister also agreed to the establishment of joint US–Vietnam technical teams, which would have free access to war records and archival materials
as well as to possible witnesses to the downing of planes or other incidents in
which members of the US armed forces disappeared in Vietnam during the
war. Nguyen Co Thach, however, pleaded a lack of sophisticated facilities to
maintain and preserve records in his country, a problem exacerbated by the
war and weather conditions, particularly high levels of humidity. In April
1991, when Vessey opened the office in Hanoi for investigating MIA cases, the
United States announced a gift of $1 million, to be channeled through hu-
manitarian groups, to provide prosthetic devices for Vietnamese war victims.

Relations with the United States improved markedly in the aftermath of
the VCP's Seventh Congress. A major landmark was the US proposal in April
1991 for a four-stage improvement of relations leading to full resumption of
diplomatic ties:

1. Discussions on normalization of relations would take place at the time of
   signing the diplomatic settlement of the Cambodian conflict. Simultaneously, the United States would approve visits by US business leaders and
   veterans groups to Vietnam.
2. With the establishment of a US transitional presence in Cambodia, the
   United States would partially lift its trade embargo against Vietnam and
   Cambodia. The second phase would also require increased accounting for
   US MIAs.
3. The third phase would begin after the UN process in Cambodia had lasted
   at least six months and would include the establishment of US and Vietnamese diplomatic offices in Hanoi and Washington, a full lifting of the US
   trade embargo against Vietnam, and an easing of US opposition to international bank lending to Vietnam. This phase would also involve further
   substantial progress in accounting for US MIAs.
4. The final phase would follow UN-supervised elections in Cambodia and
   would include full normalization of US diplomatic and economic relations
   with Vietnam and Cambodia as well as support for international bank
   lending.

Among the first positive measures was the visit of a US business delegation
led by Warren Williams, president of the US Chamber of Commerce, to Vietnam in December 1991, during which Hanoi assured him that it would reserve for the United States a stake in the country's major offshore oil fields. In
January 1992, the first US aid in the form of relief assistance to Vietnamese ty-
phoon victims arrived in Vietnam. Three months later, Washington lifted its
trade embargo on commercial sales of medicine and agricultural supplies to

meet the basic needs of the Vietnamese people. The United States also ended restrictions on the activities of US nongovernmental and nonprofit organizations, allowing them to carry out humanitarian work in Vietnam. At the same time, Hanoi released all remaining South Vietnamese detained in "reeducation" camps since 1975.

On December 12, 1992, only a few weeks before the end of his administration, President George H. W. Bush announced that US business leaders and investors would be allowed to visit Vietnam in order to prepare plans for future economic development in that country. In April 1993, when it was believed that the new US administration might abstain from voting on—if not openly vote in favor of—loans to Vietnam by the IMF at the latter's meeting toward the end of that month, an Australian researcher at Harvard University discovered a document in the Russian archives that contradicted the information on MIAs the Hanoi government had previously supplied to the United States. The document quoted Vietnamese general Tran Van Quang's speech to the VCP's Politburo on September 12, 1972, stating that North Vietnam was holding 1,205 US servicemen, a figure much higher than the 368 that North Vietnamese officials had given in December 1970. During General Vessey's visit to Vietnam in April 1993, the Vietnamese government, notably General Tran, produced evidence to show that no such Politburo meeting had taken place. Vessey closed the controversy by stating that a number of figures cited in the document were inconsistent with US records as well as the internal records of the former North Vietnamese government. Nevertheless, because the disagreement took place so soon after the publication of the US Senate's final report on prisoners of war (POWs) and MIAs, progress toward normalization of relations slowed. In July 1993, the United States announced that it would no longer veto lending to Vietnam by the IMF and other multinational agencies.

President Bill Clinton's reluctance to normalize relations dragged on through mid–1995, largely because of fears of a backlash from veterans and MIA families. The president's credentials were suspect in the eyes of these influential lobbies because he had opposed the Vietnam war while he was a student at Oxford and had obtained a draft deferral with the help of Senator William Fulbright, for whom he had worked as a junior aide. The fact that Clinton had later made himself available for the draft and that his number was not called did not seem to make a difference to these lobbies.

It appeared by the beginning of 1995 that the Vietnamese government had cooperated in full on the MIA question, the main hurdle to normalization. In March 1992, Vietnam had agreed with the United States on a five-point program to allow offshore oil exploration in Vietnam. The US Chamber of Commerce in Hong Kong reported in early 1995 that more than 150 American companies associated with the search for oil were already carrying on business in Vietnam. Even so, the unofficial US participation in Vietnam extended to no more than thirty-four out of nearly 1,000 projects. A better picture of the potential for US trade and investment was brought out in a survey by the US-ASEAN council of more than 110 American companies: It identified potential sales to Vietnam of more than $2.6 billion by 1995 and more than $8 billion by 1998.

Meanwhile, the US administration was feeling the pressure from those who supported an expeditious return to normal relations with Vietnam, including full diplomatic relations. The arguments in favor of opening a US embassy in Hanoi were several. First, it would help Americans to influence the reform process under way in Vietnam both in the economic and political spheres; second, it would offer American companies a fair share of the enormous trade and investment opportunities that other countries had been able to exploit in the wake of Vietnam's liberalization policies; third, it would enable US military attachés to assess Vietnamese and Chinese strategic plans in the Tonkin Gulf and the South China Sea.

The lifting of the US trade embargo in February 1994 removed Vietnam from the official US list of enemy countries, thereby opening the door to American trade and investment in Vietnam. The decision encouraged Western European nations, Australia, New Zealand, Japan, South Korea, Taiwan, and ASEAN states to augment their business relations with Vietnam. It appeared then that full recognition would shortly follow and that such a step would allow the United States to grant most-favored-nation trading status to Vietnam. In reality, it took another eighteen months before President Clinton, on July 11, 1995, announced normalized relations with Vietnam, a country that had waged a war and had left deep scars in the American psyche. The president said that normalization would further US interests "in working for a free and peaceful Vietnam in a stable and peaceful Asia." And although the administration denied it, there was much truth in the statement by Senator John McCain (a former POW) that the recognition would "serve as a strategic counterweight to Chinese military power in Asia."[7]

Thereafter, US–Vietnam relations continued to improve: Douglas (Pete) Peterson—a former air force pilot who had been shot down and imprisoned in the "Hanoi Hilton"—was named the first US ambassador to Vietnam in 1997. In August 1999, US Consul General Charles Ray inaugurated a new US consulate building in Ho Chi Minh City. US "national interests" in relationship with Vietnam were summarized by Stanley O. Roth, assistant secretary in the Department of State in March 1998, thus:

We have important national interests at play in Vietnam. We believe it is in our interest to promote Vietnam's economic prosperity and integration into the regional and international structures that enhance regional stability and free trade. Among these are our dialogue on human rights, and our growing cooperation on counter-narcotics. Economic normalization, which we are working to advance, encompasses a range of measures to promote trade and investment so that American businessmen can take advantage of the considerable potential in this dynamic and emerging market.[8]

The development of a close US–Vietnam relationship, however, was stymied by Vietnam's questionable record in human rights. Critics of improvement in US–Vietnam relations—especially the evangelical lobby and the anticommunist Vietnamese immigrants—openly accused the Clinton administration of favoring business corporations that had enriched the Democratic Party's electoral campaign coffers by making possible their participation in the growing trade and FDI in Vietnam at the expense of human rights violations and repression of Christianity.

Pending US Congress approval of normal trade relations (NTR) status in case of Vietnam, an annual review would be required under the Jackson-Vanik amendment. In March and June 1998, President Clinton decided to waive the Jackson-Vanik amendment that, as Senator McCain said, would not only serve as "an important tool for the enhancement of American interests in Vietnam" but would also "enhance opportunities to emigrate freely." As he pointed out, Vietnam had, since the waiver, "eliminated the requirement for the ODP [Orderly Departure Program] application, including Montagnards and former re-education camp detainees, to obtain exit permits prior to being interviewed by American officials."[9] By end of June 1998, Vietnam had cleared 80 percent of all remaining Resettlement Opportunities for Vietnamese Returnees (ROVR) applicants and promised to clear the balance.

Bilateral Trade Agreement

Meanwhile, there was a parallel process in progress since 1996 toward reaching a Bilateral Trade Agreement (BTA) between the United States and Vietnam. From 1998 to 2000, President Clinton granted Vietnam a waiver from the application of the Jackson-Vanik amendment to the Trade Act of 1974 that restricted economic assistance to states with nonmarket (communist) economies and that also were restrictive in their emigration policies.

In July 1999, Vietnam and the United States agreed "in principle" on a BTA. It was not formally signed until July 2000 owing to internal opposition among the top leaders of the VCP on the merits of BTA for their country. A prime factor that weighed with Vietnamese leadership in favor of BTA was the support it would receive from the United States for its membership in the World

Trade Organization; another crucial consideration was China's impending membership of that organization. The BTA was approved by the US Congress with bipartisan support, importantly, from Vietnam war veterans: John Kerry, John McCain, and Chuck Hagel. US Trade Representative Robert B. Zoellick hailed the BTA as "an important step forward in bringing economic freedom and opportunity to Vietnam, along with providing new trade opportunities for American workers, consumers and businesses."[10]

According to US laws, the BTA would grant Vietnam the NTR status—subject, however, to annual review and a Jackson-Vanik amendment waiver by the president. After the BTA's ratification by Vietnam's National Assembly and Vietnam's president, on December 4, 2001, the BTA became effective and operational one week later.

Broadly considered, the BTA covered six major areas: market access for industrial and agricultural goods, protection of intellectual property, market access for services, investment protection, business facilitation, and transparency in trade and investment. It involved specific commitment from Vietnam to reduce tariffs on approximately 250 products, about four-fifths of them agricultural goods. The BTA would provide new markets for US-manufactured goods, agricultural products, and services. The Vietnamese government's procurement would be more "open and transparent" and would be required to adhere to a number of multilateral disciplines on customs procedures, import and licensing prevalent in the global community, mostly Western countries and Japan. All this would help Vietnam join the World Trade Organization for regular membership, for which it had applied in January 1995 and was now promised US support. By mid–2004, Vietnam had eight rounds of negotiations with the WTO on Vietnam's future trade regime.

The BTA's impact on Vietnam's import–export trade with the United States was immediate. In 2000, US exports to Vietnam—mostly of industrial machinery, fertilizers, and semiconductors—amounted to about $368 million, while Vietnamese exports to the United States accounted for $821 million. In 2002, US exports rose to $580.20 million, while the Vietnamese exports to the United States soared to $2,394.70 million, leaving a trade balance in favor of Vietnam of $1,814.50 million. In terms of total Vietnamese exports, those destined for the United States account roughly to 5 percent, with potential, however, for much more. Yet in terms of US global trade, Vietnam stands very low, ranking seventy-second in 2002.

President Clinton Visits Vietnam

History was made when the first executive-level meeting between the two former foes—Vietnam and the United States—took place in November 2000 with the visit of President Clinton, the first US president to visit Hanoi and the first to visit Ho Chi Minh City (formerly Saigon) since President Nixon's brief visit there in 1969. Indicative of the US business interest under the BTA was a high-powered trade mission accompanying the president. Organized by the US–Vietnam Trade Council, it consisted of thirty US firms already dealing with Vietnam or aspiring to do so. These included Boeing, General Motors, Lucent Technologies, Oracle, Cisco, Coca-Cola, DaimlerChrysler, Nike, Motorola, Citigroup, Federal Express, Procter and Gamble, and United Parcel Service. Of these corporations, Federal Express was the first US corporation to start business in Vietnam almost immediately after the sanctions on trade were lifted in 1994. So also was Nike, which provided employment to several thousand Vietnamese and helped the country's exports to about $1.5 billion by 2000. The trade mission's objectives were to explore further business opportunities, removal of bureaucratic obstacles, and terminating the discriminatory pricing system that made foreign firms pay much more for basic services than their domestic counterparts. They also reviewed the series of measures that the two governments would need to make the BTA effective.

Problems in US–Vietnam Relations

There have been at least two major problems in the maintenance of cordial relations between the United States and Vietnam: Vietnam's violations of human rights—particularly of the Christians among the Montagnards—and Vietnam's substantial exports of catfish to the United States at the expense of losses to US fishermen. Not coincidentally, those who have been demanding US official action against Vietnam on both issues are also those who were opposed, throughout the 1990s, to a close relationship with Vietnam.

The Montagnards Issue

Many of the Montagnards—the ethnic minorities in the central highlands of Vietnam—had fought with US troops, including the Special Forces, during the Vietnam conflict. At the end of the war, some escaped Communist captivity and fled into the jungle, where they joined a resistance movement called the United Front for the Liberation of Oppressed Races, known as FULRO (acronym for the French name); some operated on the Thai-Cambodian border against the Vietnamese government.

Very few Montagnards arrived in the United States as "boat people." The majority of the more than 1,600 Montagnards who were admitted to the United States as refugees were processed under the UN's Orderly Departure Program

(ODP). In 1985, the year when the United States began maintaining records that identified Montagnards specifically, 2,504 Montagnards were determined to be eligible for consideration for admission to the United States as refugees because of their pre–1975 association with the US or South Vietnamese governments. Of this number, 1,024 were approved by the Immigration and Naturalization Service for admission, and 893 were scheduled for interviews but failed to appear, presumably because of their inability to secure their exit visas from the Vietnamese government. This could be due to poor communication from the highlands to Ho Chi Minh City, but could also be attributed to the involvement of their relatives with FULRO. In November 1986, some 201 Montagnard resistance fighters were processed for admission to the United States and resettled in North Carolina; in 1992, an additional 395 Montagnard resistance fighters discovered by the UN peacekeeping forces in northeastern Cambodia were also processed and moved to North Carolina. After 1997, the question of Montagnard refugee processing was taken up with the Vietnam government actively by US Ambassador Peterson and by Julia Taft of the Department of State, who visited Vietnam in May 1997 and testified before the Senate Foreign Relations Committee in March of the following year.

While the Vietnamese constitution explicitly provides for the freedom of religion, it also states that all aspects of the polity and society are controlled by the VCP as the "vanguard of the Vietnamese working class," and allows the government to impose restrictions in the interests of the state and the VCP. In April 1999, a government decree specifically defined the government's authority to prevent "all activities using religious belief in order to oppose the State of the Socialist Republic of Vietnam," and to punish those who "prevent the believers from carrying out their civic responsibilities." The decree required all religious organizations to register and secure the approval of the "relevant levels of government" for their specific activities, including production and export and import of religious literature. The government was empowered to approve the nomination, ordination, and transfer of clergy and lay specialists. All religious organizations would be required to report to the Bureau of Religious Affairs their "interactions with foreign organizations and individuals and their activities abroad." The US International Commission on Religious Freedom (ICRF) Report of May 2001 alleged that Vietnam often used national security and threats to national unity as excuses for "administrative detention" without trial up to two years. The report recommended that the US Congress ratify the US–Vietnam Bilateral Trade Agreement only after calling for the Vietnamese government to "make substantial improvements in the protection of religious freedom or after the Vietnamese government undertakes obligations to the United States to make such improvements." These should include release from imprisonment, detention, or house arrest of those who are restricted due to their religious "identities or activities," and permit "unhindered access" to religious leaders—the ICRF and UN Special Rapporteur on Religious Intolerance.

The Montagnards and several church groups in the United States, notably the Lutheran Church in the Carolinas, accused the Vietnamese government for seizure of the Montagnards' ancestral lands, allowing an influx of lowland Vietnamese settlers on them and denying the Montagnards—particularly members of the unrecognized Protestant churches—their religious freedom as well as rights to education in their native languages. Following a vicious military attack with tanks and helicopter guns on peaceful protesters on February 21, 2001, thousands of Montagnards fled to Cambodia, where many were arrested. The Vietnamese government also persecuted relatives of the Montagnards already in the United States, including of the head of the South Carolina-based Montagnard Foundation, Kok Ksor; and despite appeals from international human rights groups as well as from the UN High Commissioner for Refugees (UNHCR), Cambodia continued to forcibly turn over the asylum-seeking Montagnards to the Hanoi government on grounds that they were not refugees but "economic migrants." Such returnees faced torture and long terms of imprisonment after secret trials in Vietnam. United States pressure resulted in the settlement of about 1,000 Montagnards in 2002 and 2003, mostly in the Carolinas through the Lutheran Family Services and assistance from the former Green Berets.

In April 2004, the Vietnamese government came down strongly on Montagnard protesters, some of whom again fled to Cambodia. This time, the Phnom Penh government reluctantly agreed to allow the UNHCR—the UN refugee agency—to open its offices in the northeastern provinces of Rattanakiri and Mondulkiri, warning, however, that it will not allow the UNHCR to run long-term refugee camps for the Montagnards. The Cambodian government, anxious not to hurt relations with Hanoi, also announced that it would use force if the Montagnards attempted to set up clandestine bases inside Cambodia, agitating for a separate homeland in Vietnam.

Human Rights Violations

Apart from religious intolerance, the Vietnamese government came under censure from human rights, including Amnesty International and the Human Rights Watch, for the severe curbs placed on freedom of expression and use of the Internet. These accelerated during 2002 with the approach of Vietnam's National Assembly elections and the use of the media and the Internet by dissidents calling for pluralism to replace Vietnam's single-party system. In January, the police in Ho Chi Minh City confiscated and burned seven tons of books and magazines, including books published abroad and those written by Vietnamese dissidents. In the aftermath of the elections, dissent increased and so did the government's coercive measures. In July, police in Hanoi destroyed 40,780 compact discs, 810 videotapes, and 3,000 books. In the following month, two issues of the *Far Eastern Economic Review* were banned because of their coverage of a Vietnamese corruption scandal and review of a biography of Ho Chi Minh and his alleged love affairs. The government increased its monitoring of the Internet, denied the public access to international television programs broadcast by satellite, and arrested a number of dissidents for using the Internet to publicize their ideas. In July 2002, the government instructed the Ministry of Culture and Information (MoCI) to tighten controls at 4,000 Internet coffeehouses to prevent people from accessing state secrets, pornography, or "reactionary" documents. The government blocked approximately 2,000 web sites, including those managed by Vietnamese dissidents abroad. In August, the MoCI instructed the country's only Internet gateway, the state-owned Vietnam Data Communications Company, to obstruct subversive web sites based on the lists compiled by government ministries. And two months later, the MoCI ordered Vietnam's state-owned Internet service providers to block "politically and morally unacceptable" web content. In the same year, world attention was drawn to the death, in suspicious circumstances, of a well-known Vietnamese dissident, Tran Do, and the trial of Li Chi Quang, leader of a group of pro-democracy advocates in the country. A bill approved with overwhelming majority in the US House of Representatives in 2002 prohibiting any increase in nonhumanitarian assistance until Vietnam has made significant progress in releasing political and religious prisoners and in treating the Montagnards failed for lack of support in the Senate. In July 2003, however, the Vietnam Human Rights Act was passed by both houses of Congress. It established a seventeen-member commission to "monitor and report" on Vietnam's human rights position and required the secretary of state to assess Vietnam's performance and report. Predictably, the measure ignited a controversy in Hanoi, where the Politburo has been divided for years on the extent of closeness with the United States.

The "Catfish War"

A major trade dispute endangering the broader relations between the United States and Vietnam occurred a little more than one year after the BTA became operative on the question of large-scale Vietnamese exports of catfish to the United States. The catfish lobby—representing farmers and processors in Mississippi, Arkansas, and Louisiana—approached the US Department of

Commerce, pleading severe financial losses caused by the cheap Vietnamese imports. In mid–2003, when the US International Trade Committee (ITC) upheld the Commerce Department's ruling of the previous month that the exports in question constituted "dumping," Vietnam felt it had lost the "catfish war." Following the ITC ruling, the Commerce Department raised the tariff on catfish from 5 percent to 64 percent effective July 30, 2003. It also stipulated that out of 2,000 catfish varieties, only the US-born family Ictaluridae could be called catfish, and that the Vietnamese varieties did not qualify as catfish; they could be marketed in the United States using the Vietnamese terms of *basa* and *tra*, which belonged to the Pangasudae family.

Vietnam countered that the ITC ruling was unfair because the ITC's pricing formula was based on the production cost of catfish in India and not in Vietnam, where its low price was attributed to a far lower unit labor cost than in India or the United States. Vietnam's foreign ministry charged that the ITC ruling was contrary to "the free trade promotion policy and the spirit of fair competition that the US always talks about." The Vietnam Association of Seafood Exporters and Producers condemned the ruling for being unfair, "a protectionist measure, which goes against free trade and equal competition in the increasingly expanded globalization trend." In the United States, Senator John McCain called the labeling ban "an offensive trade barrier" and Virginia Foote, head of the US–Vietnam Trade Council, moaned that the United States changed the rules "so soon after the rules were first established."[11]

Although Vietnamese imports of catfish in the United States amounted to no more than 1 percent of the total catfish in the US market, the industry was very important for Vietnam, affecting some 400,000 to 500,000, principally in the An Giang province in the Mekong Delta, which accounted for three-quarters of the national produce. The United States was the largest importer of Vietnamese catfish; the imports rose from $39 million in 2001 to $55 million in 2002. The ITC ruling affected the imports bringing them down to below $20 million in 2003.

The defeat in the catfish war disturbed the Vietnamese government, particularly those in the top leadership who had argued for years in favor of closeness to the United States, free trade, FDI, and globalization. They rightly feared that the next in line to be attacked by US interests would be the shrimp industry. Although this would target other countries, such as Brazil, China, India, and Thailand, Vietnam was on the short list of countries accused of dumping. Shrimp constituted the third largest export item for Vietnam after crude oil and garments; shrimp exports to the United States totaled $467 million in 2002, accounting for 48 percent of Vietnam's global shrimp exports. The final ruling on the shrimp issue will be delivered by the US Department of Commerce and International Trade Commission on January 8, 2005.

The Vietnamese Refugee Problem

The Issue

Though not arising directly out of the Vietnam–China conflict, the mass exodus between 1978 and 1980 of Vietnamese, principally of Chinese ethnic origin, tarnished Vietnam's international image. A second wave of Vietnamese refugees became an issue of international concern a decade later. Soon after the fall of Saigon in 1975, a relatively small number of people left Vietnam's shores in small boats. In the following two years, the total remained below 20,000, most of them absorbed by Malaysia, Thailand, and Hong Kong. In 1978, the number rose sharply to more than 85,000. The crisis peaked in 1979–1981, as refugees of Chinese descent, many of them North Vietnamese, fled either to China or Hong Kong. By the middle of 1979, China alone received 250,000 refugees, Hong Kong 62,000, France 61,000, and the United States 150,000; more than 368,000 were awaiting resettlement in transit camps in Thailand, Malaysia, and Indonesia. At least half that number were presumed to have died of starvation on the high seas or drowned because of leaking boats. From the refugees' accounts, it appeared certain that the Vietnamese government "officially" blessed the exodus—but not before the refugees had each paid in gold the equivalent of $5,000, the government netting nearly $4 billion in the process. Between 1975 and 1990, over 1.5 million Vietnamese, Lao, and Cambodian refugees were resettled, most in Western Europe, North America, and Australia.

Traditionally, refugee resettlement has been a regional concern that has led to a regional solution. Thus most African refugees are resettled in neighboring African countries, refugees from Eastern Europe are settled in Western Europe and by their ethnic relatives in the United States, and so on. The Vietnamese refugee problem, however, was considered an international matter involving intercontinental resettlement. This was as much because of a guilty global conscience as because of the pleas made by pro-Western ASEAN countries to reduce the burden of refugees who had arrived on their shores as boat people. With the exception of China, the neighboring countries—notably Malaysia, Thailand, and Indonesia (and after 1988, the Philippines)—accepted the refugees on condition that they would be resettled permanently in Western Europe, North America, or Australia. The neighboring countries thus served as first-asylum countries, accommodating the refugees in transit camps but unwilling to provide them a permanent home on grounds that the immigrants would create social and economic problems on a large scale. The non-Communist Southeast Asian countries regarded the refugees not only as a heavy economic burden on their scarce resources but as a potential security risk. This was particularly true of Malaysia, which feared that the influx of Vietnamese Chinese refugees would upset the already delicate racial balance there.

The Causes of Migration

The causes of the massive emigration from Vietnam were economic, social, and political. During 1975–1977, Vietnam suffered a series of bad harvests. The subsequent two years were marked by natural disasters, and crops in the Mekong Delta suffered from insect pests and fungus diseases. The nonavailability of foodstuffs and their exorbitant price caused great hardship. In both north and south, the urban population had swelled enormously during the long war; it suffered from inadequate food, large-scale unemployment, and the disruptive government attempts at compulsory resettlement in NEZs, particularly in the south. The economic situation was worsened by the war in Cambodia and with China. Additionally, the conscription was extended in 1978 to include sixteen- to thirty-five-year-olds, and the period of mandatory service went from three to five years. The war itself produced a large number of refugees willing to try their fortunes on the high seas. Finally, the exodus of Hoa, ethnic Chinese, from South Vietnam was prompted by the government's policy of abolition of private trade in April 1978 and by the growing tension between Vietnam and China in early 1979. Around that time, about 250,000 Hoa, whose ancestors had lived in North Vietnam for generations, fled across the land border into China. Vietnam alleged that many of them had acted as spies in guiding the Chinese invaders along back trails to attack the Vietnamese defenders in the rear. The statement of Deputy Premier Deng Xiaoping of China to Secretary General Kurt Waldheim of the UN in April 1979, that China might teach Vietnam "another lesson," made the Vietnamese apprehensive of the remaining Hoa, particularly those in the strategic port city of Haiphong and the coastal coal-mining towns of Hongay-Campha further north. Vietnam did not want to take chances, and therefore expelled ethnic Chinese from those areas and from Hanoi. Of all the refugees and boat people, 80 percent were of Chinese origin.

The Solutions

Several international conferences in which the United Nations High Commissioner for Refugees was involved discussed the crisis in 1979. In May, at the ASEAN-sponsored meeting in Jakarta, attended by representatives of twenty-five countries, including Vietnam, Malaysia proposed that a refugee-processing center for 200,000 be established in the United States or a US-controlled territory. In response to calls for organized emigration, Vietnam agreed to send the emigrants directly to the countries of resettlement at the rate of 10,000 a month. Anyone who wished to leave the country would be allowed to do so, except those who were of age for military conscription, knew state secrets, or were awaiting trial on criminal charges.

At the UN-sponsored conference in Geneva in July, attended by representatives of sixty-five countries and international agencies, most Western countries and Japan announced their financial contributions as well as quotas for resettlement of refugees. The United States accepted the bulk of the responsibility. In May 1982, the Geneva-based Inter-Governmental Committee for Migration stated that of the almost 700,000 Indochinese refugees who had been resettled since 1975, more than two-thirds (477,000) were accepted by the United States, 82,000 by France, and 60,000 by Canada. The United States operated a refugee processing program within the ambit of the UN Orderly Departure Program (ODP), which did not always work in an orderly fashion because of periodic acrimonious exchanges between Washington and Hanoi over the modalities of emigration. In April 1982, the US government announced that Indochinese nationals would be allowed to emigrate to the United States either as refugees under the Refugee Act of 1980 or as holders of immigrant visas under the Immigration and Naturalization Act. Those with close relatives in the United States, former US government employees, and those formerly connected with US activities or with a former non-Communist government in Indochina and who had a specific reason to fear persecution would be allowed to enter the country. Indochinese nationals already in the United States could apply to the ODP for their close family members in Indochina.

The government of Vietnam periodically gave to the UNHCR lists of persons with permission to depart Vietnam. The UNHCR's office forwarded the lists to the ODP, which checked them against its own lists to determine applicants' eligibility for admission to the United States. Names appearing on both American and Vietnamese lists were then placed on a joint list and the applicants called for an interview with the UNHCR representative in Ho Chi Minh City. They would undergo a final interview with US officials at the airport in Ho Chi Minh City, where the departure papers would be signed before the refugees were allowed to fly to Bangkok. There, the ODP's local office would decide who should fly directly to the United States and who should be sent to a Special Refugee Processing Center in Indonesia or in the Philippines for three months of training in English language and cultural orientation. By 1982, the emigration by small boats had declined sharply to about 30,000 annually; between 1984 and 1986, there was only a trickle.

By September 1983, the United States had admitted a total of 678,057 refugees from Southeast Asia. Nearly two-thirds entered the United States between 1979 and 1982; Vietnamese refugees accounted for two-thirds of all Southeast Asian refugees in the United States.

Suddenly, in mid–1987, Thailand, Malaysia, and Hong Kong reported alarmingly rapid arrivals of Vietnamese refugees. Thailand related that a large number had traveled by land to the Cambodian port of Kompong Som, where they had chartered small boats operated by Thai and Cambodian smugglers for destinations on Thai shores. This time, there were no fountains of sympathy for Vietnamese refugees. Vietnam's ASEAN neighbors, Hong Kong, and the Western countries were allegedly affected by "compassion fatigue"—as even after thirteen years of the Communist victory, there seemed no end to the refugee exodus out of Vietnam. In the wake of *glasnost,* the Western world had new priorities for settlement of refugees and emigrants from Eastern Europe and the Soviet Union. Malaysia, Thailand, and Hong Kong—who had an excellent record thus far of offering first asylum to refugees from Indochina—complained that most of the new refugees were not political targets but economic migrants: peasants, fishermen as well as professionals, most from North Vietnam, who were leaving the country in search of economic opportunities in the West. Although its policy did not change officially, in January 1988, Thailand began to push back into the sea the boats that brought new refugees to its shores. Hong Kong announced that June 1988 would be the cutoff date after which refugees would be screened to sort out the genuine ones from the economic migrants, and that the latter would be forcibly repatriated to Vietnam. In April 1988, Malaysia served one year's notice to the effect that its transit camp on the rocky island of Pulau Bidong off the Trengganu coast—which since its opening in 1978 had processed 230,000 refugees as well as its transit camp at Sungei Besi near Kuala Lumpur—would be closed after March 1989.

At the insistence of Hong Kong, an international conference was held in June 1989 in Geneva, where sixty nations and international agencies adopted a comprehensive plan to work out the special difficulties of the countries of first asylum. The plan included measures to discourage clandestine departures from Vietnam, regional screening in the first-asylum countries to identify genuine political refugees, speedier resettlement of refugees in the West and Australia, and voluntary repatriation for nonpolitical refugees. Although the Soviet Union, Vietnam, and the United Nations all had reservations about compulsory repatriation, the United States was the strongest opponent of the policy.

Despite US protests, the British government proceeded to negotiate with Vietnam and sign a memorandum of understanding on involuntary repatriation, under which it sent a group of economic migrants to Vietnam. The latter buckled under British pressure to draw a semantic distinction between forced and voluntary repatriation, arguing that there was a "quiet majority" among the refugees who were not for voluntary repatriation but who were not against repatriation as such. In October 1989, Vietnamese foreign minister Nguyen Co Thach declared that if such refugees were repatriated with financial help, his government would not regard the action as forcible repatriation. This allowed the UN-sponsored voluntary repatriation scheme to return to Vietnam some 867 refugees by the end of 1989, giving each person a subsidy of $1,000. The program continued for ten years until 1997, bringing the total of voluntarily repatriated Vietnamese to 57,000. Hong Kong officially closed its last Vietnamese refugee camp in 2000. Four years previously, Malaysia and Indonesia had closed their refugee camps, sending to Vietnam the "holdouts" among the boat people. Thailand followed suit the following year.

Meanwhile, the United States held bilateral negotiations with Vietnam in July 1989 and announced on January 5, 1990, that it would accept a total of between 400,000 and 450,000 Vietnamese. The figure would include a large number of former Vietnamese reeducation-camp inmates who had served the South Vietnamese and US governments before 1975. They would be admitted under the Special Release Reeducation Center Detainee Resettlement Program, commonly known as the Humanitarian Program, or simply H.O. Program. The United States agreed not to encourage such emigrants to engage in anti-Vietnamese activities.

Refugee Settlement in the United States

Prior to 1975, when South Vietnam came under Communist rule, there were only 18,000 Vietnamese Americans in the United States. These were, for the most part, spouses of American businessmen or armed forces personnel who had lived for varying periods in South Vietnam. The bulk of Vietnamese migration to the United States occurred within the first five years after the fall of Saigon in April 1975.

Vietnamese Americans are distinguishable from most other migrants to the United States because an overwhelming majority came as refugees instead of immigrants. As James Freeman observed in *Hearts of Sorrow*, "Immigrants choose to come to a new life, whereas refugees are forced to flee—often for their lives. Vietnamese refugees left their old life, not freely, but because they were persecuted or feared being persecuted. . . . Had they not felt threatened they would not have left."[12] In that sense, Vietnamese refugees fell in the same category as the nearly 400,000 refugees who migrated from Europe to the United States after World War II or the 30,000 political refugees from Hungary in the 1950s.

Between 1975 and September 1991, a total of 1,034,159 refugees from Indochina were admitted into the United States, of which 61.2 percent came from Vietnam, 23.3 percent from Laos, and 15.5 percent from Cambodia.[13] Until the passage of the Refugee Act in 1980, admission of refugees from former Indochina was governed by ad hoc policies. Between April and December 1975, the United States admitted 130,400 people from Vietnam, Laos, and Cambodia, of which 125,000 were Vietnamese. Initially, the US government had planned for only 17,600 refugees, principally former government employees and American dependents. The list was subsequently extended to admit a large number of relatives of US citizens and permanent residents, South Vietnamese government employees and military personnel, and about 4,000 orphans. It also included some Chams and Montagnards from Vietnam and Meo and Hmong tribals from Laos who had assisted the US war effort in Vietnam. A large number of the first wave of Vietnamese refugees were well educated, knew English fairly well (because of their work experience in various US agencies), and were, by virtue of their professional backgrounds and relatively sophisticated lifestyles, capable of easy adjustment to American life.

The second wave, beginning in 1978, included large numbers of Vietnamese of Chinese origin, most of whom had migrated as boat people to Malaysian camps before their resettlement in Europe or the United States. Compared to the first wave of Vietnamese refugees, those who migrated between 1978 and 1981 were less educated, poorer, and deficient in skills needed for absorption in advanced societies such as the United States. A study of Vietnamese refugees carried out by the US Social Security Administration pointed out that the 1979 cohort differed from the preceding ones in background characteristics.

> More frequently Sino-Vietnamese with a noticeable proportion of the people born in China and largely Buddhist, this cohort includes a larger proportion of people previously engaged in trading and merchandising ventures of one sort or another. Educational levels were considerably lower for the 1979 group than for earlier arrivals and effective English-speaking capability was rare in this group.[14]

During the second wave of refugees between 1978 and 1980, the attorney general of the United States authorized a number of parole programs in response to the dire news of large numbers of boat people who had landed in neighboring countries of Southeast Asia and Hong Kong. The parole programs brought into the United States more than a quarter million new refugees from Indochina: 20,397 in 1978, 80,678; in 1979; and 166,727 in 1980.

In early 1979, in the wake of the Vietnamese invasion and occupation of Cambodia, thousands of Cambodians fled across the western border into Thailand in the hope of being resettled in a safer milieu, particularly the

United States. They were physically and psychologically in worse condition than other arrivals from the region; few had any knowledge of English or were even literate, or had relatives in the United States who could provide them initial support.

The 1980 Refugee Act—the first comprehensive legislation on the subject since 1900—treated refugees and immigrants as two distinct categories: Potential immigrants needed sponsors in the United States and had to await the full processing of their immigrant visas before entering the United States, whereas refugees could be admitted on the basis of on-site processing overseas. The act included regulations for the selection and admission of refugees, taking into account the possible impact—political, economic, and social—on the host communities where they would be settled. It recommended measures to avoid destabilization of existing communities by excessive immigration of new ethnic groups. The act empowered the president to decide, in consultation with Congress, the eligibility of individuals who would be offered a refuge and to establish numerical limits on the admission of refugees from different parts of the world. Under the new law, by the end of 1981 a total of 166,727 refugees were admitted from Indochina, of which 95,200 were Vietnamese. The number dropped dramatically to 42,600 for 1982 and to an average of 22,000 thereafter until 1988, when only 17,958 were admitted. As Vietnamese Americans became eligible for US citizenship, cases of immigrants sponsored by Vietnamese American citizens increased, raising the numbers of immigrants from Vietnam in 1989 to 30,800, in 1990 to 41,000, and in 1991 to 45,000. (See table 10.1.)

Amerasians, or Bui Doi

A major concern for the United States in the 1980s was the fate of tens of thousands of Amerasians, the offspring of US soldiers and Vietnamese women. These were a "visible impression of the time" that US soldiers spent in Vietnam. Photos of young Amerasians selling cigarette butts on Ho Chi Minh City's streets pricked America's conscience in the late 1970s. The Vietnamese pejoratively called them *bui doi*, or "the dust of life." Such children were not wanted by anybody in Vietnam—neither by the society nor the government, most often not even by their families.

Why were these children so badly discriminated against? To the new rulers of Vietnam, they were "children of the enemy"—reminders of a detested past when American men in uniform "abused" Vietnamese women, who were accused for "consorting with the enemy." Vietnamese people, in general, regarded mothers of Amerasians—many of them bar girls or call girls—as ordinary prostitutes, although a majority of such mothers were educated,

Table 10.1   Refugees from Vietnam, Cambodia, and Laos into the United States, 1975–1991 (Rounded to Hundreds)

	Cambodia	Laos	Vietnam	Remarks
1975	4,600	800	125,000	First wave
1976	1,100	10,700	3,200	
1977	300	400	1,900	
1978	1,300	8,000	11,100	
1979	6,000	30,200	44,500	Second wave
1980	16,000	55,500	95,200	Invasion of Cambodia
1981	27,100	19,300	86,000	
1982	20,100	9,400	42,600	
1983	13,200	3,000	23,000	
1984	19,900	7,200	25,000	
1985	19,200	5,200	25,400	
1986	10,000	12,900	22,400	
1987	2,000	15,600	22,600	
1988	2,900	14,600	18,000	
1989	2,200	12,800	30,800	
1990	2,300	8,700	41,000	
1991	200	9,200	45,000	

SOURCE: Based on US Department of Health and Human Services, Office of Refugee Resettlement, *Refugee Settlement Program, Report to the Congress* (Washington, DC: US Department of Health and Human Services, 1992), p. A16.

working-class women before they offered sexual favors or services to US soldiers for money.

Amerasians easily could be ostracized owing to their appearance—white or black—setting them apart from society. Many Amerasian children, regardless of whether they looked white or black, became targets for mocking and senseless beating. They ended up on the streets without an education. Those who enrolled in school were compelled by incessant ridicule and not infrequent physical abuse to abandon education. Consequently, they grew up illiterate, without counseling and unqualified to hold any job. The emotional scars on their minds were so severe that some became suicidal.

To the South Vietnamese, however, the *bui doi* were reminders of a cataclysmic war and desertion by the United States. The communist government disclaimed any responsibility, because it regarded Amerasians deriving their identity from their fathers—and, therefore, the responsibility of their fathers in America and of the US government.

In 1982, bowing down to pressures from a number of American fathers who had remained in touch with their children in Vietnam, the US Congress somewhat belatedly acknowledged its responsibility for Amerasian children, some of whom by then had become young adults—and although Hanoi initially permitted some Amerasian children to emigrate under the UN Orderly Departure Program, it used the Amerasians as a "bargaining chip" in its negotiations to establish diplomatic relations with the United States or to extract funds for reconstruction from its former enemy. Finally in 1988, when it signed an agreement allowing Amerasians to migrate to the United States, Vietnam agreed to search for and register Amerasian children, many of whom lived on the streets and had no definite address.[15] In the same year, the US Congress approved special legislation called the Amerasian Homecoming Act, under which petitions on behalf of Amerasian children could be filed in the United States.

The Homecoming Act made all Amerasians born in Vietnam between January 1, 1962, and January 1, 1976, eligible to migrate to the United States, accompanied by either immediate family, guardians or a spouse. An Amerasian would have to establish during the course of an interview process with US officials that he or she was, indeed, fathered by a US citizen. The Homecoming Act of 1988 created a black market for Amerasians in Vietnam, where people vied to qualify themselves as guardians of Amerasian children or contract marriages to qualify as spouses for immigration to the States. Suddenly, the once unwanted Amerasians became the most desirable persons. They were now called the "golden visas" or "living passports." There were numerous cases of people with means who bribed Vietnamese officials to obtain exit permits and then be paired with an Amerasian as a "family." The family relationship lasted only until the immigration papers were successfully processed.

Not all Amerasians could establish their identity, because so many of them did not know the names of their fathers or their whereabouts. This was particularly so of those who were abandoned by their real mothers and cared by some other people. Despite the Homecoming Act, thousands of Amerasians were left behind in Vietnam. By the end of 1991, only about 75,000 Amerasian children and their relatives had been admitted into the United States with the status of "legal permanent residents" or, in common parlance, green card holders.

A final chapter in the status of Amerasians in the United States will have been written with the passing of the Amerasian Naturalization Act. Sponsored by Representative Zoe Lofgren of California and nineteen other members of the House of Representatives on October 21, 2003, it was at the committee stage in July 2004. The measure seeks to provide "automatic" US citizenship for "lawful" immigrants residing in the United States and who were fathered by a US citizen and born in Vietnam between 1962 and 1975. Under the existing Child Citizenship Act, any child fathered by a US citizen and born overseas is entitled to US citizenship, provided that "fathers take steps necessary to achieve their children's citizenship." Lofgren pointed out that this has not been possible for some fathers to do in the case of Amerasians. With the passing of the Amerasian Naturalization Act of 2003, he added, it would be possible "to finally close a chapter" in US history that has "too long denied Amerasians the opportunity to become US citizens and be recognized as the Americans that they are."[16]

Secondary Migration

For most of the 1970s and 1980s, refugees from Vietnam, Laos, and Cambodia, unlike most other immigrants, did not have members of their own ethnic communities in the United States eligible to sponsor them. Humanitarian associations and church groups therefore agreed to undertake financial responsibility for many such migrants. By and large, the sponsors were located near the holding centers, some of them air force bases such as Camp Pendleton, the first and largest holding center for the Indochinese refugees in the country. Others included Travis Air Force Base in California and Fort Indiantown Gap near Harrisburg, Pennsylvania.

In most cases, the migrants had little opportunity to choose their entry point to the United States or the location where they wanted to settle down on a long-term basis. The whole process lacked coordination, often separating and dispersing families to different states. Through the years, a secondary migration occurred as these broken families tried to reunite. By 1980, 45 percent of the first wave of migrants from Vietnam, Laos, and Cambodia had moved from their state of entry to a different state.

There was far less secondary migration among refugees of the second wave, with a few notable exceptions, such as the relocation of about 30,000 Hmongs from different parts of the United States to Fresno, California, between 1980 and 1986. By that time the US administration had become aware of the hardship caused to divided families and the futility of the policy to promote dispersion of migrants. In 1981, under the new Refugee Act, the official policy was not to discourage formation of ethnic clusters. The government acknowledged that ethnic coalescence was not only a fact of life but that it could be beneficial as long as the clusters were not so large as to overburden local services. By that time, too, some of the new immigrants had ethnic sponsors from the previous wave of refugees who welcomed the resettlement of the new refugees in their midst.

Adjustment in the United States

The Vietnamese refugees who arrived in the United States had to discover a comfortable compromise between the ways of their adopted country and those of the homeland they were compelled to flee. Most were unaccustomed to almost all aspects of American life and encountered enormous social, economic, and emotional hardships. Paul Rutledge described how the refugees were shocked, for example, by the lack of herbal remedies in American medical practice and the whiteness of hospital rooms, because white to Vietnamese was "symbolic of sorrow, death and mourning. . . . They interpreted the symbols to mean that hospitals are places you go to die, not places you go to recover."[17] The language barrier, shortage of good jobs, professional demotions, unavailability of certain foods, and hostility on the part of some locals made many Vietnamese Americans loathe their new condition in the first few years.

The need for adjustment to the United States most affected the Vietnamese elders. Many had had prestigious positions in South Vietnam, but because they knew only Vietnamese, many had to accept lower-status jobs in the United States. The 1980 census showed that 13.3 percent of Vietnamese Americans held professional, managerial, or executive positions before their migration; the percentage for the first wave of refugees from April through December 1975 was much higher. As mentioned earlier, a large number were well educated and had lived in big cities such as Saigon, now Ho Chi Minh City.

In the United States, as they adapted to American society, older Vietnamese also had to modify their traditional family roles, causing depression, isolation, and feelings of helplessness. They were particularly affected by the rapid acculturation of their children and grandchildren. First-generation immigrants generally put a high premium on retaining old customs and values. Their children, however, tended to take up the values and ways of life of their adopted country by imitating their school peers. As communication between the generations became impaired, the traditional authority, respect, and status accorded to elders eroded. Contrary to the expectation that children would look after them in their old age, many elderly people found themselves abandoned when their grown-up children moved to wherever employment opportunities took them. There seemed to be constant disagreement between the generations, the parents lamenting that the young people were not Vietnamese enough and children regretting that the older people were too traditional. Generational conflict among the Vietnamese immigrants was predictable and inevitable. In this respect, perhaps, the Vietnamese experience was not much different from that of any other immigrant community.

After the initial wave of sympathy, Vietnamese-American refugees faced a country that was skeptical and often unsupportive of their presence in the United States. Americans' attitudes toward the Vietnamese wavered between a sense of obligation to those who supported them in a war they lost together and an often overwhelming desire to forget the uncomfortable realities of the past. A Gallup poll taken in May 1975 showed that 54 percent of Americans were opposed to admitting Vietnamese refugees to the United States. Most cited economic reasons: The immigrants took away their jobs and needed public assistance. Besides, for most Americans, Vietnam connoted—and still does—something negative: an unwanted, brutal war that cost young lives and created prostitutes and Amerasian progeny.

Of course, the Vietnamese Americans preferred living in communities that accepted their culture and traditions. Although the new refugees were interested in meeting the challenge of assimilation into American culture, they were even more concerned with preserving the legacy of their homeland. Yet the US Refugee Task Force favored, at least until 1980, a policy of dissipating the refugees throughout the country to prevent the formation of ghettos and to facilitate cultural assimilation. The Vietnamese have historically cherished a proud ethnic identity. Despite a millennium of Chinese rule and a protectorate status for eight centuries, they successfully maintained their social institutions and traditional habits, refusing to capitulate to Chinese cultural domination.

In the United States, however, they found their youth quickly succumbing to the inexorable force of a dominant American culture that seemed to threaten Vietnamese cultural identity. It was no surprise, then, that the Vietnamese immigrants soon created ethnic clusters and community organizations in some preferred locations such as southern California, Texas, Virginia, Washington, and Louisiana.[18] Table 10.2 shows Vietnamese-American clusters in different counties in 1999.

In 1998, more than 1 million Vietnamese resided in communities of at least 10,000 in twenty states. The largest Vietnamese community outside Vietnam was in Westminster in Orange County, California, which has emerged as the economic and cultural capital of the emigrés. In the short span of a decade, the refugees converted former bean fields into a bustling business district popularly known as Bolsa and officially named Little Saigon. By 1990, the Vietnamese Chamber of Commerce listed some 1,500 businesses in Orange County operated by its members, providing 30,000 jobs and contributing $60

Table 10.2   Vietnamese Americans, by County, 1999

County	Vietnamese Americans
Orange (CA)	102,522
Los Angeles (CA)	81,587
Santa Clara (CA)	75,522
Harris (TX)	52,472
San Diego (CA)	31,641
Fairfax (VA)	18,607
Alameda (CA)	18,596
Dallas (TX)	16,724
King (WA)	16,530
Tarrant (TX)	15,128

SOURCE: *Los Angeles Times*, 24 April 2000, p. A14.

million annually to the county's economy. On the cultural side, the Vietnamese community built several temples for the nearly 80 percent of its population that is Buddhist, and a network of Sunday schools where their children can learn to speak, read, and write Vietnamese.

In 1990, forty-two newspapers and magazines in Orange County served the Vietnamese community, and two television stations broadcast hourlong programs in Vietnamese every week.[19] Other areas that Vietnamese Americans have dramatically transformed into business-cum-residence clusters, with numerous small hotels and mom-and-pop businesses, include San Francisco's red-light district in Union Square, skid row in Los Angeles, and downtowns in San José, Santa Ana, and Arlington, Virginia.

Yet Vietnamese Americans do not form a homogeneous community. They tend to associate with the Khmer Vietnamese, who are considered close to "mainstream" Vietnamese, but they do not mix socially with the Chams and the Montagnards. In the United States, as in Vietnam, Vietnamese look down on Amerasians.

Many Vietnamese Americans, not unlike migrants from other non-Western lands, fear that their family structure is being undermined by American influences. Accustomed to a Confucian tradition, those who were born in Vietnam view the younger generation of Vietnamese—most of them born in the United

States—as undisciplined, individualistic, and self-centered, bereft of time-honored Vietnamese values.[20]

At the same time, even the older generation has assimilated some of the ways of American life. And although they love to visit their homeland, they complain that people back in Vietnam consider them foreigners because they appear "fatter, paler," and relatively affluent. After more than two decades of life in the United States, many of those who migrated from Vietnam feel as if they are in cultural limbo, caught between two societies without quite belonging to either; but they have demonstrated their faith in *tran can cu,* combining "hard work, patience and tenacity into a relentless drive to survive or to be successful in an alien land."[21]

Vietnamese Americans—particularly the so-called 1.5 generation and the second generation—have made impressive advances in education. Vietnamese parents have succeeded in instilling in their children their traditional love of learning. A study of education among Indochinese refugee children in the late 1970s and early 1980s gave much credit to the older generation for the academic success of their youngsters:

> For the most part, the perspectives and values embedded in the cultural heritage of the Indochinese had been carried with them to the U.S. . . . Cultural values played an important role in the educational achievement of their children. Conserved values constituted a source of motivation and direction as the families dealt with contemporary problems set in a country vastly different from their homeland. The values formed a set of cultural givens with deep roots in the Confucian and Buddhist traditions of East and Southeast Asia.[22]

Achievements of Vietnamese Americans

Despite the trauma of escaping from Vietnam, the consequent disruption of life, loss of formal schooling while living in relocation camps, and the handicap of little or no prior knowledge of English, young Vietnamese Americans excelled at all levels—school, college, and university. By 1990, Vietnamese Americans constituted 12.6 percent of the freshman class of 2,344 students of the University of California at Irvine (close to Westminster), with the highest grade point average of any ethnic group. Most of them—not unlike children of other Asian immigrant groups—preferred the better-paying fields of business and the sciences to humanities or the social sciences. In 1997, some 1,500 students at UCLA, most in the sciences and professional schools, claimed Vietnamese ethnic origin.

The 1.5 and second generation of Vietnamese Americans boast a number of achievements. In 1988, Tue Nguyen set a record at the Massachusetts Institute of Technology by earning seven undergraduate degrees. In 1992, Dr. Eugene Trinh became the first Vietnamese American in space. A NASA astronaut, he was a primary payload specialist on the forty-eighth shuttle launch of the Space Shuttle *Columbia*. Le Ly Hayslip's autobiography, providing the perspective of a Vietnamese American woman, was the subject of the popular 1993 film *Heaven and Earth*; and in 1997, Thang Barrett became the first Vietnamese American judge to sit on a court of general jurisdiction in the United States. In sports, Dat Nguyen—the "most productive linebacker" in Texas A&M University—became the first Vietnamese American drafted into the National Football League. In his second year, he became the starting middle linebacker with the Dallas Cowboys. Three Vietnamese Americans—Tawny Binh, Michelle Do, and Khoa Nguyen—participated in the 2000 Summer Olympics in Sydney as members of the US Olympic Team in table tennis. Binh and Nguyen were gold medalists at the 1999 Pan American games, while Do at seventeen was the 1998 Nationals Under 22 Women's Singles Champion.

The Vietnamese-American experience became the focus of study on numerous US campuses. Of note are the Vietnam Centers at Texas Tech University, opened in 1989, and at San Francisco State University in 1997. The 1.5 and second generation of Vietnamese Americans have also distinguished themselves in information technology. An estimated 10,000 Vietnamese Americans were involved in the IT industry in Silicon Valley, at least fifteen of them as CEOs. Many have established companies in Vietnam and engaged an estimated 20,000 employees in outsourcing projects.

The Viet Kieu and Their Home Country

Judging from the opinion polls conducted by newspapers, such as the *Orange County Register*, and accounts in ethnic Vietnamese publications, the strong sentiment among the first generation of Vietnamese Americans against normalization of relations with the country of their origin diminished over time in its passion. It was considerable in mid–1995, immediately after relaxation of trade restrictions in 1994 and around the time of the establishment of official US–Vietnam relations the following year.

There had always been some contacts between individuals in the immigrant community and their relatives in Vietnam. They sent cash and packets of much-needed food items, which earned the Communist government hard foreign exchange. Noting the importance that the Vietnamese Americans had attained in the IT industry in Silicon Valley and elsewhere in the United

States, the Vietnamese government held the first of numerous dialogues with them in New York in July 2000. It offered to establish hi-tech industrial parks in Ho Chi Minh City with state-of-the-art, low-priced Internet connections and tax breaks. The government also assured the establishment of IT training facilities for local Vietnamese so that the investors among the Viet Kieu will not lack IT personnel for outsourcing and other projects.

In the eight years following the normalization of relations, the numbers of Viet Kieu returning to Vietnam as visitors increased dramatically from about 13,000 in 1995 to some 360,000 (including 20,000 from Canada) in 2003. This was largely facilitated by the passing of a landmark resolution in that year by the Communist government luring the Viet Kieu with promises of bureaucratic changes, assurance of property rights, and even Vietnamese language classes for those who had no chance to learn the language in the States. By mid–2004, reports indicated that about 1,000 commercial and industrial ventures in Ho Chi Minh City belonged to the Viet Kieu. The government encouraged the construction of gated communities of large homes, such as in the Saigon International Resort, with all the creature comforts to which returning Vietnamese from the United States, Canada, and Australia were accustomed. In 2003, remittances from overseas Vietnamese totaled $2.7 billion. The government allows them not only to do business in Vietnam but to buy property and enjoy local rates for hotels and airline tickets. The visit to Vietnam in January 2004 of arguably the most prominent Vietnamese American—former premier Nguyen Cao Ky—attracted widespread publicity both in the United States and in Vietnam. He was given red carpet treatment by the Communist government. His call for the Vietnamese American community to put the past behind them and assist the economic development in Vietnam in the hope that it would promote political reforms there evoked mixed reaction. He asked the Viet Kieu to "celebrate Asia's next economic dragon." Opponents charged him for legitimizing a government known for gross violation of human rights.

Chronology

c. 10,000 BC	Mesolithic Age (Hoa-Binh culture)
c. 3,000 BC	Neolithic Age (Bac-son)
c. 2,000 BC	Bronze Age (Phung-Nguyen)
700 BC–300 AD	Dong-son culture
257 BC	Kingdom of Au Lac founded
208 BC	Zhao Tuo, a Chinese general, conquers Au Lac and styles himself emperor of Nam Viet
111 BC–AD 939	Nam Viet ruled by China as the province of Giao Chi
AD 39–43	Trung sisters rebel against China, establish an independent state lasting two years
192	Champa (or Lin-yi) founded after the overthrow of Chinese rule
284	Champa sends its first delegation to China
802	Khmer empire founded in the Angkor region
939	Vietnamese, under Ngo Quyen's leadership, overthrow the Chinese in the Tongking region, send tribute to China
939–968	Ngo dynasty
968	Dinh Bo Linh overthrows Ngo dynasty, calls his state Dai Co Viet
968–980	Dinh dynasty
1010–1225	Ly dynasty
1225–1400	Tran dynasty
1282	Mongols attack Champa
1284–1287	Vietnamese defeat the Mongols
1400–1407	Ho dynasty
1414–1428	Vietnam under Chinese rule
1428	Le Loi overthrows Chinese rule, establishes Le dynasty (1428–1788)
1431	Thais sack Angkor; Khmers send tribute to Ayuthaya (Thailand)
1461–1497	Reign of Le Thanh Thong; major legal and administrative reforms
1471	Vietnamese conquest of Champa

1545	Civil war divides Vietnam; China mediates
1603	Establishment of the French East India Company
1615	French Jesuits open a mission at Fai Fo
1627	Alexandre de Rhodes devises *quoc-ngu* to adapt Vietnamese language to roman script
1720	Vietnamese absorb the remnant of Champa
1772–1802	Tayson rebellion
1787	Bishop Pigneau de Béhaine in France to obtain support for Prince Nguyen Anh
1802–1819	Nguyen Anh becomes Emperor Gia Long, unifies the country; reconstruction and reform
1802–1945; 1945–1955	Nguyen dynasty
1820–1841	Reign of Minh Mang
1825	Minh Mang forbids his subjects' conversion to Catholicism, bans Catholic institutions
1836	Minh Mang closes ports to European shipping
1841–1847	Reign of Thieu Tri
1846	French blockade and bombardment of Tourane (Da Nang)
1847–1883	Reign of Tu Duc
1858	Franco-Spanish expedition to Vietnam to save missionaries
1862	Vietnam cedes three provinces of Cochin China to France
1863, August 11	French protectorate over Cambodia
1866, June	De Lagrée-Garnier Mekong expedition begins
1867	Franco-Thai treaty recognizes French protectorate over Cambodia
1884	Vietnam signs protectorate treaty with France
1885, June 9	Franco-Chinese treaty establishing a French protectorate over Annam and Tongking
1887	France creates the Indochinese Union, consisting of Cochin China, Annam, Tongking, and Cambodia
1890	Ho Chi Minh born
1893	France extends protectorate over Laos
1900	Boxer Uprising
1913	Ho Chi Minh leaves for Europe, remains out of Vietnam for three decades; Phan Boi Chau establishes the Association for the Restoration of Vietnam
1919	Ho Chi Minh, at Versailles peace conference, tries to present a petition demanding self-determination for Vietnam
1920	Ho Chi Minh joins the French Communist Party

1923	Ho Chi Minh goes to Moscow to attend an international conference and remains there
1924	Ho Chi Minh accompanies Borodin to China and stays on to organize a movement against French rule in Vietnam
1925	Ho Chi Minh forms the Association of Vietnamese Revolutionary Youth; Bao Dai becomes emperor of Annam; Phan Boi Chau sentenced to life imprisonment
1927	Vietnam Nationalist Party founded
1930, January	Ho Chi Minh unites Vietnamese Communist groups into one Communist Party, later to be named the Indochina Communist Party
1930, February 10	Yen Bay uprising; VNQDD suppressed; leaders flee to China
1930, May 1	ICP organizes strikes in plantations and factories; French repress ICP-led rebellions; leaders flee to China
1932, September	Prince Bao Dai returns from France
1940, August	Japan occupies Indochina but leaves the pro-Vichy French officials in charge
1941, May	Viet Minh established
1944, December	Vo Nguyen Giap founds the Viet Minh army
1945, March	Japan assumes direct control of French Indochina, interns French officials
1945, August 7	Japan surrenders; the Viet Minh elects a national liberation committee to serve as a provisional government
1945, August 25	Bao Dai abdicates in favor of the provisional government
1945, August 29	Ho Chi Minh proclaims provisional government with Bao Dai as supreme counselor
1945, September	China occupies Vietnam north of the 16th parallel; British troops occupy Vietnam south of the 16th parallel
1945, September 2	Democratic Republic of Vietnam proclaimed
1945, November 11	ICP dissolved and replaced by Association of Marxist Studies
1946, March 6	Franco–Viet Minh agreement; France recognizes Vietnam as a "free state" within the French union; French allowed to return to North Vietnam as China agrees to withdraw its troops
1946, November 23	French bombing of Haiphong
1946, December 19	Viet Minh attack French troops in Hanoi; DRV government moves out of Hanoi
1946–1954	First Indochina War

1949, March 8	Elysée agreement signed by France and Bao Dai creates the "state" of Vietnam as an associated state within the French union
1949, October	People's Republic of China established
1950	Franco-US treaty; United States aids France directly in Indochina
1950, January 14	China and the Soviet Union recognize the Democratic Republic of Vietnam
1950, February 7	Britain and the United States recognize Bao Dai's government
1951, February	Ho Chi Minh founds the Lao Dong (Workers') Party
1953, March 5	Stalin dies
1953, October	France grants Laos "full independence" as a member of the French union
1953, November 9	Prince Sihanouk declares Cambodia independent
1954, May 7	Viet Minh defeat the French at Dien Bien Phu
1954, May 8	Geneva conference on Indochina opens
1954, June 16	Ngo Dinh Diem appointed premier of the "state" of Vietnam
1954, June 17	Pierre Mendès-France becomes premier of France, vows to resign if a settlement on Indochina is not reached by July 20
1954, July 21	Geneva agreements on Indochina signed
1954, September 8	Southeast Asia Treaty Organization founded
1955, February 19	President Eisenhower offers Diem unconditional support
1955, October 23	Diem becomes president of the Republic of Vietnam
1960	Birth of the National Liberation Front
1963, May 8	Buddhist agitation begins
1963, November 1	Diem and Nhu assassinated
1964–1975	Second Indochina War
1964, August 2	United States charges that the USS *Maddox* and *C. Turner Joy* were attacked by North Vietnam
1964, August 5	US Congress passes the Gulf of Tonkin Resolution, giving the president extraordinary powers to act in Southeast Asia
1965, February 7	Viet Cong attack US base at Pleiku
1965, February 24	United States launches Operation Rolling Thunder; sustained bombing of North Vietnam
1967, September 3	Nguyen Van Thieu elected president of South Vietnam, with Nguyen Cao Ky as vice president
1968, January 31	Tet offensive begins
1968, March 28	President Johnson announces decision not to seek re-election
1968, June 8	First withdrawal of US troops announced

1969, July 25	Nixon Doctrine enunciated in Guam
1969, September 3	Ho Chi Minh dies
1970, February 20	Kissinger begins secret talks in Paris with Le Duc Tho
1970, March 18	Sihanouk overthrown; Lon Nol establishes a pro–US government
1970, April 30	US and South Vietnamese forces invade Cambodia in search of Communist sanctuaries
1971	Withdrawal of US forces from Vietnam begins
1971, July	Sino-US rapprochement begins; Kissinger visits Beijing
1971, October 3	Thieu re-elected president of South Vietnam
1972, February	Nixon visits China
1973, January 27	Paris peace accords signed; cease-fire in Vietnam, Laos, and Cambodia
1973, March 29	Withdrawal of US troops from Vietnam completed
1973, September	South Vietnam incorporates the Spratly Islands
1974, January	China occupies the Paracel Islands
1975, April 17	Khmer Rouge overthrows the Lon Nol regime; Cambodia renamed Kampuchea
1975, April 21	Thieu resigns and leaves South Vietnam; neutralist government established under General Duong Van Minh
1975, April 30	Communists take over Saigon and assume power in South Vietnam
1976, January 2	Vietnam formally reunited
1976, April	Elections held for the National Assembly of all Vietnam
1976, July	Establishment of the Socialist Republic of Vietnam
1977, January	Kampuchea attacks Vietnam's border provinces
1978, May	Special minority status of the Vietnamese Chinese abolished
1978, May	Integration of currencies of North and South Vietnam
1978, June 29	Vietnam joins the Moscow-dominated COMECON
1978, July	China terminates all aid to Vietnam, closes its borders with Vietnam
1978, November 3	Soviet-Vietnamese treaty of friendship and cooperation signed
1978, December 25	Vietnam invades Kampuchea
1979, February–March	China invades Vietnam
1980	SRV adopts new constitution; Council of State established
1982	Fifth Congress of the Vietnamese Communist Party
1986, July 10	Le Duan dies; Truong Chinh becomes secretary-general of the VCP
1986, December	Sixth Congress of the VCP; policy of *doi moi* adopted
1987, December 29	Law on foreign investment adopted

1988, March 10	Pham Hung, premier since June 1987, dies
1988, June 22	Du Muoi becomes premier
1988, September 30	Truong Chinh, president since 1981, dies
1989, June 13–14	Geneva conference on Indochinese refugees
1989, July–August	Nineteen-nation conference on Cambodia in Paris
1989, September	Vietnam completes withdrawal of troops from Cambodia
1990, July 18	United States withdraws support of CGDK seat in the UN
1990, August 28	UN approves framework for peace in Cambodia
1991, April	United States opens office in Hanoi for investigation of MIAs, offers Vietnam $1 million in aid to those injured in the war
1991, June	Seventh Congress of the VCP
1991, October 23	Cambodian peace agreements signed in Paris
1991, November	Do Muoi and Vo Van Kiet visit Beijing; relations with China normalized
1992, July	Vietnam granted ASEAN observer status; Vietnam and Laos sign a treaty of amity and cooperation with ASEAN
1992	SRV's constitution revised; Council of State abolished
1993, May 23–28	General elections in Cambodia
1993, September 24	Cambodia adopts new constitution, restores monarchy; Sihanouk becomes king
1994, February	US trade embargo lifted
1995, January	United States and Vietnam agree to open reciprocal liaison offices
1995, July	ASEAN admits Vietnam as a member; United States and Vietnam establish full diplomatic relations
1996, June	Eighth Congress of the VCP; Do Muoi, Le Duc Anh, and Vo Van Kiet re-elected secretary-general, president, and premier for five years
1997, May	First US ambassador to Vietnam, Douglas Peterson, arrives
1997, July	Coup in Cambodia; first prime minister Ranaridh ousted
1997, July	Laos admitted as a member of ASEAN
1997, August	Former emperor Bao Dai dies
1998, December	Hanoi hosts ASEAN conference
2000, April	Pham Van Dong dies
2000, July	Vietnam–US Bilateral Trade Agreement (BTA) signed
2000, November	President Clinton visits Vietnam
2001, February	President Putin visits Vietnam; signs agreement
2004, January	Nguyen Cao Ky, former premier, visits Vietnam.

Notes

Chapter One

1. Georges Coedès, *The Making of South East Asia* (Berkeley: University of California Press, 1966), p. 79.

2. David Marr, *Vietnamese Anti-Colonialism, 1885–1925* (Berkeley: University of California Press, 1971), p. 9.

3. Lê Thanh Khoi, *Le Viet-Nam, histoire et civilisation* (Paris: Editions de Minuit, 1955), p. 86, refutes the theory that the Viets are the only ancestors of the Vietnamese.

4. Quoted in Thomas Hodgkin, *Vietnam: The Revolutionary Path* (London: Macmillan, 1981), p. 21.

5. King C. Chen, *Vietnam and China, 1938–1954* (Princeton: Princeton University Press, 1969), p. 12.

6. Hodgkin, *Vietnam*, p. 29.

7. Jean Chesneaux, *Contribution à l'histoire de la nation vietnamienne* (Paris: Editions Sociales, 1962), pp. 26–27.

8. Joseph Buttinger, *Vietnam: A Political History* (New York: Praeger, 1968), p. 29.

Chapter Two

1. Quoted in Ralph Smith, *Viet-Nam and the West* (London: Heinemann, 1968), p. 9.

Chapter Three

1. Charles Maybon, *Histoire moderne du pays d'Annam, 1592–1820* (Paris: Plon-Nourrit, 1919).

2. Translations of this edict vary. One version reads, "The wicked religion of the Western people casts its malicious spell on the minds of the people; the Catholic missionaries wrong the people's mind, violate the country's good customs and result in a great harm for the nation." See Marvin E. Gettleman, ed., *Vietnam: History, Documents and Opinions on a Major World Crisis* (Greenwich, CT: Fawcett, 1965), p. 28; and Georges Taboulet, *La Geste française en Indochine*, vol. 1 (Paris: Adrien-Maisonneuve, 1956), pp. 328–329.

3. John F. Cady, *The Roots of French Imperialism in Eastern Asia* (Ithaca, NY: Cornell University Press, 1954), p. 29.

4. Joseph Buttinger, *The Smaller Dragon: A Political History of Vietnam* (New York: Praeger, 1958), p. 133.

5. *Catholic Digest,* February 1962, p. 17.

6. Henri Blet, *France d'Outre-mer,* vol. 2 (Paris: Arthaud, 1950), p. 281.

7. Bernard Fall, *The Two Viet-Nams: A Political and Military Analysis,* 3d ed. (New York: Praeger, 1967), p. 16.

8. Lê Thanh Khoi, *Le Viet-Nam, histoire et civilisation* (Paris: Editions de Minuit, 1955), p. 365.

9. Francis Garnier, *Voyage d'exploration en Indochine* (Paris: Librairie Hachette, 1885), 2 vols.

10. H. I. Priestley, *France Overseas: A Study of Modern Imperialism* (New York: Appleton-Century, 1938), p. 217.

11. Ella S. Laffey, "French Adventurers and Chinese Bandits in Tonkin: The Garnier Affair in Its Local Context," *Journal of Southeast Asian Studies* 6 (March 1975), p. 41.

12. Ibid., p. 39.

13. Taboulet, *La Geste française,* vol. 2, p. 709.

14. M. Dutreb, *L'Amiral Dupré et la conquête du Tonkin* (Paris: E. Leroux, 1924), pp. 94–96.

15. Lois E. Bailey, *Jules Ferry and French Indo-China* (Madison: University of Wisconsin Press, 1946), p. 24.

16. Thomas F. Power Jr., *Jules Ferry and the Renaissance of French Imperialism* (New York: Octagon Books, 1966), p. 191.

Chapter Four

1. David Marr, *Vietnamese Anti-Colonialism, 1885–1925* (Berkeley: University of California Press, 1971), p. 4.

2. Truong Buu Lam, *Patterns of Vietnamese Response to Foreign Intervention, 1858–1900* (New Haven: Yale University Press, 1967), p. 3.

3. For a detailed analysis along these lines, see Marr, *Vietnamese Anti-Colonialism,* pp. 95–97.

4. Hoang Van Chi, *From Colonialism to Communism* (New York: Praeger, 1964), p. 18; P. J. Honey, ed., *North Vietnam Today: Profile of a Communist Satellite* (New York: Praeger, 1962), p. 4.

5. King Chen has compiled a list of Ho's nineteen aliases, some repeated at different times in his life. King C. Chen, *Vietnam and China, 1938–1954* (Princeton: Princeton University Press, 1969), pp. 37 and 40, footnotes.

6. Pham Van Dong and the Committee for the Study of the History of the Vietnamese Workers' Party, *President Ho Chi Minh* (Hanoi: Foreign Languages Publishing House, 1960), pp. 41–42.

7. M. E. Gettleman, ed., *Vietnam* (New York: Penguin, 1965), p. 37.

8. Ibid., p. 39.

9. Vinh Sinh and Nicholas Wickenden, trans., *Overturned Chariot, The Auto-biography of Phan Boi Chau* (Honolulu: University of Hawaii Press, 1999), pp. 260–262.

10. Ibid., p. 262.

11. Quoted from a Viet Minh pamphlet by Jean Lacouture, *Ho Chi Minh: A Political Biography* (New York: Vintage Books, 1968), p. 88.

12. Quoted in Ellen Hammer, *The Struggle for Indochina* (Stanford: Stanford University Press, 1954), p. 102.

13. At this point, the Indochina Communist Party is believed to have had 5,000 members. The number jumped to 210,000 in 1946 and to 365,000 in the following year. According to Joseph Buttinger, these 365,000 became the "founding members" of the Lao Dong (Workers' Party), the name under which the Vietnamese Communist Party was officially reformed on March 3, 1951. *Vietnam: A Political History* (New York: Praeger, 1968), p. 336.

14. Quoted in David Halberstam, *Ho* (New York: Vintage Books, 1971), pp. 84–85.

15. Milton E. Osborne, *Region of Revolt: Focus on Southeast Asia* (Rushcutters Bay, Australia: Pergamon Press, 1970), p. 100.

16. *Le Monde*, 24 August 1949.

17. New China News Agency, Daily News Release, 23 November 1949.

18. US Department of State, *Department of State Bulletin* 22 (13 February 1950), p. 244.

19. The Geneva agreements were signed in the early hours of July 21. The French premier's plane engines were buzzing at that time, ready to take him from Geneva to Paris to submit his resignation in case the talks failed.

Chapter Five

1. For a detailed study of the commission's work, see D. R. SarDesai, *Indian Foreign Policy in Cambodia, Laos and Vietnam, 1947–1964* (Berkeley: University of California Press, 1968).

2. Statement of the US representative at Geneva, Bedell Smith, as given in United Kingdom, Foreign Office, *Further Documents Relating to the Discussions of Indochina at the Geneva Conference*, Cmd. 9239 (London: Her Majesty's Stationery Office, 1954), pp. 6–7.

3. The five principles were mutual respect for each other's territorial integrity and sovereignty, nonaggression, noninterference in each other's internal affairs, equality and mutual benefit, and peaceful coexistence. The Sino-Indian agreement of 1954 began a friendship between the two Asian countries that lasted until 1962. The principles outlined in the accords were later included in numerous agreements between communist and nonaligned countries.

4. Victor Bator, *Vietnam: A Diplomatic Tragedy* (New York: Oceana, 1965), p. 172.

5. US Senate, Committee on Foreign Relations, *Report on Indochina by Senator Mike Mansfield, October 15, 1954*, 82d Cong., 2d sess., p. 14.

6. *New York Times*, 18 November 1954. See also Robert Sheer, *How the United States Got Involved in Vietnam* (Santa Barbara, CA: Center for the Study of Democratic Institutions, 1965), quoted in Marvin E. Gettleman, ed., *Vietnam: History, Documents and Opinions on a Major World Crisis* (Greenwich, CT: Fawcett, 1965), p. 241.

7. President Eisenhower to Bao Dai, 19 February 1955, in *Department of State Bulletin* 32 (14 March 1955), p. 423.

8. Graham Greene, "Last Act in Indo-China," *New Republic* 132, 9 May 1955, p. 10.

9. Republic of Vietnam, Ministry of Information, *The Problem of Reunification of Viet-Nam* (Saigon: 1958), p. 29.

10. Dwight D. Eisenhower, *Mandate for Change, 1953–56* (New York: Signet Books, 1965).

11. Douglas Pike, *Viet Cong* (Cambridge: MIT Press, 1966), p. 76.

12. George M. Kahin and John W. Lewis, *The United States in Vietnam* (New York: Dial Press, 1967), p. 119.

13. Frances Fitzgerald, *Fire in the Lake* (New York: Vintage, 1972), p. 18.

14. Ibid.

15. Stanley Karnow, *Vietnam, A History* (New York: Penguin, 1983), p. 261.

16. Paul Mus, "The Buddhist Background to the Crisis in Vietnamese Politics," New Haven, Southeast Asia Studies Program, Yale University. Mimeo. Quoted in Fitzgerald, *Fire in the Lake*, pp. 177–178.

17. Ibid., p. 179.

18. Ibid., p. 180.

19. US Department of State, *A Threat to the Peace* (Washington, DC: Government Printing Office, 1961), p. iii.

20. *Pentagon Papers*, vol. 2 (New York: Bantam Books, 1971), p. 75.

21. NSC's memo of 11 May 1961, quoted in Maxwell D. Taylor, *Swords and Ploughshares* (New York: Norton, 1972), p. 274.

22. Ibid., pp. 225–226.

23. *Pentagon Papers*, pp. 446–447.

24. Cable from Maxwell Taylor to Kennedy from Baguio, Philippines, 1 November 1961, in *Pentagon Papers*, p. 147.

25. *Pentagon Papers*, p. 181.

26. Robert Shaplen, *The Lost Revolution* (New York: Harper and Row, 1965), p. 210.

27. Fitzgerald, *Fire in the Lake*, p. 183.

28. *New York Times*, 15 November 1963, cited in ibid.

Chapter Six

1. JCS Memorandum to the secretary of defense, 22 January 1964, *Pentagon Papers*, vol. 3, pp. 496–499.

2. Robert S. McNamara, *In Retrospect: The Tragedy and Lessons of Vietnam* (New York: Random House, 1995), p. 109.

3. McNamara's interview with Peter Hackes of NBC-TV, *Sunday Show*, 29 March 1964.

4. McNamara, *In Retrospect*, p. 114.

5. Of the two well-known international limits for territorial waters, the French, during colonial rule, adopted a three-mile limit, while China observed a twelve-mile limit. In mid–1964, there was no exact knowledge of what North Vietnam observed as its limit.

6. John Galloway, *The Gulf of Tonkin Resolution* (Cranbury, NJ: Associated University Press, 1970), pp. 36–37.

7. Stanley Karnow, *Vietnam, A History* (New York: Penguin, 1984), p. 373.

8. George W. Ball, *The Past Has Another Pattern: Memoirs* (New York: Norton, 1982), pp. 399–409.

9. Karnow, *Vietnam*, p. 435.

10. Ibid., p. 436.

11. *New York Times*, 1 February 1966.

12. Karnow, *Vietnam*, p. 506.

13. Ibid., p. 505.

14. The United States was helped by token forces from its allies: New Zealand (500), Australia (7,000), the Philippines (no combat troops, only a hospital corps and an engineer battalion), South Korea (10,000), and Thailand (2,500).

15. McNamara, *In Retrospect*, p. 110.

16. Ibid.

17. Clark Clifford, "A Vietnam Reappraisal," *Foreign Affairs* 47 (July 1969), p. 612.

18. Dean Rusk's statement in Ted Gittinger, ed., *The Johnson Years: A Vietnam Roundtable* (Austin: University of Texas, 1993), pp. 183–186.

19. Raymond L. Garthoff, *Détente and Confrontation: American-Soviet Relations from Nixon to Reagan* (Washington, DC: Brookings Institute, 1985), pp. 69–70.

20. Henry Kissinger, *The White House Years* (Boston: Little, Brown, 1979), p. 216.

21. John G. Stoessinger, *Henry Kissinger: The Anguish of Power* (New York: Norton, 1976), pp. 51–52.

22. For an analysis of the US policy of the time, see Stephen P. Gilbert, "Implications of the Nixon Doctrine for Military Aid Policy," *Orbis* 16, 3 (Fall 1972), pp. 660–681. See also Richard Nixon, *U.S. Foreign Policy for the 1970's: A New Strategy for Peace—A Report to the Congress*, 18 February 1970 (Washington, DC: Government Printing Office, 1970), pp. 55–56.

23. Whittle Johnston, "Containment and Vietnam," in John N. Moore, ed., *The Vietnam Debate, A Fresh Look at the Argumentation* (Lanham, MD: University Press of America, 1990), p. 234.

24. Norodom Sihanouk, "Cambodia Neutral: The Dictate of Necessity," *Foreign Affairs* 36 (July 1958), pp. 582–586.

25. For short biographies of the eight most prominent members of the Khmer Rouge high command, see John Barron and Anthony Paul, *Murder of a Gentle Land: The Untold Story of Communist Genocide in Cambodia* (New York: Reader's Digest Press, 1977), pp. 43–45.

26. Pol Pot's speech, 28 September 1977, *BBC Summary of World Broadcasts*, 3 October 1977.

27. Norodom Sihanouk, *My War with the CIA* (Harmondsworth, England: Penguin, 1973).

28. Nguyen Cao Ky, *How We Lost the Vietnam War* (New York: Stein and Day, 1984), p. 108.

Chapter Seven

1. For detailed statistical information on postwar South Vietnam, see Huynh Kim Khanh, "Restructuring the Economy of South Vietnam," *Southeast Asian Affairs* (1976), pp. 467–484.

2. Huynh Kim Khanh, "Year One of Post-Colonial Vietnam," *Southeast Asian Affairs* (1977), p. 290.

3. Ibid., p. 291.

4. The conversion rate was 1.2 dongs to the dollar in 1980.

5. *Nhan Dan*, 1 November 1983.

6. *Saigon Newsreader*, September 1986, p. 7.

7. *The Economist* (London), 6 May 2004.

8. Based on ASEAN Secretariat and World Bank, *Annual Report 2002–2003*.

9. Ibid.

10. Larry W. Croce, *Vietnamese Economic Reform: How Important to U.S.–Vietnam Trade Relations* (Washington, DC: Worldfact Book, 2000), p. 8.

11. Quoted in *Far Eastern Economic Review*, 11 July 1996, p. 14.

12. Quoted in *Time Asia*, 21 January 2002.

Chapter Eight

1. William Shawcross, "The Third Indochina War," *New York Review of Books*, 6 April 1978, p. 16. Shawcross was a correspondent in Vietnam and the author of the well-known book *Sideshow*.

2. Nayan Chanda, *Brother Enemy: The War After the War—A History of Indochina Since the Fall of Saigon* (San Diego: Harcourt Brace Jovanovich, 1986), pp. 72–73.

3. For details, see Ben Kiernan, *How Pol Pot Came to Power: A History of Communism in Kampuchea, 1930–1975* (London: Verso, 1985).

4. Speech by Deng Xiaoping, vice premier of the People's Republic of China, as reported by the New China News Agency, 30 June 1975.

5. *Straits Times* (Singapore), 31 July 1975.

6. William S. Turley, "The Khmer War: Cambodia After Paris," *Survival* 32, 5 (September–October 1990), pp. 437–451.

Chapter Nine

1. Mike Yeong, "New Thinking in Vietnamese Foreign Policy," *Contemporary Southeast Asia* 14, 3 (December 1992), pp. 257–258.

2. Chang Pao-min, *The Sino-Vietnamese Territorial Dispute* (New York: Praeger, 1986), p. 28.

3. Charles McGregor, *The Sino-Vietnamese Relationship and the Soviet Union* (London: International Institute for Strategic Studies, 1988), pp. 23–24.

4. *Bangkok Post*, 1 April 1993.

5. Yeong, "New Thinking," p. 265.

6. Denny Roy, "Consequences of China's Economic Growth for Asia-Pacific Security," *Security Dialogue* 24, 2 (1993), pp. 181–191.

7. Ibid.

Chapter Ten

1. *Department of State Bulletin*, 15 December 1975, p. 847.

2. Ibid.

3. *New York Times*, 24 March 1977.

4. Zbigniew Brzezinski, *Power and Principle: Memoirs of the National Security Advisor, 1977–1981* (New York: Farrar, Straus and Giroux, 1983), pp. 227–229.

5. Gareth Porter, "Vietnamese Policy and the Indochina Crisis," in *The Third Indochina Conflict*, ed. David W. P. Elliott (Boulder, Colo.: Westview Press, 1981), p. 108.

6. Christopher Goscha, "Letter from Reagan: U.S. Encourages Private Aid to Vietnam and Presses MIA Issue," *Far Eastern Economic Review*, 21 January 1988, pp. 29–30.

7. Full text of President Clinton's announcement in the *New York Times*, 12 July 1995; Senator McCain's statement in *Keesing's Contemporary Archives*, July 1995, p. 40,643.

8. Stanley O. Roth, Assistant Secretary for East Asian and Pacific Affairs, statement before the Senate Foreign Relations Committee, 10 March 1998.

9. Senator John McCain's testimony before the International Trade Subcommittee hearing in support of the Jackson-Vanik Waiver, 7 July 1998, at www.mccain.senate.gov/

10. Robert B. Zoellick, in DPC.Senate.gov: S.J. Res 16, a joint resolution approving the extension of nondiscriminatory treatment to the products of the Socialist Republic of Vietnam.

11. Tran Dinh Tranh Lam, "U.S. 'Catfish War' Defeat Stings Vietnam," *Asian Times*, 31 July 2003.

12. James M. Freeman, *Hearts of Sorrow: Vietnamese American Lives* (Palo Alto: Stanford University Press, 1989), p. 11.

13. Refugee figures in this section are based on US Department of Health and Human Services, Office of Refugee Resettlement, *Refugee Resettlement Program, Report to the Congress* (Washington, DC: US Department of Health and Human Services, 1992), tables A–15 to A–19.

14. US Department of Health and Human Services, Social Security Administration, *Survey of the Social, Psychological and Economic Adaptation of Vietnamese Refugees in the U.S., 1975–1979* (Washington, DC: US Department of Health and Human Services, 1982), p. 7.

15. *Newsweek*, 14 March 1988, p. 34.

16. Zoe Lofgren introducing the bill on 21 October 2003, at: www.house.gov/apps/list/press/Ca16_lofgren/peterrobert_031022_Amerasian.html.

17. Paul J. Rutledge, *The Vietnamese Experience in America* (Bloomington: Indiana University Press, 1992), p. 101.

18. US Immigration Commission, *Asian American Encyclopaedia*, vol. 6 (New York: Marshall Cavendish, 1995), p. 1626.

19. Jim Cooper, "Refugees Made It a Remarkable 15 Years," *Los Angeles Times*, 3 May 1990, p. B3, Orange County edition.

20. Ronald Takaki, *Strangers from a Different Shore: A History of Asian-Americans* (New York: Penguin Books, 1989); Nazli Kibria, *Family Tightrope: The Changing Lives of Vietnamese Americans* (Princeton: Princeton University Press, 1993).

21. Rutledge, *Vietnamese Experience*, p. 45.

22. Nathan Caplan, Marcella H. Choy, and John K. Whitmore, "Indochinese Refugee Families and Academic Achievement," *Scientific American*, February 1992, p. 39.

Bibliography

Vietnam and Southeast Asia—General

Beresford, Melanie. *Vietnam: Politics, Economics, and Society.* London: Pinter, 1988.

Buttinger, Joseph. *Vietnam: A Political History.* New York: Praeger, 1968.

———. *The Smaller Dragon: A Political History of Vietnam.* New York: Praeger, 1958.

Elliott, Duong Van Mai. *The Sacred Willow: Four Generations in the Life of a Vietnamese Family.* New York: Oxford University Press, 1999.

Hickey, Gerald C. *Village in Vietnam.* New Haven: Yale University Press, 1964.

Hodgkin, Thomas. *Vietnam: The Revolutionary Path.* London: Macmillan, 1981.

Karnow, Stanley. *Vietnam: A History.* New York: Viking, 1983.

Lê Thanh Khoi. *Le Viet-Nam, histoire et civilisation.* Paris: Editions de Minuit, 1955.

Pelley, Patricia M. *Postcolonial Vietnam: New Histories of the National Past.* Durham, NC: Duke University Press, 2002.

SarDesai, D. R. *Southeast Asia, Past and Present.* 5th ed. Boulder, CO: Westview Press and London: Macmillan, 2003

Smith, Ralph. *Viet-Nam and the West.* London: Heinemann, 1968.

Reference Works

Anderson, David L., ed. *The Columbia Guide to the Vietnam War.* New York: Columbia University Press, 2002.

Duiker, William J. *Historical Dictionary of Vietnam.* Metuchen, NJ: Scarecrow Press, 1989; 2d ed., Lanham, Md.: Scarecrow Press, 1999.

Hillstrom, Kevin, and Laurie Collier. *The Vietnam Experience: A Concise Encyclopedia of American Songs and Films.* Westport, CT: Greenwood Press, 1998.

Kutler, Stanley I., ed. *Encyclopedia of the Vietnam War.* New York: Macmillan, 1996.

Moise, Edwin E. *Historical Dictionary of the Vietnam War.* Lanham, MD: Scarecrow Press, 2001.

Summers, Harry G., Jr. *Historical Atlas of the Vietnam War.* Boston: Houghton Mifflin, 1995.

Tucker, Spencer C., ed. *Encyclopedia of the Vietnam War: A Political, Social, and Military History.* 3 vols. Santa Barbara, CA: ABC-CLIO, 1998; New York: Oxford University Press, 2000.

Young, Marilyn B., and Robert Buzzanco, eds. *A Companion to the Vietnam War.* Malden, MD: Blackwell, 2002.

Prehistoric and Traditional Vietnam

Adams, J., and N. Hancock. "Land and Economy in Traditional Vietnam." *Journal of Southeast Asian History* 1, 2 (1970).

Benedict, Paul. "Analysis of Annamese Kingship Terms." *Southwestern Journal of Anthropology* 3 (1947), pp. 371–391.

Coedès, Georges. *The Indianized States of Southeast Asia.* Honolulu: East-West Center Press, 1968.

———. *The Making of South East Asia.* Berkeley: University of California Press, 1966.

Elman, Benjamin A., John B. Duncan, and Herman Ooms, eds. *Rethinking Confucianism: Past and Present in China, Japan, Korea and Vietnam.* Los Angeles: UCLA Asian Pacific Monograph Series, 2002.

Janse, J. M. *Archaeological Research in Indo-China: The Ancient Dwelling Site of Dong-S'on.* Cambridge: Harvard University Press, 1958.

Le May, Reginald. *The Culture of South-East Asia.* London: Allen and Unwin, 1954.

Li, Tana. *Nguyen Cochinchina: Southern Vietnam in the Seventeenth and Eighteenth Centuries.* Ithaca, NY: Southeast Asia Program, 1998.

———. *Southern Vietnam Under the Nguyen: Documents in the Economic History.* Singapore: Institute of Southeast Asian Studies, 1993.

Nguyen Ngoc Huy. *The Le Code: Law in Traditional Vietnam.* Athens: Ohio University Press, 1987.

Nguyen The Anh. "Buddhism and Vietnamese Society Throughout History." *Southeast Asia Research* (London) 1, 1 (March 1993), pp. 98–114.

O'Harrow, S. "From Co-loa to the Trung Sisters' Revolt: Viet-Nam as the Chinese Found It." *Asian Perspectives* 22, 2 (1979), pp. 140–164.

Pham Minh Huyen. "Various Phases of the Development of Primitive Metallurgy in Viet Nam." In D. T. Bayard, ed., *Southeast Asian Archaeology at the XV Pacific Science Congress.* Dunedin, New Zealand: Otago University, 1984.

Quaritch-Wales, H. G. *The Making of Greater India.* 2d ed. London: Bernard Quaritch, 1961.

Ta Van Tai. "The Status of Women in Traditional Vietnam: A Comparison of the Code of Le Dynasty (1428–1788) with the Chinese Code." *Journal of Asian History* 15 (1981), pp. 7–41.

Taylor, Kenneth W. "The Literati Revival in Seventeenth Century Vietnam." *Journal of Southeast Asian Studies* 18 (March 1987), pp. 1–23.

———. *The Birth of Viet Nam.* Berkeley: University of California Press, 1983.

Taylor, Kenneth W., and John K. Whitmore, eds. *Essays into Vietnamese Pasts.* Ithaca, NY: Cornell University Southeast Asia Program, 1995.

Vella, Walter Francis, ed. *Aspects of Vietnamese History.* Honolulu: University of Hawaii Press, 1973.

Whitmore, John K. *Vietnam, Ho Quy Ly and the Ming (1371–1421).* New Haven: Center for International and Area Studies, Yale University, 1985.

———. "Social Organization and Confucian Thought in Vietnam." *Journal of Southeast Asian Studies* 15 (September 1984), pp. 298–308.

Woodside, Alexander. "Medieval Vietnam and Cambodia: A Comparative Comment." *Journal of Southeast Asian Studies* 15 (September 1984), pp. 315–319.

———. *Vietnam and the Chinese Model.* Cambridge: Harvard University Press, 1970.

Young, Stephen B. "The Law of Property and Elite Prerogatives During Vietnam's Le Dynasty, 1428–1788." *Journal of Asian History* 10 (1976), pp. 1–48.

Yu, Insun. *Law and Society in Seventeenth and Eighteenth Century Vietnam.* Seoul: Korea University, 1990.

The French Period

Bailey, Lois E. *Jules Ferry and French Indo-China.* Madison: University of Wisconsin Press, 1946.

Betts, R. F. *Assimilation and Association in French Colonial Theory, 1890–1914.* New York: Columbia University Press, 1961.

Buttinger, Joseph. *A Dragon Embattled: A History of Colonial and Post-Colonial Vietnam.* 2 vols. New York: Praeger, 1967.

Cady, John F. *The Roots of French Imperialism in Eastern Asia.* Ithaca, NY: Cornell University Press, 1954.

DeCaro, Peter Anthony. *Rhetoric of Revolt: Ho Chi Minh's Discourse for Revolution.* Westport, CT: Praeger, 2003.

Ennis, Thomas E. *French Policy and Development in Indochina.* Chicago: University of Chicago Press, 1936.

Garnier, Francis. *Voyage d'exploration en Indochine.* 2 vols. Paris: Librairie Hachette, 1885.

Honey, P. J. "French Historiography and the Evolution of Colonial Vietnam." In D. G. E. Hall, ed., *Historians of Southeast Asia.* London: Oxford University Press, 1961.

Marsot, Alain G. *The Chinese Community in Vietnam Under the French.* San Francisco: Edwin Mellon Press, 1993.

McLeod, Mark W. *The Treaty of Saigon and the Vietnamese Response to French Intervention, 1862–1874.* New York: Praeger, 1991.

Murray, Martin J. *The Development of Capitalism in Colonial Indochina, 1870–1940.* Berkeley: University of California Press, 1980.

Ngo Vinh Long. *Before the Revolution: The Vietnamese Peasants Under the French.* Cambridge: Harvard University Press, 1973.

Norman, C. B. *Tonkin, or France in the Far East.* London: Chapman and Hall, 1884.

Osborne, Milton E. *The French Presence in Cochin-China and Cambodia: Rule and Response, 1859–1905.* Ithaca, NY: Cornell University Press, 1969.

Pham Cao Duong. *Vietnamese Peasants Under French Domination, 1861–1945.* Berkeley: University of California Press, 1989.

Pham, David Lan. *Two Hamlets in Nam Bo: Memoirs of Life in Vietnam Through Japanese Occupation, the French and American Wars, and Communist Rule, 1940–1986.* Jefferson, NC: McFarland, 2000.

Phan, Peter C. *Mission and Catechesis: Alexandre de Rhodes and the Inculturation in Seventeenth Century Vietnam.* Maryknoll, NY: Orbis Books, 1998.

Power, Thomas F., Jr. *Jules Ferry and the Renaissance of French Imperialism.* New York: Octagon Books, 1966.

Priestley, H. I. *France Overseas: A Study of Modern Imperialism.* New York: Appleton-Century, 1938.

Robequain, Charles. *The Economic Development of French Indo-China.* London: Oxford University Press, 1954.

Roberts, Stephen H. *The History of French Colonial Policy, 1870–1925.* 2 vols. London: P. S. King, 1929.

Sinh, Vinh, and Nicholas Wickenden, trans. *Overturned Chariot: The Autobiography of Phan Boi Chau.* Honolulu: University of Hawaii Press, 1999.

Smith, Ralph. *Viet-Nam and the West.* London: Heinemann, 1968.

Taboulet, Georges. *La Geste française en Indochine.* 2 vols. Paris: Adrien-Maisonneuve, 1955–1956.

Thompson, Virginia. *French Indochina.* New York: Macmillan, 1937.

Truong Buu Lam. *Patterns of Vietnamese Response to Foreign Intervention, 1858–1900.* New Haven: Yale University Press, 1967.

Tuck, Patrick J. N., ed. *French Catholic Missionaries and the Politics of Imperialism in Vietnam, 1857–1914.* Liverpool: Liverpool University Press, 1987.

Nationalist and Communist Movements to Dien Bien Phu and Geneva

Artaud, Denise, and Lawrence Kaplan, eds. *Dienbienphu: The Atlantic Alliance and the Defense of Southeast Asia.* Wilmington, DE: Scholarly Resources, 1989.

Billings-Yun, Melanie. *Decision Against War: Eisenhower and Dien Bien Phu, 1954.* New York: Columbia University Press, 1988.

Cable, James. *The Geneva Conference of 1954 on Indochina.* New York: St. Martin's Press, 1986.

Chen, King C. *Vietnam and China, 1938–1954.* Princeton: Princeton University Press, 1969.

Chesneaux, Jean. *Contribution à l'histoire de la nation vietnamienne.* Paris: Editions Sociales, 1962.

Devillers, Philippe, and Jean Lacouture. *End of a War: Indochina, 1954.* New York: Praeger, 1969.

Duiker, William J. *The Rise of Nationalism in Vietnam, 1900–1941.* Ithaca: Cornell University Press, 1976.

———. *The Comintern and Vietnamese Communism.* Athens: Ohio University Southeast Asia Program, 1975.

———. *Ho Chi Minh.* New York: Hyperion, 2000.

Fall, Bernard B. *Hell in a Very Small Place: The Siege of Dien Bien Phu.* Philadelphia: Lippincott, 1967.

———, ed. *Ho Chi Minh on Revolution: Selected Writings, 1920–1966.* New York: Praeger, 1967.

Fischer, Ruth. "Ho Chi Minh: Disciplined Communist." *Foreign Affairs* 33 (October 1954), pp. 86–97.

Gardner, Lloyd C. *Approaching Vietnam: From World War II Through Dienbienphu, 1941–1954.* New York: Norton, 1988.

Halberstam, David. *Ho.* New York: Vintage Books, 1971.

Hammer, Ellen J. *The Struggle for Indochina.* Stanford: Stanford University Press, 1956.

Hoang Van Chi. *From Colonialism to Communism.* New York: Praeger, 1964.

Ho Chi Minh. *Prison Diary.* Trans. Aileen Palmer. Hanoi: Foreign Languages Publishing House, 1961.

Huynh Kim Khanh. *Vietnamese Communism, 1925–1945.* Ithaca: Cornell University Press, 1986.

Irving, Ronald E. *The First Indochina War: French and American Policy, 1945–1954.* London: Croom Helm, 1975.

Lacouture, Jean. *Ho Chi Minh: A Political Biography.* New York: Vintage Books, 1968.

Lancaster, Donald. *The Emancipation of French Indochina.* London: Oxford University Press, 1961.

Marr, David G. *Vietnam 1945: The Quest for Power.* Berkeley: University of California Press, 1995.

———. *Vietnamese Tradition on Trial, 1920–1945.* Berkeley: University of California Press, 1981.

———. *Vietnamese Anti-Colonialism, 1885–1925.* Berkeley: University of California Press, 1971.

McAlister, John T., Jr. *Vietnam: The Origins of Revolution.* New York: Knopf, 1969.

McAlister, John T., Jr., and Paul Mus. *The Vietnamese and Their Revolution.* New York: Harper and Row, 1970.

Mus, Paul. *Viet-Nam, sociologie d'une guerre.* Paris: Editions du Seuil, 1952.

———. "The Role of the Village in Vietnamese Politics." *Pacific Affairs* 23 (September 1949), pp. 265–272.

O'Ballance, Edgar. *The Indo-China War, 1945–54: A Study in Guerrilla Warfare.* London: Faber and Faber, 1964.

Patti, Archimedes. *Why Vietnam?* Berkeley: University of California Press, 1980.

Pike, Douglas. *History of Vietnamese Communism, 1925–1976.* Palo Alto: Hoover Institution Press, 1978.

Post, Ken. *Revolution and Socialism and Nationalism in Vietnam.* 5 vols. Aldershot, England: Dartmouth, 1989–1994.

Quinn-Judge, Sophie. *Ho Chi Minh: The Missing Years, 1919–1941.* Berkeley: University of California Press, 2002.

Rotter, Andrew J. *The Path to Vietnam: Origins of American Commitment to Southeast Asia.* Ithaca: Cornell University Press, 1987.

Roy, Jules. *The Battle of Dien Bien Phu.* Trans. Robert Baldick. New York: Harper and Row, 1965.

Sacks, Milton. "Marxism in Vietnam." In Frank Trager, ed., *Marxism in Southeast Asia.* Stanford: Stanford University Press, 1959.

———. *Political Alignments of Vietnamese Nationalists.* Washington, DC: US Department of State, 1949.

Sainteny, Jean. *Histoire d'une paix manquée: Indochine.* Paris: A. Dumont, 1953.

Tai Hue-Tam. *Radicalism and the Origins of the Vietnamese Revolution.* Cambridge: Harvard University Press, 1992.

Tanham, George K. *Communist Revolutionary Warfare: The Vietminh in Indo-China.* New York: Praeger, 1961.

Truong Buu Lam. *Patterns of Vietnamese Response to Foreign Intervention, 1858–1900.* New Haven: Yale University Press, 1967.

Truong Chinh. *The August Revolution.* Hanoi: Foreign Languages Publishing House, 1958.

Truong Chinh and Vo Nguyen Giap. *The Peasant Question, 1937–1938.* Trans. Christine Peltzer White. Ithaca: Cornell University Center for Southeast Asian Studies, 1974.

Vo Nguyen Giap. *People's War, People's Army.* New York: Praeger, 1962.

Warbay, William. *Ho Chi Minh and the Struggle for a Free Vietnam.* London: Merlin Press, 1972.

Young, Marilyn. *The Vietnam Wars, 1945–1990.* New York: HarperCollins, 1991.

Vietnam from the Geneva Conference to 1975

Anderson, David L. *Facing My Lai: Moving Beyond the Massacre.* Lawrence: University Press of Kansas, 1998.

Anderson, Desaix. *An American in Hanoi: America's Reconciliation with Vietnam.* White Plains, NY: EastBridge, 2002.

Ang, Cheng Guan. *The Vietnam War from the Other Side: The Vietnamese Communists' Perspective.* London: Routledge Curzon, 2002.

Ashmore, Harry S., and William C. Baggs. *Mission to Hanoi.* New York: G. P. Putnam, 1968.

Asselin, Pierre. *A Bitter Peace: Washington, Hanoi, and the Making of the Paris Agreement.* Chapel Hill: University of North Carolina Press, 2002.

Ball, Moya Ann. *Vietnam-on-the-Potomac.* New York: Praeger, 1992.

Bator, Victor. *Vietnam: A Diplomatic Tragedy.* New York: Oceana, 1965.

Berman, Larry. *Lyndon Johnson's War.* New York: Norton, 1989.

———. *Planning a Tragedy: The Americanization of the War in Vietnam.* New York: Norton, 1982.

Berman, William C. *William Fulbright and the Vietnam War: The Dissent of a Political Realist.* Kent, OH: Kent State University Press, 1988.

Bibby, Michael, ed. *The Vietnam War and Postmodernity.* Amherst, MA: University of Massachusetts Press, 2000.

———. *Hearts and Minds: Bodies, Poetry and Resistance in the Vietnam Era.* New Brunswick, NJ: Rutgers University Press, 1996.

Bodard, Lucien. *The Quicksand War: Prelude to Vietnam.* Boston: Little, Brown, 1967.

Brown, T. Louise. *War and Aftermath in Vietnam.* New York: Routledge, 1991.

Brune, Lester H. *America and the Indochina Wars, 1945–1990.* Claremont, CA: Regina Books, 1992.

Bui, Diem. *In the Jaws of History.* Paris: Editions Sudasie, 2000.

Bui, Tin. *From Enemy to Friend: A North Vietnamese Perspective on the War.* Trans. Nguyen Ngoc Bich. Annapolis, MD: Naval Institute Press, 2002.

Burrows, Larry. *Vietnam.* New York: Alfred A. Knopf, 2002.

Butler, David. *The Fall of Saigon: Scenes from the Sudden End of a Long War.* New York: Simon and Schuster, 1985.

Buzzanco, Robert. *Masters of War: Military Dissent and Politics in the Vietnam Era.* Cambridge: Harvard University Press, 1996.

Catton, Philip E. *Diem's Final Failure: Prelude to America's War in Vietnam.* Lawrence: Kansas University Press, 2002.

Clarke, Jeffrey J. *Advice and Support: The Final Years, 1965–1973.* Washington, DC: Center for Military History, 1988.

Clifford, Clark. "A Vietnam Reappraisal." *Foreign Affairs* 47 (July 1969), pp. 601–622.

Clymer, Kenton J., ed. *The Vietnam War: Its History, Literature and Music.* El Paso: Texas Western Press, 1998.

Cooper, Chester L. *The Lost Crusade: America in Vietnam.* New York: Dodd Mead, 1970.

Dacy, Douglas C. *Foreign Aid, War, and Economic Development: South Vietnam, 1955–1975.* Cambridge: Cambridge University Press, 1986.

Dickerson, James. *North to Canada: Men and Women Against the Vietnam War.* Westport, CT: Praeger, 1999.

Duiker, William. "Waging Revolutionary War: The Evolution of Hanoi's Strategy in the South, 1958–1965." In J. S. Warner and L. D. Huynh, eds., *The Vietnam War: Vietnamese and American Perspectives.* Armonk, NY: M. E. Sharpe, 1993.

———. *The Communist Road to Power in Vietnam.* Boulder, CO: Westview Press, 1981.

Eisenhower, Dwight D. *Mandate for Change, 1953–56.* New York: Signet Books, 1965.

Elliott, David. *NLF-DRV Strategy and the 1972 Spring Offensive.* Ithaca: Cornell University International Relations of East Asia Project, 1974.

Ellsberg, Daniel. *Secrets: A Memoir of Vietnam and the Pentagon Papers.* New York, Viking, 2002.

Ely, John Hart. *War and Responsibility: Constitutional Lessons of Vietnam and Its Aftermath.* Princeton: Princeton University Press, 1993.

Englemann, Larry. *Tears Before the Rain: An Oral History of the Fall of South Vietnam.* New York: Oxford University Press, 1990.

Falk, Richard A., ed. *The Vietnam War and International Law.* Princeton: Princeton University Press, 1968.

Fall, Bernard B. *The Two Viet-Nams: A Political and Military Analysis.* 3d ed. New York: Praeger, 1967.

———. *Last Reflections on a War.* New York: Doubleday, 1963.

Fifield, Russell H. *Americans in Southeast Asia: The Roots of Commitment.* New York: Thomas Crowell, 1973.

Fitzgerald, Frances. *Fire in the Lake.* New York: Vintage Books, 1972.

Fulbright, J. William. *The Arrogance of Power.* New York: Random House, 1967.

Galloway, John. *The Gulf of Tonkin Resolution.* Cranbury, NJ: Associated University Press, 1970.

Gardner, Lloyd C. *Pay Any Price: Lyndon Johnson and the Wars for Vietnam.* Chicago: Ivan R. Dea, 1995.

———. *Approaching Vietnam: From World War II Through Dienbienphu, 1941–1954.* New York: Norton, 1988.

Garthoff, Raymond L. *Détente and Confrontation: American-Soviet Relations from Nixon to Reagan.* Washington, DC: Brookings Institution, 1985.

Gettleman, Marvin E. *Vietnam and America: Documented History.* New York: Grove Press, 1985.

———, ed. *Vietnam.* New York: Penguin, 1965.

———, ed. *Vietnam: History, Documents and Opinions on a Major World Crisis.* Greenwich, CT: Fawcett, 1965.

Gibbons, William Conrad. *The U.S. Government and the Vietnam War: Executive and Legislative Roles and Relationships.* Princeton: Princeton University Press, 1986.

Gilbert, James W. *The Perfect War: The War We Couldn't Lose and How We Did.* Boston: Atlantic Monthly Press, 1986.

Gilbert, Marc Jason, ed. *Why the North Won the Vietnam War.* New York: Palgrave, 2002.

Gittinger, Ted, ed. *The Johnson Years: A Vietnam Roundtable.* Austin, TX: Lyndon Baines Johnson Library, 1993.

Goodman, Allan. *The Lost Peace: America's Search for a Negotiated Settlement of the Vietnam War.* Stanford: Stanford University Press, 1978.

Griffiths, Philip Jones. *Agent Orange: "Collateral Damage" in Vietnam.* London: Trolley, 2003.

Gruening, Ernest, and Herbert W. Beaser. *Vietnam Folly.* Washington, DC: National Press, 1968.

Gustainins, J. Justin. *American Rhetoric and the Vietnam War.* Westport, CT: Praeger, 1993.

Halberstam, David. *The Making of a Quagmire: America and Vietnam During the Kennedy Era.* New York: Random House, 1965.

Hamilton, Donald W. *The Art of Insurgency: American Military Policy and the Failure of Strategy in Southeast Asia.* Westport, CT: Praeger, 1998.

Hammer, Ellen J. *A Death in November: America in Vietnam, 1963.* New York: E. P. Dutton, 1987.

Harrison, James P. *The Endless War: Fifty Years of Struggle in Vietnam.* New York: Free Press, 1982.

Head, William, and Lawrence E. Grinter, eds. *Looking Back on the Vietnam War.* Westport, CT: Praeger, 1993.

Herring, George C. *LBJ and Vietnam: A Different Kind of War.* Austin: University of Texas Press, 1994.

———. *America's Longest War: The United States and Vietnam, 1950–1975.* Philadelphia: Temple University Press, 1986.

Herrington, Stuart. *Silence Was a Weapon: The Vietnam War in the Villages.* Novato, Calif.: Presidio Press, 1982.

Hess, Gary R. *Vietnam and the United States: Origins and Legacy of War.* Boston: Twayne, 1990.

Hickey, Gerald Cannon. *Window on a War: An Anthropologist in the Vietnam Conflict.* Lubbock: Texas Technical University Press, 2002.

Honey, P. J. *Communism in North Vietnam: Its Role in the Sino-Soviet Dispute.* Cambridge: MIT Press, 1963.

Hunt, Richard A. *Pacification: The American Struggle for Vietnam's Hearts and Minds.* Boulder, CO: Westview Press, 1995.

Isaacs, Arnold R. *Without Honor: Defeat in Vietnam and Cambodia.* Baltimore: Johns Hopkins University Press, 1983.

Joes, Anthony James. *The War for South Vietnam, 1945–1975.* New York: Praeger, 1989.

Johnston, Whittle. "Containment and Vietnam." In John N. Moore, ed., The *Vietnam Debate: A Fresh Look at the Argumentation.* Lanham, MD: University Press of America, 1990.

Jones, Howard. *Death of a Generation: How the Assassinations of Diem and JFK Prolonged the Vietnam War.* New York: Oxford University Press, 2003.

Kahin, George M. *Intervention: How America Became Involved in Vietnam.* New York: Knopf, 1986.

Kahin, George M., and John W. Lewis. *The United States in Vietnam.* New York: Dial Press, 1967.

Karnow, Stanley. *Vietnam, a History: The First Complete Account of Vietnam at War.* New York: Viking, 1983.

Katsiaficas, George, ed. *Vietnam Documents: American and Vietnamese Views of the War.* Armonk, NY: M. E. Sharpe, 1990.

Kattenburg, Paul. *The Vietnam Trauma in American Foreign Policy, 1945–1975.* New Brunswick, NJ: Transaction Books, 1980.

Kissinger, Henry. *The White House Years.* Boston: Little, Brown, 1979.

———. *Ending the Vietnam War: A History of America's Involvement in and Extrication from the Vietnam War.* New York: Simon and Schuster, 2003.

Kolko, Gabriel. *Anatomy of a War: Vietnam, the United States, and the Modern Historical Experience, 1930–1975.* Armonk, NY: M. E. Sharpe, 2002.

Kurland, Gerald, ed. *Misjudgment or Defense of Freedom? The United States in Vietnam.* New York: Simon and Schuster, 1975.

Lacouture, Jean. *Vietnam Between Two Truces.* New York: Vintage Books, 1966.

Le Duan. *Letters to the South.* Hanoi: Foreign Languages Publishing House, 1986.

———. *On the Socialist Revolution in Vietnam.* 2 vols. Hanoi: Foreign Languages Publishing House, 1965.

Lee, J. Edward, and H. C. "Toby" Haynsworth. *Nixon, Ford, and the Abandonment of South Vietnam.* Jefferson, NC: McFarland, 2002.

Levy, David W. *The Debate over Vietnam.* Baltimore, MD: Johns Hopkins University Press, 1991.

Lind, Michael. *Vietnam, the Necessary War: A Reinterpretation of America's Most Disastrous Military Conflict.* New York: Free Press, 1999.

Lomperis, Timothy J. *From People's War to People's Rule: Insurgency, Intervention and the Lessons of Vietnam.* Chapel Hill: University of North Carolina Press, 1996.

Maclear, Michael. *The Ten Thousand Day War.* New York: St. Martin's Press, 1981.

Mahony, Phillip, ed. *From Both Sides Now: The Poetry of the Vietnam War and Its Aftermath.* New York: Scribner, 1998.

Mangold, Tom. *The Tunnels of Cu Chi.* London: Hodder and Stoughton, 1985.

McCulloch, Jock. *The Politics of Agent Orange.* Richmond, Australia: William Heinemann, 1984.

McNamara, Robert. *In Retrospect.* New York: Vintage Books, 1995.

McNamara, Robert, James G. Blight, and Robert K. Brigham. *Argument Without End: In Search of Answers to the Vietnam Tragedy.* New York: Public Affairs, 1999.

Merom, Gil. *How Democracies Lose Small Wars: State, Society, and the Failures of France in Algeria, Israel in Lebanon and the United States in Vietnam.* Cambridge: Cambridge University Press, 2003.

Moore, John Norton, and Robert F. Turner, eds. *The Real Lessons of the Vietnam War: Reflections Twenty-Five Years After the Fall of Saigon.* Durham, NC: Carolina Academy Press, 2002.

Newman, John M. *JFK and Vietnam: Deception, Intrigue and the Struggle for Power.* New York: Warner Books, 1992.

Nguyen Cao Ky. *How We Lost the Vietnam War.* New York: Stein and Day, 1984.

Norodom Sihanouk. *My War with the CIA.* Harmondsworth, England: Penguin, 1973.

———. "Cambodia Neutral: The Dictate of Necessity." *Foreign Affairs* 36 (July 1958), pp. 582–586.

Oberdorfer, Don. *Tet.* New York: Da Capo Press, 1971.

O'Nan, Stewart, ed. *The Vietnam Reader: The Definitive Collection of American Fiction and Non-Fiction on the War.* New York: Anchor Books/Doubleday, 1998.

Palmer, Bruce, Jr. *The Twenty-Five-Year War: America's Military Role in Vietnam.* Lexington: University Press of Kentucky, 1984.

Papp, Daniel S. *Vietnam: The View from Moscow, Peking, Washington.* Salisbury, NC: McFarland, 1981.

Pentagon Papers. New York: Bantam Books, 1971.

Pham, David Lan. *Two Hamlets in Nam Bo: Memoirs of Life in Vietnam Through Japanese Occupation, the French and American Wars, and Communist Rule, 1940–1986.* Jefferson, NC: McFarland, 2000.

Pham Kim Vinh. *McNamara's Vietnam War and the Untold Truth.* Fountain Valley, CA: Pham Kim Vinh Institute, 1995.

Pham Van Dong and the Committee for the Study of the History of the Vietnamese Workers' Party. *President Ho Chi Minh.* Hanoi: Foreign Languages Publishing House, 1960.

Pike, Douglas. *Viet Cong.* Cambridge: MIT Press, 1966.

Podhoretz, Norman. *Why We Were in Vietnam.* New York: Simon and Schuster, 1982.

Porter, Gareth. *A Peace Denied: The United States and the Paris Agreements.* Bloomington: Indiana University Press, 1975.

Prados, John. *The Blood Road: The Ho Chi Minh Trail and the Vietnam War.* New York: Wiley, 1999.

Race, Jeffrey. *War Comes to Long An: Revolutionary Conflict in a Vietnamese Province.* Berkeley: University of California Press, 1972.

Record, Jeffrey. *The Wrong War: Why We Lost in Vietnam.* Annapolis, MD: Naval Institute Press, 1998.

Republic of Vietnam, Ministry of Information. *The Problem of Reunification of Viet-Nam.* Saigon: 1958.

Robbins, Mary Susannah, ed. *Against the Vietnam War: Writings by Activists.* Syracuse, NY: Syracuse University Press, 1999.

Rotter, Andrew J. *The Path to Vietnam: Origins of American Commitment to Southeast Asia.* Ithaca: Cornell University Press, 1987.

Russell, Jamie. *Vietnam War Movies.* Harpenden, Hertfordshire, UK: Pockets Essentials, 2002.

Rust, William J. *Kennedy in Vietnam.* New York: Scribner, 1985.

SarDesai, D. R. *Indian Foreign Policy in Cambodia, Laos and Vietnam, 1947–1964.* Berkeley: University of California Press, 1968.

Schlesinger, Arthur M., Jr. *The Bitter Heritage: Vietnam and American Democracy, 1941–1966.* Boston: Houghton Mifflin, 1967.

Schwab, Orrin. *Defending the Free World: John F. Kennedy, Lyndon Johnson, and the Vietnam War, 1961–1965.* Westport, CT: Praeger, 1998.

Sevy, G., ed. *The American Experience in Vietnam.* Norman: University of Oklahoma Press, 1989.

Shawcross, William. *Sideshow: Kissinger, Nixon and the Destruction of Cambodia.* New York: Pocket Books, 1979.

Shultz, Richard H. *The Secret War Against Hanoi: Kennedy's and Johnson's Use of Spies, Saboteurs, and Covert Warriors in North Vietnam.* New York: Harper-Collins, 1999.

Siff, Ezra Y. *Why the Senate Slept: The Gulf of Tonkin Resolution and the Beginning of America's Vietnam War.* Westport, CT: Praeger, 1999.

Smith, Ralph B. *An International History of the Vietnam War.* Vol. 1. *Revolution Versus Containment, 1955–1961.* New York: St. Martin's Press, 1983.

Smyser, W. R. *The Independent Vietnamese: Vietnamese Communism Between Russia and China, 1955–1969.* Athens: Ohio University Press, 1980.

Spector, Ronald H. *Advice and Support: The Early Years of the United States Army in Vietnam, 1941–1960.* New York: Free Press, 1985.

Tanham, George. *Communist Revolutionary Warfare: The Vietminh in Indochina.* New York: Praeger, 1961.

Taylor, Mark. *The Vietnam War in History, Literature and Film.* Edinburgh: Edinburgh University Press, 2003.

Taylor, Sandra C. *Vietnamese Women at War: Fighting for Ho Chi Minh and the Revolution.* Lawrence: University Press of Kansas, 1999.

Terzani, Tiziano. *Giai Phong! The Fall and Liberation of Saigon.* New York: St. Martin's Press, 1976.

Thayer, Thomas C. *War Without Fronts: The American Experience in Vietnam.* Boulder, CO: Westview Press, 1985.

Thompson, Robert. *No Exit from Vietnam.* London: Chatto and Windus, 1969.

———. *Defeating Communist Insurgency: Experiences from Malaya and Vietnam.* London: Chatto and Windus, 1966.

Topmiller, Robert J. *The Lotus Unleashed: The Buddhist Peace Movement in South Vietnam, 1964–1966.* Lexington: University Press of Kentucky, 2002.

Truong Chinh. *Resolutely Taking the North Vietnam Countryside to Socialism Through Agricultural Cooperation.* Hanoi: Foreign Languages Publishing House, 1959.

Truong Nhu Tang. *Journal of a Vietcong.* London: Cape, 1986.

———. *A Vietcong Memoir.* San Diego: Harcourt Brace Jovanovich, 1985.

Turley, William S. *The Second Indochina War: A Short Political and Military History, 1954–1975.* Boulder, Colo.: Westview Press, 1986.

United Kingdom. Foreign Office. *Further Documents Relating to the Discussions of Indochina at the Geneva Conference.* Cmd. 9239. London: Her Majesty's Stationery Office, 1954.

US Department of State. *A Threat to the Peace.* Washington, DC: Government Printing Office, 1961.

US Senate. Committee on Foreign Relations. *Causes, Origins and Lessons of the Vietnam War: Hearings.* 92d Cong., 2d sess., 9, 10, 11 May 1972.

VanDeMark, Brian. *Into the Quagmire: Lyndon Johnson and the Escalation of the Vietnam War.* New York: Oxford University Press, 1991.

Vickerman, Andrew. *The Fate of the Peasantry: Premature "Transition to Socialism" in the Democratic Republic of Vietnam.* New Haven: Yale University Press, 1986.

Walton, C. Dale. *The Myth of Inevitable US Defeat in Vietnam.* London: Frank Cass, 2002.

Warner, Denis. *The Last Confucian.* New York: Macmillan, 1963.

Warner, Roger. *Back Fire: The CIA's Secret War in Laos and Its Link to the War in Vietnam.* New York: Simon and Schuster, 1995.

Well, Tom. *The War Within: America's Battle over Vietnam.* Berkeley: University of California Press, 1994.

Werner, J. S., and L. D. Huynh, eds. *The Vietnam War: Vietnamese and American Perspectives.* Armonk, NY: M. E. Sharpe, 1993.

Westmoreland, William C. *A Soldier Reports.* New York: Doubleday, 1976.

Wiest, Andrew A. *The Vietnam War, 1956–1975.* New York: Routledge, 2003.

Woods, Randall B. *Vietnam and the American Political Tradition: The Politics of Dissent.* Cambridge: Cambridge University Press, 2003.

Woodside, Alexander B. *Community and Revolution in Modern Vietnam.* Boston: Houghton Mifflin, 1976.

Wyatt, Clarence R. *Paper Soldiers: The American Press and the Vietnam War.* New York: Norton, 1993.

Vietnam and Cambodia Since 1975

Albin, David A., and Marlowe Hood, eds. *The Cambodian Agony.* Armonk, NY: M. E. Sharpe, 1987.

ASEAN Secretariat and World Bank. 2002. *Annual Report 2002–2003.*

Barron, John, and Anthony Paul. *Murder of a Gentle Land: The Untold Story of Communist Genocide in Cambodia.* New York: Reader's Digest Press, 1977.

Barry, Kathleen, ed. *Vietnam's Women in Transition.* Houndsmills, England: Macmillan, 1996.

Becker, Elizabeth. *When the War Was Over: The Voices of Cambodia's Revolution and Its People.* New York: Simon and Schuster, 1986.

Beresford, Melanie. *National Unification and Economic Development in Vietnam.* London: Macmillan, 1989.

Binh, Tran-Nam, and Chi, Do Pham, eds. *The Vietnamese Economy: Awakening the Dormant Dragon.* London: Routledge Curzon, 2003.

Borer, Douglas A. *Superpowers Defeated: Vietnam and Afghanistan Compared.* London: Frank Cass, 1999.

Burchett, Wilfred. *The China-Cambodia-Vietnam Triangle.* London: Zed, 1981.

Buzzanco, Robert. *Masters of War: Military Dissent and Politics in the Vietnam Era.* Cambridge: Harvard University Press, 1996.

Campagna, Anthony. *The Economic Consequences of the Vietnam War.* New York: Praeger, 1991.

Cargill, Mary Terrell, and Jade Quang Huynh, eds. *Voices of Vietnamese People: Nineteen Narratives of Escape and Survival.* Jefferson, NC: McFarland, 2000.

Carney, Timothy M., ed. *Communist Party in Kampuchea, Documents and Discussion.* Ithaca: Cornell University Southeast Asia Program, 1977.

Chan, Anita, Benedict J. Tria Kerkvliet, and Jonathan Unger. *Transforming Asian Socialism: China and Vietnam Compared.* Lanham, MD: Rowman and Littlefield, 1999.

Chanda, Nayan. *Brother Enemy: The War After the War—A History of Indochina Since the Fall of Saigon.* San Diego: Harcourt Brace Jovanovich, 1986.

Chandler, David P. *The Tragedy of Cambodian History: Politics, War and Revolution Since 1945.* New Haven: Yale University Press, 1991.

———. *Revolution and Its Aftermath in Kampuchea.* New Haven: Yale University Press, 1983.

Chandler, David P., Ben Kiernan, and Chanthou Boua, eds. *Pol Pot Plans the Future: Confidential Leadership Documents from Democratic Kampuchea, 1976–1977.* New Haven: Yale University Press, 1988.

Chang Pao-min. *The Sino-Vietnamese Territorial Dispute.* New York: Praeger, 1986.

———. *Kampuchea Between China and Vietnam.* Singapore: Singapore University Press, 1985.

———. *Beijing, Hanoi and the Overseas Chinese.* Berkeley: Center for Chinese Studies, University of California, 1982.

Croce, Larry W. *Vietnamese Economic Reform: How Important to U.S.–Vietnam Trade Relations.* Washington, DC: Worldfact Book, 2000.

Curtis, Grant. *Transition to What? Cambodia, UNTAC and the Peace Process.* Geneva: United Nations Research Institute for Social Development, 1993.

Dahm, Henrich. *French and Japanese Economic Relations with Vietnam Since 1975.* Richmond, Surrey: Curzon, 1999.

Daum, Andreas W., Lloyd C. Gardner, and Wilfried Mausbach, eds. *America, the Vietnam War and the World: Comparative and International Perspectives.* New York: Cambridge University Press, 2003.

Dellinger, David T. *Vietnam Revisited: From Covert Action to Invasion to Reconstruction.* Boston: South End Press, 1986.

Duiker, William J. *China and Vietnam: The Roots of Conflict.* Berkeley: University of California Press, 1986.

———. *Vietnam Since the Fall of Saigon.* Athens: Ohio University Center for International Studies, 1985.

Ebihara, May M. *Cambodian Culture Since 1975.* Ithaca: Cornell University Press, 1994.

Elliott, David W. P., ed. *Indochina: Social and Cultural Change.* Claremont, CA: McKenna College, 1994.

———. *The Third Indochina Conflict.* Boulder, CO: Westview Press, 1981.

———. *The Vietnamese War: Revolution and Social Change in the Mekong Delta, 1930–1975.* Armonk, NY: M. E. Sharpe, 2002.

Elman, Benjamin A., John B. Duncan, and Herman Ooms, eds. *Rethinking Confucianism: Past and Present in China, Japan, Korea and Vietnam.* Los Angeles: UCLA Asian Pacific Monograph Series, 2002.

Etcheson, Craig. *The Rise and Demise of Democratic Kampuchea*. Boulder, CO: Westview Press, 1984.

Evans, Grant. *Red Brotherhood at War: Vietnam, Cambodia and Laos Since 1975*. London: Verso, 1990.

Fforde, Adam. *The Agrarian Question in North Vietnam, 1974–1979*. Armonk, NY: M. E. Sharpe, 1989.

Fforde, Adam, and Stefan Vylder. *From Plan to Market: The Economic Transition in Vietnam*. Boulder, CO: Westview Press, 1996.

Freeman, James M. *Hearts of Sorrow: Vietnamese American Lives*. Palo Alto: Stanford University Press, 1989.

Frings, K. Viviane. *Allied and Equal: The Kampuchean People's Revolutionary Party's Historiography and Its Relations with Vietnam, 1979–1991*. Clayton, Australia: Center for Southeast Asian Studies, Monash University, 1994.

Frost, Frank. *The Peace Process in Cambodia*. Queensland, Australia: Griffith University, 1993.

———. *Vietnamese Territorial Disputes*. New York: Praeger, 1986.

Griffin, Keith, ed. *Economic Reform in Vietnam*. New York: St. Martin's Press, 1998.

Heder, Stephen R. *Kampuchean Occupation and Resistance*. Bangkok: Institute of Asian Studies, Chulalongkorn University, 1980.

Hildebrand, George C. *Cambodia: Starvation and Revolution*. New York: Monthly Review Press, 1976.

Hodd, Stephen. *Dragons Embattled: Indochina and the China–Vietnam War*. Westport, CT: Praeger, 1993.

Human Rights Watch. *Repression of Montagnards: Conflicts over Land and Religion in Vietnam's Central Highlands*. New York, Human Rights Watch, 2002.

Huynh Kim Khanh. "Year One of Post-Colonial Vietnam." *Southeast Asian Affairs, 1977* (Singapore: Institute of Southeast Asian Studies, 1977).

———. "Restructuring the Economy of South Vietnam." *Southeast Asian Affairs, 1976* (Singapore: Institute of Southeast Asian Studies, 1976).

Jackson, Karl D., ed. *Cambodia, 1975–1978: Rendezvous with Death*. Princeton: Princeton University Press, 1989.

Kenny, Henry J. *Shadow of the Dragon: Vietnam's Continuing Struggle with China and the Implications for U.S. Foreign Policy*. Washington, DC: Brassey's, 2002.

Khanh Tran. *The Ethnic Chinese and Economic Development in Vietnam*. Singapore: Institute of Southeast Asian Studies, 1993.

Kibria, Nazli. *Family Tightrope: The Changing Lives of Vietnamese Americans*. Princeton: Princeton University Press, 1993.

Kiernan, Ben. *The Pol Pot Regime*. New Haven: Yale University Press, 1993.

———. *How Pol Pot Came to Power: A History of Communism in Kampuchea, 1930–1975*. London: Verso, 1985.

Kiljunen, Kimmo, ed. *Kampuchea: Decade of the Genocide*. London: Zed, 1984.

Kimura, Tetsusaburo. *The Vietnamese Economy, 1975–1986, Reforms and International Relations*. Tokyo: Institute of Developing Economies, 1989.

Klintworth, Gary. *Vietnam's Withdrawal from Cambodia.* Canberra: Australian National University, 1987.

Kokko, Ari. *Step by Step: Economic Reform and Renovation in Vietnam Before 9th Party Congress.* Stockholm: International Development Cooperation Agency, 2001.

Lamb, David. *Vietnam Now: A Reporter Returns.* New York: Public Affairs, 2002.

Leifer, Michael. *Cambodian Conflicts: The Final Phase?* London: Center for Security and Conflict Studies, 1989.

Litvack, Jennie I., and Dennis A. Rondinelli. *Market Reform in Vietnam: Building Institutions for Development.* Westport, CT: Quorum, 1999.

Ljunggren, Boerje, ed. *The Challenge of Reform in Indochina.* Cambridge: Harvard University Press, 1993.

Long, Robert Emmet, ed. *Vietnam Ten Years After.* New York: Wilson, 1986.

Luong, Hy V., ed. *Postwar Vietnam: Dynamics of a Transforming Society.* Lanham, MD: Rowman and Littlefield, 2003.

Marr, David G., and Christine P. White, eds. *Post-War Vietnam: Dilemmas in Socialist Development.* Ithaca: Cornell University Southeast Asia Program, 1988.

Martin, Marie Alexandrine. *Cambodia: A Shattered Society.* Berkeley: University of California Press, 1994.

May, Someth. *Cambodian Witness: The Autobiography of Someth May.* Ed. James Fenton. London: Faber, 1986.

McGregor, Charles. *The Sino-Vietnamese Relationship and the Soviet Union.* London: International Institute for Strategic Studies, 1988.

McKelvey, Robert S. *The Dust of Life: America's Children Abandoned in Vietnam.* Seattle: University of Washington Press, 1999.

———. *A Gift of Barbed Wire: America's Allies Abandoned in South Vietnam.* Seattle: University of Washington Press, 2002.

Morris, Stephen J. *Why Vietnam Invaded Cambodia: Political Culture and the Causes of War.* Palo Alto: Stanford University Press, 1999.

Ngor Haing S. *Surviving the Killing Fields: The Cambodian Odyssey.* London: Chatto and Windus, 1988.

Nguyen Khac Vien. *Southern Vietnam, 1975–1985.* Hanoi: Foreign Languages Publishing House, 1985.

Nguyen Van Kanh. *Vietnam Under Communism, 1975–1982.* Palo Alto: Stanford University Press, 1983.

Nguyen-Vo Tho-Huong. *Khmer-Viet Relations and the Third Indochina Conflict.* Jefferson, NC: McFarland, 1992.

Norodom Sihanouk. "A Passion for Cambodia: Norodom Sihanouk and the Khmer Factions—A Reply." *Indochina Reports* 13 (October–December 1987).

Pham, David Lan. *Two Hamlets in Nam Bo: Memoirs of Life in Vietnam Through Japanese Occupation, the French and American Wars, and Communist Rule, 1940–1986.* Jefferson, NC: McFarland, 2000.

Picq, Laurence. *Beyond the Horizon: Five Years with the Khmer Rouge.* New York: St. Martin's Press, 1989.

Pike, Douglas. *Vietnam and the Soviet Union: Anatomy of an Alliance.* Boulder, Colo.: Westview Press, 1987.

Ponchaud, François. *Cambodia, Year Zero.* New York: Holt and Rinehart, 1977.

Porter, Gareth. *Vietnam: The Politics of Bureaucratic Socialism.* Ithaca: Cornell University Press, 1993.

―――. "Vietnamese Policy and the Indochina Crisis." In David W. P. Elliott, ed., *The Third Indochina Conflict.* Boulder, CO: Westview Press, 1981.

Ross, Robert S. *The Indochina Tangle: China's Vietnam Policy, 1975–1979.* New York: Columbia University Press, 1988.

Rutledge, Paul J. *The Vietnamese Experience in America.* Bloomington: Indiana University Press, 1992.

Salemink, Oscar. *The Ethnography of Vietnam's Central Highlanders: A Historical Contextualization, 1850–1990.* New York: Routledge Curzon, 2003.

Schanberg, Sydney Hillel. *The Death and Life of Dith Pran.* New York: Penguin, 1985.

Shawcross, William. *The Quality of Mercy: Cambodia, Holocaust and Modern Conscience.* New York: Simon and Schuster, 1984.

Stern, Lewis M. *The Vietnamese Communist Party's Agenda for Reform: A Study of the Eighth National Party Congress.* Jefferson, NC: McFarland, 1998.

Stuart-Fox, Martin. *The Murderous Revolution: Life and Death in Pol Pot's Kampuchea.* Denver: Alternate Publishing Company, 1986.

Sutter, Robert G. *The Cambodian Crisis and U.S. Policy Dilemmas.* Boulder, CO: Westview Press, 1991.

Tadashi, Mio, ed. *Indochina in Transition: Confrontation or Co-Prosperity?* Tokyo: Japan Institute of International Affairs, 1989.

Takaki, Ronald. *Strangers from a Different Shore: A History of Asian-Americans.* New York: Penguin Books, 1989.

Tan Teng Lang. *Economic Debates in Vietnam: Issues and Problems in Reconstruction and Development (1975–84).* Singapore: Institute of Southeast Asian Studies, 1985.

Tetreault, Maryann. *Women and Revolution in Vietnam.* East Lansing: Michigan State University, 1992.

Tho Tran Van, ed. *The Economic Development of Vietnam in an Asian Pacific Perspective.* Tokyo: Japan Center for Economic Research, 1990.

Thrift, Nigel, and Dean Forbes. *The Price of War: Urbanization in Vietnam, 1954–1985.* London: Allen and Unwin, 1985.

Tran Dang T. *Vietnam: Socialist Economic Development.* San Francisco: Institute for Contemporary Studies Press, 1994.

Tran Van Don. *Our Endless War: Inside South Vietnam.* Novato, CA: Presidio Press, 1978.

Tran Van Hoa, ed. *Prospects in Trade, Investment, and Business in Vietnam and East Asia.* New York: St. Martin's Press, 2000.

Turley, William S. "The Khmer War: Cambodia After Paris." *Survival* 32, 5 (September–October 1990).

―――, ed. *Confrontation or Coexistence: The Future of ASEAN–Vietnam Relations.* Bangkok: Chulalongkorn University, 1985.

Turley, William S., and Mark Selden, eds. *Reinventing Vietnamese Socialism: Doi Moi in Comparative Perspective.* Boulder, CO: Westview Press, 1993.

US Department of Health and Human Services. Office of Refugee Resettlement. *Refugee Resettlement Program, Report to the Congress.* Washington, DC: US Department of Health and Human Services, 1992.

———. Social Security Administration. *Survey of the Social, Psychological and Economic Adaptation of Vietnamese Refugees in the U.S., 1975–1979.* Washington, DC: US Department of Health and Human Services, 1982.

US House. Committee on Foreign Affairs. Subcommittee on Asian and Pacific Affairs. *Issues Affecting the Question of U.S. Relations with Vietnam: Hearings.* 101st Cong., 1st sess., 17 November 1989.

US Immigration Commission. *Asian American Encyclopaedia.* New York: Marshall Cavendish, 1995.

US Library of Congress. Congressional Research Service. Foreign Affairs and National Defense Division. *Vietnam's Future Policies and Role in Southeast Asia.* Washington, DC: Government Printing Office, 1982.

US Senate. Committee on Foreign Relations. Subcommittee on East Asian and Pacific Affairs. *U.S. Policy Toward Vietnam: Hearings Before the Subcommittee on East Asian and Pacific Affairs.* 103d Cong., 1st sess., 21 July 1993.

Vickery, Michael. *Kampuchea: Politics, Economics, and Society.* London: Pinter, 1986.

———. *Cambodia, 1975–1982.* Boston: South End Press, 1984.

Vo Than Tri. *Vietnam's Economic Policy Since 1975.* Singapore: Institute of Southeast Asian Studies, 1990.

Yang, Sam. *Khmer Buddhism and Politics from 1954 to 1984.* Newington, CT: Khmer Studies Institute, 1987.

Young, Kenneth B. *Vietnam's Rice Economy: Developments and Prospects.* Fayetteville, AR: Agricultural Experiment Station, 2002.

Young, Marilyn. *The Vietnam Wars, 1945–1990.* New York: HarperCollins, 1991.

Zasloff, Joseph, ed. *Post-War Indochina: Old Enemies and New Allies.* Washington, DC: Government Printing Office, 1989.

Reference

Anderson, David L., ed. *The Columbia Guide to the Vietnam War.* New York: Columbia University Press, 2002.

Duiker, William J. *Historical Dictionary of Vietnam.* 2d ed. Lanham, MD: Scarecrow Press, 1999.

Kutler, Stanley I., ed. *Encyclopedia of the Vietnam War.* New York: Macmillan, 1996.

Moise, Edwin E. *Historical Dictionary of the Vietnam War.* Lanham, MD: Scarecrow Press, 2001.

Summers, Harry G., Jr. *Historical Atlas of the Vietnam War.* Boston: Houghton Mifflin, 1995.

Tucker, Spencer C., ed. *Encyclopedia of the Vietnam War: A Political, Social, and Military History.* 3 vols. Santa Barbara; ABC-CLIO, 1998; New York: Oxford University Press, 2000.

Index